Secrets of Service Level Management
A process owner's guide

London: TSO

information & publishing solutions

Published by TSO (The Stationery Office) and available from:

Online
www.tsoshop.co.uk

Mail, Telephone, Fax & E-mail
TSO
PO Box 29, Norwich, NR3 1GN
Telephone orders/General enquiries: 0870 600 5522
Fax orders: 0870 600 5533
E-mail: customer.services@tso.co.uk
Textphone: 0870 240 3701

TSO@Blackwell and other Accredited Agents

First published 2013

Second impression 2016

ISBN 9780113313525

Printed in the United Kingdom for The Stationery Office, London

P002468774   c8   03/13

Contents

List of figures

List of tables

About the authoring team

THE AUTHOR

Ami Nahari

As an expert in the field of IT service management (ITSM), ITIL® and service level management (SLM), Ami Nahari has assessed and implemented SLM processes for Fortune 100 companies. In addition to his 15 years of experience, he brings first-rate project management skills, a creative approach and proven leadership to his role as author.

PMI and ITIL V3 Expert certified, Ami has written articles and spoken extensively about the methodology he developed relating to IT service performance measurements and service level manager responsibilities. He holds a BS (Hons) in Political and Management Science from Bar Ilan University, Ramat Gan, Israel, and shows real commitment and enthusiasm in all his chosen fields.

Ami has lived in Israel, Toronto, Ireland and San Francisco, and he currently resides in New York City.

THE CONTRIBUTORS

Craig J. LaCava

Craig J. LaCava has been an IT management and business consultant for more than 16 years. During his career, Craig has specialized in ITSM, IT strategy and planning, business continuity and IT governance. Craig has consulted with Fortune 100 companies across North America, Europe and Asia.

Craig earned the ITIL IT Service Manager certificate with distinction from the Information Systems Examination Board (ISEB) in 2005 and now holds the ITIL V3 Expert certificate. He specializes in helping IT organizations to achieve more effective and efficient operations and governance through the adaptation of ITIL, ISO 20000 and other best-practice frameworks.

Craig holds a BS (Hons) in Computer Science from the Georgia Institute of Technology and lives in Atlanta, Georgia.

Joe Fennis

Joe Fennis is a highly skilled SLM solutions designer and architect. Joe has worked in the ITSM domain for more than 12 years, specializing in service level agreement (SLA) management, and focusing on metric, key performance indicator (KPI) and SLA calculations. Joe has consulted and implemented several ITSM projects for companies in Australia, Europe and the United States.

Joe holds a Bachelor degree in information technology from Griffith University, Australia, and now lives and works in Belgium.

Acknowledgements

AUTHOR ACKNOWLEDGEMENTS

Special thanks to Tanya Benson and Kim Donica, who spent hours upon hours editing my chapters to ensure that the writing standards were high and that the guidance contained in this publication would be clear to all audiences. Beyond editing capabilities, both Tanya and Kim provided highly skilled ITSM feedback which helped the author immensely.

Other contributors include Khaled Aly, Eli Anhang, Mike Cartoscelli, Mike Efstathiou, Tzachi Golan, Molnar John, Yakov Kogan, Pascal Marat, Larissa Montrose, Kevin Mullen, Eitan Rafael, Eric Reich, Ross Richardson, Loren Shumway, Mark Stadtmueller, Kathy Steinway, Drew Terranova, Lloyd Turner, Mark Walter, Martin Williamson, Scott Wilson, Ivri Yair and David Zemon.

PUBLISHER ACKNOWLEDGEMENTS

The Stationery Office (TSO) would like to thank itSMF for its help in the quality assurance of this publication. Thanks are also due to those people who generously donated their time in reviewing this title, including George Kinnear of The Grey Matters, Paul Wigzel of Paul Wigzel Training and Consultancy, and Dot Tudor of TCC.

Preface

People ask me if I like to travel. Well, I like meeting new people and visiting new cultures, and I like escaping my daily routine and going on vacation, but all of these usually involve going through numerous airport security checks, which I don't like at all.

Recently, I flew from New York to Toronto. My flight was scheduled to depart at 6:30 p.m. and arrive at 8:00 p.m. The chaos in the airport was unbearable: it was difficult to get hold of the desk attendant; flights were being cancelled; and departure gates were being changed by the minute. Our plane finally left the gate at 7:00 p.m., and then taxied for more than an hour and a half until we were airborne at 8:30 p.m., to land in Toronto at 9:30 p.m. Many people missed their connecting flights and were forced to stay the night in the airport. Toronto was my destination but I, too, was delayed a while longer, as local immigration officials decided to take me through some additional inspection. Needless to say, my plans for the evening were ruined.

Examined through service management standards, my flight experience failed every single metric: response time, resolution time, performance, availability and, above all, customer satisfaction. This happened for one simple reason: there was no alternative service.

The objective of service level management (SLM) is to defy precisely that outcome. The process goal is to interface with the customer and ensure their satisfaction. SLM is a core ITIL[1] process because it examines the actual quality of service as the customer perceives it and how happy the customer is with it. 'Happy' is not an IT term and cannot be tracked by a monitoring tool, and that is why SLM is different from other processes.

You can have a service level agreement (SLA) report showing 100% scores for every objective, but if your customer satisfaction is lagging, you must start a new record in your continual service improvement (CSI) register and prioritize this item. Likewise, you may have an SLA report indicating warnings and even breaches in some of your objectives, but if your customers are happy, you must be doing something right.

To be a successful service level manager, you will need to be attentive to your customers' needs, maintain complete and relevant documentation, and negotiate and track your SLAs to improve your process. In this publication I will show you how. I will take you step by step through the necessary action for successful implementation of SLM. I will help you to foresee coming challenges, and learn how to overcome them. I will also reveal the

---

1 Readers wishing to understand more about ITIL and the ITIL service lifecycle are advised to refer to the five core publications on IT service management: *ITIL Service Strategy*, *ITIL Service Design*, *ITIL Service Transition*, *ITIL Service Operation* and *ITIL Continual Service Improvement*. See www.axelos.com for more details.

'secrets of the trade', providing you with behind-the-scenes experiences, recorded by first-hand practitioners.

The air travel nightmare that I mentioned earlier required the cooperation of three different entities – security, airport and airline – to produce and maintain its unusual level of customer stress and discomfort. But, unlike airline passengers, your customers have alternatives. If you want them to continue using you as their service provider, they must experience a positive service performance. You have no choice but to establish a best-practice SLM process. Your competition does.

This book is dedicated to my parents, Yehiel and Ora Nahari.

Service level
management overview

1

1 Service level management overview

1.1 UNDERSTANDING SERVICE LEVEL MANAGEMENT

1.1.1 Defining service level management

Service level management (SLM) is the process that provides the main channel of communication between the customer and the service provider regarding the quality of service provision. In a utopian world, service providers provide services to the customer that support their business activities, meet agreed service level targets, and are cost-effective. However, we don't live in a utopian world. A formal process is needed to provide a continual dialogue with the customer regarding the fitness for purpose and achieved service levels of delivered services, and to ensure customer satisfaction on the one hand is balanced against efficient service provision on the other.

ITIL defines SLM as the process responsible for negotiating achievable service level agreements (SLAs) and ensuring that these are met. It is responsible for ensuring that all IT service management processes, operational level agreements (OLAs) and underpinning contracts (UCs) are appropriate for the agreed service level targets. SLM monitors and reports on service levels, holds regular service reviews with customers, and identifies required improvements. Although the definition identifies the core activities and more tangible elements of the process, there are other underlying elements that this publication details. When I lecture on SLM, I emphasize additional topics such as relationships, communication, customer perception and other relevant abstract elements – topics that are fundamental to SLM and should be defined and transformed into concrete activities within the process.

Documenting, negotiating, agreeing and monitoring the quality of services, while important, are merely activities that support the overall objective of managing the relationship between the customer and the service provider regarding the provision of services. Relationships, communications and customer perceptions, when integrated with these activities, are the key to building a truly productive relationship based on trust and quality.

1.1.2 Service level management and ITIL

SLM is considered one of the core processes in any IT service management framework. While incident management and the service desk function are usually the first to be implemented in organizations wishing to advance their ITIL maturity level, today we see an increasing number of organizations realizing the significance and value of SLM in accelerating their efforts and, as such, moving the SLM process up the queue for process implementation.

Many ITIL consultants and practitioners recommend implementing or improving SLM prior to any other process. This might sound extreme at first, but those who have experience with implementing SLM will agree that it exposes gaps in the service delivery environment, including gaps in established processes. For example, an organization that initially implements incident management will utilize best practice and customize the process to meet the specific needs of the organization while at the same time assuming that, with time, the process will adjust to meet those needs. Unfortunately this is seldom the case, and often process implementations stagnate or even deteriorate as time passes.

With an established SLM process, important inputs from the process would have assisted in getting the incident management process right first time. For example, a detailed understanding of customer requirements, critical services, and service improvement prioritization are only a few of the many important inputs that would focus the efforts of implementing an incident management process – or, for that matter, any ITIL process. I will refrain from stating that SLM is the most important process in ITIL; however, it is the process that has the closest relationship with the customer and continually monitors not only the actual quality of service but the customer's perceptions of quality and value for money.

The SLM process belongs to the service design stage of the lifecycle, but it's important throughout the operational stage as well. ITIL defines a service lifecycle that positions SLM in the design phase. This is a very interesting discussion point. Services are strategized through processes such as service portfolio and demand management, which clearly belong to the service strategy phase. Service catalogue and availability management assist in completing the design of the services addressed in service strategy. SLM is indeed a process that assists in the design phase and in fact is one of the primary factors in developing the service catalogue.

Not to dispute the fact that SLM belongs in service design, it is imperative to understand that SLM is an important factor in the service operations arena too. SLA monitoring and service review are prominent operational activities, along with assisting with critical incidents and developing root cause analysis of incidents and problems. The service desk works closely with SLM to interface with end users on an operational level. Therefore, when analysing SLM, make sure to define the process as two-pronged: a process that defines services but also supports the ongoing delivery of services.

Finally, in consideration of the continual service improvement stage of the service lifecycle, I should explain my use of the terms 'continual process improvement' and 'continual service improvement'. When talking about ongoing improvements to the SLM process (and not the wider service), I use the term 'continual process improvement'. However, when describing the activity in the context of the ITIL service lifecycle, I use 'continual service improvement', in keeping with the correct name for that lifecycle stage.

1.1.3 Scope of service level management

Traditionally, SLM was the process that owned the SLA, generated service performance reports, and developed the OLAs and UCs. As important as those components are, you will learn that the scope of SLM has matured in recent years, promoting it to the level of vital contributor to a healthy service management environment. The service level manager is no longer an analyst expected to document services and their performance. The service level manager today is expected to carry out management tasks, such as building a relationship with the customer, and negotiating terms and conditions of service quality, and is a respected figure amongst the technical delivery teams.

Example

A customer uses an application which stores financial elements to support the business. The customer expects to have the application available 24/7. The service level manager works with the service provider to detail the resources required to support the customer's service level expectations. The service level manager discusses with the customer the true requirements of the service. The meetings with both sides (customer and service provider) reveal that the business requires only 9 a.m. to 5 p.m. availability and that the cost of support for the application increases significantly during the weekends. The service provider also indicates that providing support for the application between 5 p.m. and 8 p.m. does not require additional resources. When the customer realizes the increased cost for weekends and night hours (after 8 p.m.), it declines the offer and agrees for the services to be provided during normal working hours only. This type of 'negotiation' results in availability of the application from 7 a.m. to 8 p.m. during weekdays.

SLM ensures that services are designed to perform as required by the business and governs those who provide the services to ensure that services are provided as agreed with the customer. This point is important to understand. SLM does not strive for 100% availability of a service but, rather, strives to meet the agreed availability level. The customer will always want a 100% performance for all services; however, it is the responsibility of SLM to agree on service levels that encompass not only the customer's requirements but also two other important attributes: business requirements and cost (see example provided).

The example illustrates the essence of SLM. This is a process that no longer concerns itself only with maintaining the SLA and generating reports. SLM ensures that services are provided according to the business needs, promote efficiency and are cost-effective. This is achieved through an effective communication platform that SLM provides.

1.1.4 The service level management process

In this publication, the SLM process is broken down into five steps, as shown in Figure 1.1.

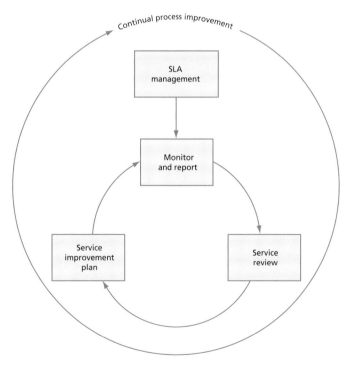

Figure 1.1 Service level management process

Each step in the process is considered a process in its own right, or a sub-process of SLM. As Figure 1.1 shows, the SLM process is made up of five interconnecting sub-processes or activities, which are described as follows:

- **SLA management** The SLA management sub-process focuses on agreements of service level measurements, targets and conditions. The goal of this process is to create a formal documented agreement between the customer and the service provider regarding the quality of service provision from the customer's perspective. The resulting SLA defines the critical service levels and key measurements of the overall service provision. This process does not end with the signing of the SLA; rather, it is an iterative process in which the SLA is continually reviewed, adjusted and agreed to ensure quality measurements are relevant throughout the service provision period. The SLA management sub-process utilizes OLAs, UCs and service level requirements (SLRs) to support the SLA.

- **Monitor and report** Monitoring and reporting service quality is based directly and strictly on the conditions defined in the SLA. This activity is one of the three ongoing activities of the SLM process, the other two being service review and the service improvement plan (SIP). The three of them are essentially integrated and coordinated throughout the SLA review period (typically a month). SLM reports achieve service levels against agreed service level targets, which are presented and reviewed in the service review meeting. Service review meetings result in items for improvement that are subsequently managed through the SIP.

The monitoring and reporting activity collects, correlates and aggregates operational data in order to generate calculations and reports for review of service performance. Monitoring and reporting owns the report catalogue and is a primary actor in defining the metrics and measurements.

- **Service review** The service review meeting is not just another regular meeting that is placed on the customer's and the service level manager's calendar. Service review meetings are essential to the overall process and provide an opportunity for both parties to build and maintain strong relationships, review SLA results and follow up on service improvement activities. There are specific inputs and outputs for the service review sub-process and a structured agenda to the meeting, and it cannot be stressed enough how important it is to design this process as effectively and productively as possible.

- **Service improvement plan** The SIP sub-process is designed to allow the service level manager to effectively convey to the customer what is being completed regarding degraded or disrupted services. The SIP utilizes the continual service improvement (CSI) register to communicate to the service provider the customer's expectations and prioritization of action items.

- **Continual process improvement** All aspects of SLM are subject to process improvement. Improvements are not only performed at regular intervals but can also occur reactively, being triggered by operational events or proactive measurements such as assessments and a key performance indicator (KPI) review. These improvement activities are considered to be background processes that are aimed at improving the overall effectiveness of the SLM process.

In Part 2, which deals with service design, you will find elaborate definitions of the above processes, and in Part 4 on service operation, each process is defined in terms of its functions, goals and activities. Finally, Part 5 on continual service improvement details the theories and practical activities involved in continually improving the SLM process.

1.1.5 Outsourcing engagement versus enterprise

SLM provides the means of communication between a service provider and its customer. The basic assumption is that within any service environment we can identify a function, a process or personnel that provide services. Within the same environment we can identify a function, a process or personnel that receive the services. The structure and size may differ but the main two actors in the service arena are the service provider and the customer.

This publication provides one standard SLM process that strives to fit all organization structures. However, there are two service structures that sometimes require special attention: outsourcing engagement and enterprise. They are defined as follows:

- **Outsourcing engagement** In this type of an environment the customer is an organization that outsources services to an external service provider. For example, a financial institution contracts with a large IT service provider to supply internet access, security services and operational support.

- **Enterprise** In this type of an environment the organization utilizes an internal service provider for its IT services.

When considering SLM, ignoring the difference between these two service structures (outsourcing engagement and enterprise) is nothing short of reckless. However, it is important to note that SLM as a process is almost identical in both environments and, when a difference does occur, I will point it out and guide you on how to address the matter, whether in an outsourcing engagement or in an enterprise.

1.2 PUBLICATION OBJECTIVES AND TARGET AUDIENCE

1.2.1 Who should read this publication?

Secrets of Service Level Management serves service level managers, ITIL practitioners, IT service management consultants or any individual who aspires to implement or improve SLM as a process. It is *not* an ITIL theoretical or foundation publication; rather, it includes advanced material that will allow practitioners to precisely design and implement elements that support SLM.

1.2.2 How this publication is different

Many publications that provide guidance on the ITIL framework focus on defining the processes, activities and objectives. Here I provide you with practical guidance on how to implement the process and activities and how to achieve your objectives.

In this publication I approach an element, define it, and continue with detailed guidance on how to achieve the ideal implementation of that element. I have made the text easy to read, drawing on the knowledge of practitioners with years of experience of how to do and, sometimes more importantly, how not to do something.

Secrets of Service Level Management is a practitioner guide on how to successfully implement an effective SLM process, how to take the theory of ITIL and convert it into practice, and how to plan and execute process improvement. I also explain what the challenges are, how to anticipate them and how to overcome them.

1.3 HOW TO USE THIS PUBLICATION

1.3.1 Publication structure

This publication adopts the ITIL service lifecycle approach. It assumes that in order to implement a process the same steps must be followed as when implementing a service. Firstly the process must be strategized, providing input into the design activities of the process. The subsequent design is then transitioned into its operational state, where the process activities are being executed. The process of implementation is not complete even in its operational state. ITIL suggests a cyclical structure to its lifecycle, signifying that continual service improvement is performed throughout in order to ensure that the process is adjusted for ever-changing service environments and the improvement of local failures (see Figure 1.2).

The chapters of this publication are arranged in accordance with ITIL lifecycle phases. The following describes the content that can be found in each lifecycle phase.

■ **Service strategy (Part 1)** Chapters 2–4 provide an overall understanding of SLM and how to position it within the IT service management framework. In Chapter 3, you will find the tools to define the vision and the objectives of the process, and learn how to produce key deliverables including the process charter, service level manager job description, critical success factors (CSFs) and key performance indicators (KPIs). Chapter 4 provides a practical roadmap for implementation, based on a gap assessment.

■ **Service design (Part 2)** When you reach this phase, it is assumed that your strategic elements have been established, and that you have defined your vision and the process objectives.

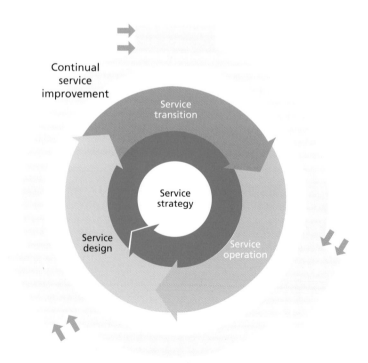

Figure 1.2 ITIL service lifecycle

In Chapters 5–11 we examine process elements, including the overall SLM process, resources and functions, SLA structure, service performance measurements and much more. At the end of Part 2, you will hold precise definitions for all tools and procedures of SLM. The design chapters recognize that each organization has its own culture, requirements, procedures and constraints. The guidance provided here will allow you to customize processes and deliverables according to your specific needs.

- **Service transition (Part 3)** A completion of your design activities does not necessarily mean that you can start executing the activities that you define. Service transition assists you with transitioning those elements that were designed in service design into their operational state. Service transition typically takes the form of a project and therefore many of the activities and terminologies are borrowed from the project management world. Part 3 (Chapters 12–13) will help you organize all the tools, templates and activities that must be addressed before they are utilized in production.

- **Service operation (Part 4)** Chapters 14–19 detail those activities that are performed on an ongoing basis by SLM. The chapters address SLA management, service review meetings, SIP, service reporting and much more. Part 4 also includes detailed procedures and guidelines to manage the process through risk management and stakeholder management.

- **Continual service improvement (Part 5)** SLM is continually subjected to improvement needs. Reactive improvements may be carried out to fix an activity or a product that is underperforming locally. Proactive improvements are activities carried out to prevent failures that may put the

process at risk. Part 5 (comprising Chapter 20) provides you with frameworks to assist with ensuring that SLM is always on the right path and is continually improving the service environment.

1.3.2 Publication language

I have written this guide in a straightforward and personal style, attempting to 'talk' to the practitioner and explain the matter at hand. I aim to act as a mentor to the practitioner and guide them through each activity, acknowledging the fact that many practitioners are international, multicultural professionals whose first language is not necessarily English.

The publication will refer to 'you' as the reader in many roles. Sometimes I will refer to 'you' as a service level manager, sometimes as project manager and sometimes as an IT service management (ITSM) practitioner. The term used in a particular instance has low significance and I recommend you not to be tied to the role referred to but rather to the method being presented.

There are many terms and definitions that are used differently across organizations, and it is not within the scope of this publication to challenge the correct usage of such terms and definitions. For example, the service provider in some organizations is the IT department or the IT operations or supplier. Similarly, customers may be broken down by functions, departments or business units; but they are still the receivers of the services and are referred to mostly as 'customers'.

In some instances an effort has been made to distinguish clearly between different meanings of terms and definitions where confusion may arise if an inappropriate connotation is likely. For example, the definitions of 'customer' and 'user' are occasionally confused. The customer represents a group of users (or end users), signs agreements and pays for the services. The user consumes and merely uses the service on a day-to-day basis.

1.3.3 Reference guide

Secrets of Service Level Management covers all aspects of SLM and positions the activities in a logical order for implementation. It is recommended to initiate the implementation with strategic activities that will lead to effective design work and so on. In an ideal world the reader will read the entire publication from start to finish in sequential order. However, this publication dedicates chapters and sections to address process-essential aspects. This allows you to go directly to the chapter that addresses the issue you are looking to learn about. For example, if you are interested in establishing an SLA according to best practice, it is not necessary to read from the beginning until you reach Chapter 8. You are encouraged to use the table of contents or the index to search for topics of interest.

1.3.4 Secrets of the trade

I wrote *Secrets of Service Level Management* with the help of SLM practitioners, solution architects and consultants who dedicated time, outside their daily work, to document the actual practices of implementation of the SLM process. In this publication you will find 'secrets of the trade' that allow me to share the personal experiences and perspective of these practitioners on the topic in hand. 'Secrets of the trade' show an insight into the world of those experts, providing you with tips regarding the practicality of implementing SLM, and on tackling and overcoming unforeseen challenges.

Secrets of the trade

As a subject-matter expert, I have been engaged by many organizations to oversee SLM implementation projects. The conclusion that I have drawn from the many projects I have worked on is that every organization introduces its own definitions and expectations of SLM. My early aspirations to standardize the concepts of SLM across organizations have proven to be futile. As I matured through education and experience, I learned to appreciate this fact and to see the positive in it. Ultimately, organizations develop their own unique culture and seek their own unique targets.

Being aware of this has led to a change in my strategy as a consultant. Rather than attempting to convert my customer's view of SLM, I began to adjust existing procedures towards the vision of the organization.

1.4 IMPLEMENTING SERVICE LEVEL MANAGEMENT

My mother is a great cook. My friends used to enjoy many dinners at my house. My friends' mothers used to ask my mother for recipes that ended up not tasting the same. When my mother was asked about it, she always delivered the same clichéd statement, 'Love is the secret ingredient'.

Effective SLM is much more than a comprehensive SLA, colourful reports and elegantly formatted documents. All those instruments are simply enablers of the process objective, which is to provide channels of communication between the service provider and the customer and to increase customer satisfaction. The process instruments, which are essential, will not lead to a successful process without the secret ingredient – relationship.

If you are a practitioner or service level manager preparing for process implementation, always keep in mind the overall goal of the process: positive customer perception of service provision. The processes and functions that you design must be the basis of this approach.

Prior to the initiation of the implementation, you should consider the following guidelines:

- **Communication** SLM must align its activities with the strategy of the company. Therefore you must establish a channel of continual communication with senior management, utilizing business relationship management, service review and service relationship management. You must ensure that a process is in place for information to flow both ways, from senior management to SLM and vice versa.
- **Service lifecycle** This publication offers you best-practice implementation methods based on the ITIL service lifecycle: strategy, design, transition, operation and continual service improvement. It is tempting to skip activities that are not familiar to you – assessment, envisioning, CSFs, KPIs etc. – and start directly with common activities (SLA structure, service review). However, the activities documented here are based on experience that is both practical and beneficial. Each chapter starts with a theoretical discussion explaining the added value the chapter is providing. You are recommended to read through the introductions and overviews, and determine whether the

activity suits your organization and whether it will generate the desired results before deciding to omit it.

- **Budget** The scope of implementation is inevitably constrained by the budget allocated for the project. It is realized that some activities cannot be performed due to lack of funding. For example, assessment and envisioning requires the outsourcing of external consulting groups and the advanced SLA compliance report entails the procurement of expensive software. Your challenge is to work around your budget and define those activities that are short-term goals to start working on, and those that are considered expensive and to be aimed for as long-term achievements.
- **SLM financials** Advanced service management practice demands that service provision should be tied to sound cost management. The chargeback system and service level penalties are direct results of this approach. In Chapter 10, you will find detailed and comprehensive guidance on how to establish those financial practices that are required by SLM. You should keep in mind that those activities do not exist in a void: your organization must provide supporting processes and functions to enable costs for services to be recovered or to penalize service providers for breaching agreed service level targets. We witness many service level managers who have battled unsuccessfully against organizational culture and senior management. In this case, and in any case that causes resistance, prepare yourself for the long ride, which will include the development of a business case, stakeholder management, internal politics and plenty of patience.

It is hoped that this publication will help you appreciate SLM as a process that, beyond tracking service levels, provides a platform of communication and networking, influences customer perception, and is a key contributor to the overall health of the service management environment. Good luck in your forthcoming design and implementation activities, and let's get to work.

PART 1
Service strategy

Introduction to process strategy

2

2 Introduction to process strategy

This publication guides the user through the implementation of the service level management (SLM) process. Most chapters concentrate on a deliverable or an activity that will eventually create the design and deployment of the process. This chapter is different. It sets the stage and proposes basic principles for those of you who either own an existing SLM process or who are assigned to lead the implementation of the process.

The chapter takes more of a philosophical role than a practical one in order to set the stage for the upcoming activities that implement the SLM process.

2.1 SERVICE LEVEL MANAGEMENT STRATEGY – OVERVIEW

This publication is divided into five main parts which follow the ITIL lifecycle. The first part of the service lifecycle (Part 1) relates to service strategy and contains three chapters (Chapters 2–4). The three chapters are organized as stages, opening with basic concepts and continuing with envisioning the process, which can then enable a maturity assessment for SLM:

■ **Process strategy** This chapter takes us through the journey of establishing the strategy of the organization's SLM process (see Figure 2.1). It discusses the issues and challenges that need to

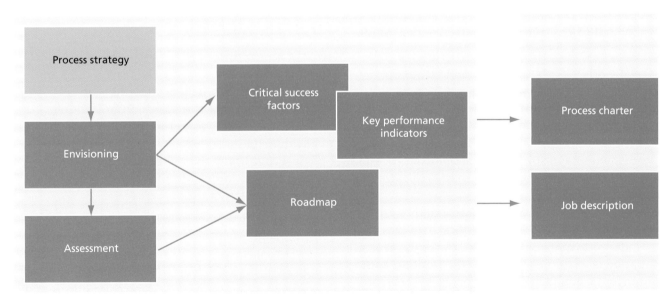

Figure 2.1 SLM strategy activities – process strategy

be considered, and this sets the stage for the subsequent activities that will execute the service strategy phase.

- **Process envisioning** Chapter 3 provides guidance on aligning the SLM process with the business, to ensure SLM delivers the organization's desired results. The chapter develops critical success factors (CSFs) and key performance indicators (KPIs), and it concludes with a sample process charter and job description for the service level manager.

- **Maturity assessment** Chapter 4 helps evaluate current process maturity compared with best practice. Although the envisioning exercise produced a roadmap, the suggested maturity assessment produces a more practical and tangible roadmap that will be used throughout the implementation of the process.

Both the maturity assessment and the process envisioning are inputs to the process charter, service level manager job description and roadmap. If all the steps are executed correctly, these deliverables will provide an excellent source for the next stage of the lifecycle, namely service design.

Like any other process or function in IT service management (ITSM), SLM must establish its strategy. Ideally, the process owner is assigned in the early stages, allowing the owner to participate in the critical formative activities such as establishing process vision and strategy, developing a process charter and then continuing with the development of process design documentation. However, in many cases an owner is already assigned to an existing process, where those critical activities are considered to be completed. The challenge in this situation is to step back, review the position and improve the capabilities of the process. Therefore,

regardless of whether this is a new process or an existing one, our starting point continues to be strategy development.

The primary goal of any strategy activity is to provide guidance and give direction. The deliverables of SLM strategy include ITIL/SLM maturity assessment, envisioning the process, creating a process roadmap and establishing CSFs, all of which are detailed in the next two chapters. These deliverables will provide us with the guidance and direction needed to begin the process lifecycle.

This chapter addresses different matters to consider when it comes to defining the strategy of SLM, ITSM structure, organizational structure, and customer–provider relationship types. Let's begin by reviewing the general approach to SLM strategy and how to implement it.

2.2 POSITIONING SERVICE LEVEL MANAGEMENT IN THE ORGANIZATION

If SLM is new to your IT organization, it is important to decide where these new roles and responsibilities will be placed within the organizational structure. Your organization's executive IT management must not only select an individual (or individuals) who will manage the process, but that person must decide where the process is positioned within the overall organization structure.

The IT executive management may need to carry out some restructuring in order to accommodate the SLM role. If this is the first step towards a higher ITIL maturity level, this could mean a major reorganization is required. Some chief information officers (CIOs) fully embrace the ITIL service lifecycle and organize IT into service strategy, service design, and service transition and service operations groups. Others are organized by the lines of business and the major classes of IT services. Still others are organized by technologies. All of these organizational options are viable as long as IT is well structured to meet the needs of the business.

Figure 2.2 is an example of IT organization within an enterprise that is organized in accordance with the ITIL service lifecycle. The CIO made a strategic decision to fully embrace ITIL and ensured his organization mirrored the service lifecycle. In this

scenario there was a single service level manager, indicated by the darker box, who had a staff of two people to assist with the execution of the process on a daily basis.

There are other IT organizations with a similar structure but with multiple service level managers assigned to specific IT service portfolios which are large enough to warrant their own service level manager.

Figure 2.3 was taken from an IT organization that was organized around IT service portfolios instead of the five stages of the ITIL service lifecycle. The business it serviced happened to be part of the

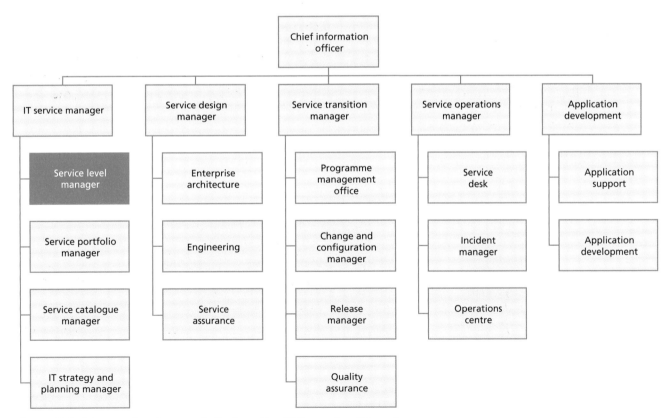

Figure 2.2 IT organization modelled on the ITIL service lifecycle

healthcare industry. The CIO had a group of direct reports, most of whom mapped directly to the service portfolio. The vice presidents of each portfolio, shown as shaded blocks, were appointed as service level managers for their portfolios of IT services. Although Figure 2.3 breaks down SLM into four areas, and in fact there is an acting service level manager per area, the organization utilized one of them to lead the SLM process to promote consistency and standardization. In this example, the service level manager for the financial services was acting as the global service level manager.

No matter what the size of the IT organization, it is critical to ensure the role of service level manager is well positioned for success within the IT organization and that the incumbent has the staff needed to execute the process. Furthermore, these service level managers need to have counterparts on the business side of the organization. In order to be successful, a service owner or advocate from the lines of business must be appointed on the customer side and given responsibility for interacting with the service level managers.

For more about the roles and responsibilities within SLM, refer to Chapter 6 on SLM functions and processes.

2.3 ITSM GOVERNANCE AND THE SERVICE LEVEL MANAGEMENT DILEMMA

One of the main challenges during the strategy phase is to balance the SLM influence or authority in the ITSM environment. On the one hand, limiting the process to developing and reviewing service level agreement (SLA) reports will not suffice, but on the other hand we need to be careful not to over-extend the authority of SLM.

SLM has the tools to monitor performance and has the advantage over other ITIL processes in that it is integrated with other ITSM processes and functions. Given this scope, at times it is suggested that SLM should govern the entire ITSM process.

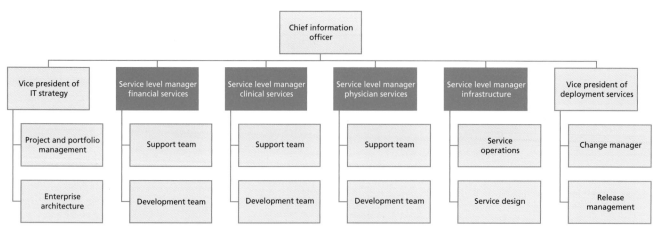

Figure 2.3 IT organization modelled on the IT service portfolio

Is that the right path to take? Should we consider SLM to be the umbrella process that coordinates and manages the other processes?

To answer these questions, let's examine the objective of SLM. The primary objective of SLM is to ensure that an agreed level of service is provided to the customer. SLM focuses on the needs of the customer and interfaces with the customer periodically to review the performance of services and ensure improvements for those services which are lacking. The customer is interested in the result of service performance and is less interested in how its activities are undertaken. For example, configuration audits are performed to ensure that no discrepancies exist between what is recorded in the configuration management database (CMDB) and the actual environment. Should SLM follow up with configuration management and monitor the execution of the audits? The answer is no: SLM is only responsible for the performance of services that were agreed upon with the customer.

However, not all situations are as simple. Consider the following scenario. The average speed to answer (ASA) is a measurement of the service desk function that monitors time elapsed to answer all calls in a given period. Is SLM responsible for tracking the performance of the ASA measurement? If we go back to the guiding principle that SLM is responsible for service levels agreed to by the customer, it will provide us with the answer: if ASA is in the SLA, then yes; but if it is not a service that was negotiated and agreed upon with the customer, it is out of the scope of SLM.

No matter what the assessment results indicate or what the CSFs are, we must first define the very basic objective of the process, which is to ensure the provision of services according to the agreement that has been signed with the customer.

Eliminating SLM as the process that controls and monitors ITIL processes and functions raises the obvious question: who in fact undertakes such control and monitoring? In this connection there are three matters to be addressed that are seemingly not covered by any of the formal ITIL processes:

- Monitoring the performance of ITIL processes and functions
- Coordinating between ITIL processes and functions
- Aligning ITIL strategy with the business strategy.

Two other aspects of ITSM governance also need to be considered, as set out next: the possible existence of a service management office, and IT governance.

2.3.1 Service management office

Although not defined in ITIL publications, many organizations that have adopted ITIL have created a service management office. Named differently in different organizations, this function acts as the link between the business and ITSM.

Secrets of the trade

The service management office takes many forms and labels, including IT management programme, project management office (PMO) and more. This function can be forced down by the CIO or developed naturally by IT operations. Organizations that have embraced systems of best practice such as ITIL, PRINCE2, PMBOK and COBIT have quickly realized that coordination between functions needs to be formalized to achieve maximum process efficiency.

The service management office optimizes the integration points between the processes and functions, thus assisting the individual processes to view the environment beyond their specific niche. In addition, allocating resources to monitor and coordinate processes allows the process owner to focus on completing operational activities.

2.3.2 IT governance

All organizations perform some form of IT governance when they use IT to support their businesses. This type of practice can fulfil the activities discussed in this section.

Control OBjectives for Information and related Technology (COBIT), which is a set of best practices for IT and IT governance, states that for ITIL to be successful in an organization, management should put an internal control system or framework in place. This system contributes by:

- Making a link to the business requirements
- Organizing IT activities into a generally accepted process model
- Identifying the major IT resources to be leveraged
- Defining the management control objectives to be considered.

Traditionalists strongly believe that IT governance is better when focused more on control and less on execution and should remain on a strategy level as a decision maker, measuring the performance of ITSM only from a business point of view. Less conservative thought extends the scope of IT governance to monitor the efficiency of ITSM, not only by decision-making, but also by ensuring activities are done correctly and efficiently.

To conclude, every organization must establish a function that will align the objective of IT service management with the business objective. This governing function will monitor the performance of ITSM and coordinate its functions and processes. This function should free up resources for the process owners to complete tasks at hand. Thus, the incident manager can ensure quick resolutions of incidents and the service level manager can focus on achieving high customer satisfaction.

2.4 SERVICE LEVEL MANAGEMENT STRATEGY FACTORS

By examining past SLM projects and practices, we learn that the process may have different forms, structures and impacts on the business environment. There are three factors that have an impact on the strategy of SLM:

- Service provider structure
- ITSM environment
- Service level manager.

2.4.1 Service provider structure

ITIL describes three different types of service provider:

- **Type I – Internal service provider** The IT department provides services to internal business units and is funded by overheads. Type I providers have the benefit of tight coupling with their owner-customers, avoiding the costs and risks associated with conducting business with external parties.
- **Type II – Shared services unit** Shared services operate within organizations by providing services to internal clients. They operate on business principles and provide internal services at a cost and quality that is acceptable to clients, when assessed against external alternatives. They are referred to as shared

services because their activities are shared by units across entire organizations, instead of duplicating similar services within each unit.

■ **Type III – External service provider** Customers may pursue sourcing strategies requiring services from external providers. The motivation may be access to knowledge, experience, scale, scope, capabilities and resources that are beyond the reach of the organization.

Each type of service provider will establish an SLM process to ensure that the quality of services delivered is as agreed. However, the strategy of the process differs according to the service provider type.

From a strategy point of view, SLM considers the shared services unit to be essentially the same as an external service provider. Shared services units and external service providers share common elements such as market-based pricing, competition, legally binding contracts, and the fact that both are subjected to comparison with other service providers.

Although the extent of service provision type can differ from company to company, SLM defines its strategy based on two organizational structures (see Figure 2.4):

■ **Enterprise** The IT department is an internal function that provides services to other internal functions.

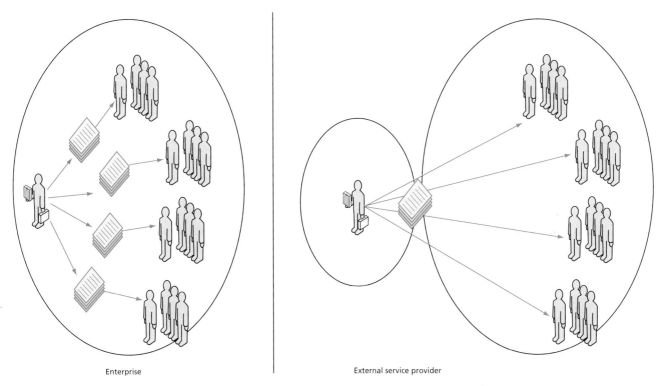

Enterprise

External service provider

Figure 2.4 Service provision: enterprise versus outsourcing engagement

- **Outsourcing engagement** A company chooses to outsource IT services to an external service provider.

In the case of an enterprise, SLM regards the internal functions as customers: human resources, accounting, marketing, sales and so on. This is very different from the outsourcing engagement, where the customers are external to the organization.

While most aspects of SLM apply equally to all types of service providers – the requirements of the customers are collected, an SLA is signed and tracked, and over time a service improvement plan (SIP) is established to ensure that gaps in the service provision are resolved – there are still many variations we must consider. In the outsourcing engagement there is much at stake if services are not provided according to the SLA. For example, penalties can be executed, bonuses will not be paid, contracts might not be extended and, in the worst-case scenario, engagements might be terminated.

In an enterprise, SLM must ensure that the internal business units are satisfied with the level of services. SLAs will be signed with the customers, and operational level agreements (OLAs) and underpinning contracts (UCs) will be signed with internal and external providers. In a more mature environment, chargebacks are carried out to recover the cost of service provision.

2.4.2 ITSM and service level management

There has been a shift in the SLM approach. Some organizations allocate a broader role for SLM in the IT service management environment, with SLM acting as the superior governor and coordinator of other service management processes and functions. Other organizations treat SLM as a process that maintains the SLA and reports on its

results. ITIL SLM is very clear on the goal of the process, which is to ensure that an agreed level of IT service is provided for all current IT services, and that future services are delivered to agreed achievable targets.

When IT service management was implemented in organizations, the need to interface with the customers, obtain their service requirements and discuss service management matters was realized. As ITSM grew and ITIL V2 was introduced, SLM became very effective in relation to the coordination between customers and service providers, and governing their services naturally transitioned into doing the same between services, processes and functions.

Definitions aside, in reality the authority of SLM is determined by each organization and its politics. Many organizations that adopted ITIL still have SLM as the coordinator and integrator of their ITSM environment. The reason for this is simple: such organizations position SLM within service strategy, when it should be positioned within service design.

When you start developing the process strategy, you will need to define the relationships with other ITSM processes. The ITIL lifecycle approach helps with this exercise. If you previously defined the relationships for each process and function, you can now define the relationship with the five phases of the lifecycle:

- **Service strategy** SLM is one of the main links between service strategy and service design. The service strategy function passes decisions regarding services via the service portfolio and, together with the service catalogue manager, details the services going into the service catalogue and SLA.

In reality, senior managers in charge of the service strategy process are in constant communication with SLM, particularly the service relationship management part of the process. In the example of an outsourcing engagement, the account management will continually enquire about customer satisfaction and service review meeting results, all under the authority of SLM.

■ **Service design** There is a direct correlation between the maturity of the ITSM environment and the bond between processes within service design. Effective coordination between service catalogue management, financial management and SLM will produce high-quality outputs of service design. The catalogue and the cost model are dependent on inputs from SLM, and the disregarding of SLM needs will leave gaps in both.

Nonetheless, the SLA is completely dependent on the outputs of service design. Organizations that produce service packages are ones in which SLM thrives.

■ **Service transition** Best practice advises the involvement of SLM in the service transition activities, but in practice unfortunately we don't do it. For example, change management suggests having the service level manager take part in change advisory board (CAB) meetings and, in some matters, the service level manager should even be involved in deployment plans.

The list of service transition activities in which SLM should be involved is not written in stone. However, a mature ITIL environment should include SLM in certain subsequent service transition activities:
● Defining/modifying change policy
● Prioritizing a forward change schedule

● Being present at CAB meetings for relevant matters
● Post-implementation review.

■ **Service operation** The objective of service operations is to provide services according to the level agreed with the customer. This means that the relationships between all processes and functions within service operations must remain tight and consistent. When a service desk operator logs an incident, the service level target should be communicated to the end user. For example, if a printer is down, the operator might tell the end user that the incident at hand is set to Priority 3 and ask the end user to allow six hours for restoring the service, as documented in the relevant SLA. When a decision is being made whether to initiate the problem management process, one of the primary considerations is the service level for responding and for restoring the service.

■ **Continual service improvement (CSI)** ITIL considers SLM to be a crucial part of CSI, along with the seven-step process, reporting and measuring. While CSI addresses the overall health of the ITSM environment, along with services and their components, SLM provides important inputs to CSI, including the CSI register and customer satisfaction results.

2.4.3 The unique skills of the service level manager

The service level manager is responsible for the SLM function and the process activities under its authority. They are responsible for implementing, maintaining and continually improving the process.

The service level manager is also responsible for the development of appropriate documentation, including an SLM charter and the service structure document, which defines the service providers, the services and the customers. They assist with the development of the service catalogue and cost modelling, which are both inputs to the SLA. The service level manager is the sole owner of the SLAs and is responsible for their lifecycles. They are also the owner of the SIP, and communicate its status between the customer and operations. The service level manager is responsible for the continual improvement of SLM processes and functions. However, they must possess and acquire other 'soft skills' to be successful in their mission.

A service level manager is required to have strong interpersonal skills and be respected by customers and service providers. They must have the authority as well as the ability to negotiate a balanced understanding and commitment between customer and service provider.

The service level manager communicates with the service provider and the customer and must adopt the role of a diplomat and ambassador. They strike a balance between customer requirements and the provider's service delivery capabilities.

Throughout the lifecycle of the process, there are many touch points requiring the service level manager to develop these relationships. Some of the areas and activities that need particular awareness are as follows:

- **Documentation** When creating an SLM charter, you will work with senior management to scope the process. This is a great opportunity to develop the relationship with senior managers by helping them to understand the key features of the process and how it can benefit them.
- **Contracting** If you are lucky, you will be initiated early enough to take part in the contracting phase. Here, you will be introduced to the accounts team and, most importantly, the accounts manager. The SLA negotiations and future changes will go more smoothly if your relationship with the accounts manager is positive.

- **Service level requirements (SLRs)** Clearly defined and agreed SLRs will improve your position if it comes to further negotiation around pricing. By working openly with the customer, you can in effect agree on your pricing structure together. It is also the perfect opportunity to work with your customer and understand what their business need truly is.
- **Service catalogue and cost model** The service catalogue manager should be your best friend. Also, don't forget to identify the financial manager, who will provide you with the most essential information to support the process.
- **Negotiations** Negotiating the SLA is a substantial part of the process, which will provide the opportunity to exercise your interpersonal skills. The service level manager should be prepared to drive the proactive maintenance of an SLA, also known as SLA audits, at regular intervals.
- **Reporting** Submitting reporting requirements for SLA and metric reports and communicating back to the reporting function in order to demonstrate the value of the reports for both the customer and service provider are valuable activities.
- **Service review meetings** The service review meetings are the primary execution of the communication plan between the service level manager and the customer.

■ **Service improvement plan** Including your customer in a formal SIP process is critical to its success. Sharing the agreed plans is a positive and sensible strategy that ensures customer buy-in and support.

To summarize, the personality of the service level manager is crucial for the ITSM environment. Some service level managers will follow the ITIL process as suggested but still find that they have limited influence. One of the objectives of this publication is to encourage the manager to take a more proactive role in their ITSM environment by keeping the best interests of the customer in sight, and at the same time ensuring that the interests of the business are maintained, by promoting communication, creating data transparency, and presenting improvements in a timely and professional manner.

2.5 INITIATING SERVICE LEVEL MANAGEMENT

There is a growing concern regarding the initiation of the process of SLM and transitioning it into the live environment, specifically in relation to outsourcing engagements. In many engagements, practitioners are required to assist with this issue and provide concrete recommendations on how to proceed.

To better understand this situation, let's describe the lifecycle of an outsourcing procurement process. As shown in Figure 2.5, the bidding process starts with the request for proposal (RFP), followed by the development of the statement of work, proposal evaluation service provider selection, and then contract signature. After the commencement date is determined for the provision of the service, the engagement is on its way.

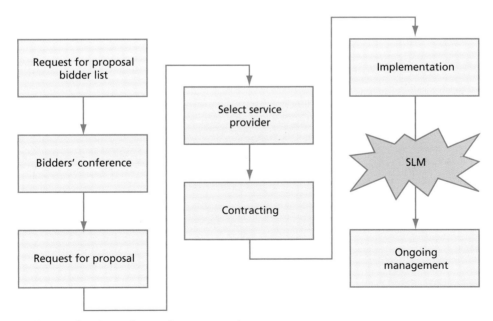

Figure 2.5 Typical introduction of SLM in outsourcing engagement

When should SLM be introduced? When do we allow the service level manager to meet the customer and understand the environment?

Unfortunately, in most cases the service level manager starts working on the day the services commence being provided. The services are already predefined by the engagement without the participation of the service level manager.

This is a common problem that needs to be addressed in outsourcing deals. This scenario forces the service level manager to manage an SLA and associated metrics that the service level manager did not work to define; instead, they were defined solely by the business. The contract, which details many of the service aspects, was completed by the contract team or by the accounts team, but the service level manager was not involved. This is far from an ideal situation for any service level manager.

The following are the primary problems created by late initiation of SLM:

- The SLA structure is not according to best practice.
- SLA metrics are not based on service management facts.
- Reporting requirements are not aligned with ITSM best practice or the SLA. The complete picture needs to be taken into account.
- Process definitions are not tailored to the specific engagement. In many contracts, definitions of SLM activities are copied from a previous contract. The SLM process must be designed and customized to the particular needs of the customer and the engagement.

The problem cannot be addressed by SLM alone. There is a need to review the procurement process. The service level manager should be introduced immediately after the first stages of the sale cycle;

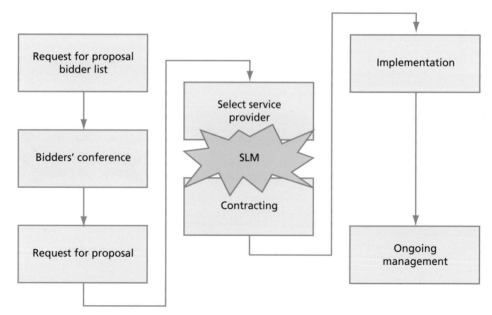

Figure 2.6 Ideal time to introduce SLM in outsourcing engagement

they must be involved in the contract and must own the SLA. The service level manager will build it with the vision of sub-processes, reporting, SLA reports and other systems in place.

Figure 2.6 shows the ideal time to introduce SLM in an outsourcing procurement process.

2.6 SUMMARY

This chapter's objective was to smooth the transition into the practicality of SLM. The chapter has ideally helped you to realize that different organizational structures and types of service provision have an impact on the strategy of the process.

Before executing the strategic activities that are detailed later in this publication, the basic elements of the organization and how they impact on the process must first be understood.

Envisioning value creation

3 Envisioning value creation

Service strategy is a phase in the service management lifecycle for providing direction and guidance to the organization. Process owners are required to make their processes uniform and transparent to facilitate acceptance, understanding and adoption within the organization. Envisioning reveals the essential strategic elements of a process and lays the foundation for the communication and implementation of the process within the broader business environment.

Practitioners will benefit from reading this chapter mainly because it introduces an effective methodology (with associated tools) that will assist in the development of a strategy for service level management (SLM) and the subsequent customization of the SLM process for specific organization needs. A practical workshop approach to the envisioning methodology is outlined.

The chapter also provides an overview of the process charter – the main output from the envisioning exercise that encapsulates the SLM process strategy. The charter defines, among other things, the scope of SLM, critical success factors (CSFs), key performance indicators (KPIs), a formal job description for SLM staff, and a roadmap for process implementation (see Figure 3.1).

3.1 ENVISIONING SERVICE LEVEL MANAGEMENT

SLM must work towards the success of the company. The question we must ask ourselves is: 'How do we define an SLM process within the overall strategic framework that promotes and supports the company's objectives?'

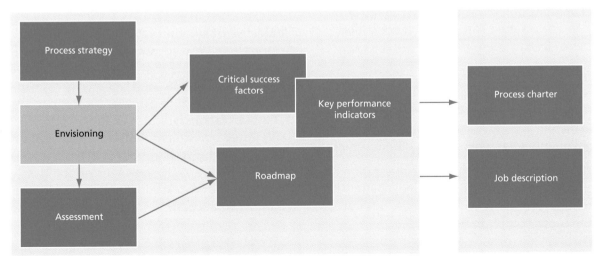

Figure 3.1 SLM strategy activities – envisioning

The envisioning approach outlined in this chapter will assist in aligning the SLM process within the business to ensure SLM delivers the desired results. The goal is to establish a 'steering wheel' through the process lifecycle in the form of a process charter and accompanying roadmap for implementation. The envisioning methodology is based on the book *Capability Cases: A Solution Envisioning Approach* by Irene Polikoff, Robert Coyne and Ralph Hodgson (2006).

The envisioning process has three modules: business value exploration, solution value exploration, and planning and closeout.

3.1.1 Business value exploration

Business value exploration (BVE) is aimed at exploring in detail the challenges of SLM. The activities typically involve interviews, collecting qualitative and quantitative data, technical analysis and financial assessments. BVE refines the specific process and builds a clearer picture of the challenges. It leads to a prioritization of the challenges and enables preliminary discussions about solutions that may help drive change and unlock business value. The following are critical activities of BVE:

■ Refining process objectives
■ Prioritizing challenges
■ Identifying gaps and providing the setting for change
■ Highlighting areas where change is not required.

Note that the BVE may result in the realization that an identified activity may be extremely beneficial and create a significant business value, but not have the support tools to be deployed.

3.1.2 Solution value exploration

The information gathered at the BVE stage enables us to determine the best way forward. Solution value exploration features a detailed comparison of industry best practice for SLM against the current state of the process. It identifies the changes required to realize new or different approaches, and it gives us the opportunity to edit, characterize and validate new approaches and concepts.

Solution value exploration will help you determine what changes may be necessary to achieve best practice in your own process. We characterize the process in conjunction with the overall strategy framework, clearly identifying gaps between the vision of the organization and the potential value that the SLM process brings. In addition, this stage will enable the development of CSFs and KPIs to determine how SLM would need to change in terms of people, processes and technology in order to realize the full potential value of the process.

Secrets of the trade

As explained in section 3.1.2, the primary objective of solution value exploration is to compare the current state of the process with best practice. Note that IT service management (ITSM) recommends an ITIL maturity assessment as the instrument to achieve this comparison. This publication dedicates Chapter 4 primarily to a suggested assessment method. This might inspire you to use the assessment as part of the solution value exploration. However, envisioning is positioned as a workshop that is limited in time and number to the activities that can be accomplished. It is up to you – practitioner, consultant or service level manager – to choose the instrument that will uncover the gaps in the process.

3.1.3 Planning and closeout

This final module creates a process charter outlining the high-level and strategic importance of SLM within the organization. This includes a plan of action, showing the phased realization of the solution (i.e. the untapped potential) to unlocking value in your process. The result is a list of reviewed CSFs and a roadmap. Planning and closeout enable you to gain the support and commitment for change from your stakeholders, and they also enable your organization to start designing and implementing the process according to the overall strategy of the organization.

3.2 THREE-DAY ENVISIONING WORKSHOP

Typical organizational constraints, such as time and cost, often form an obstacle to carrying out the envisioning exercise. To reduce the odds of neglecting this important activity, you are recommended to conduct a three-day workshop rather than initiate a project. Our goal is to create a high-level recommendation for the SLM process that will have a significant impact on the organization. Note that a successful envisioning workshop requires experienced personnel who possess creative and innovative thinking.

3.2.1 Workshop example

3.2.1.1 Pre-workshop planning
- Review mission statement, existing systems, goals, organization culture and beliefs.
- Undertake key stakeholder interviews and surveys.
- Determine workshop participants, schedules and logistics.

3.2.1.2 Day 1 – Business value exploration
- **Establish organizational business goals** Understand the high-level objectives, the business drivers, how IT service management enables the business and how SLM operates within that environment.
- **Develop CSFs** Document what defines a successful SLM process in the organization.
- **Explore possibilities** List all the potential best practices in SLM, including ITIL, documented field experience, advanced monitoring and reporting tools.
- **Possibilities selection** From the best practices (see previous bullet point) select the appropriate possibilities that are to be explored. Note that the intention is not to implement the possibilities as-is, but rather to stimulate conversation and thought-sharing.

3.2.1.3 Day 2 – Solution value exploration
- **Explore possibilities** Analyse and evaluate each possibility, utilizing techniques such as return on investment (ROI) and value on investment (VOI).
- **Explore possibility requirements** Define what it will take to implement a possibility (cost, time, culture change, organization change).
- **Review and readout** Review findings with stakeholders to ensure that you are on the right path.

3.2.1.4 Day 3 – Planning for action and closeout
- **Develop roadmap** The roadmap is one of the primary deliverables of the envisioning workshop.
- **Workshop closeout action planning and schedule** Compile your data, release resources and hand over the envisioning package.

3.2.1.5 Post-workshop final deliverables

- **Envisioning final presentation** The presentation consists of workshop objective, organizational goals and drivers, SLM process goal, current assessment, findings, recommended actions, roadmap and next steps.
- **Process charter** Capture the results of the envisioning activities in the SLM process charter (as outlined below).

3.3 PROCESS CHARTER

If we have learned anything from managing projects and implementing processes, it is not to underestimate the value of the process charter. Let me say it as bluntly as possible: the implementation of the process will not be successful without a charter. The charter:

- Provides important information regarding the process
- Details the scope of the process and, more importantly, what is out of scope
- Presents the authority of the process owner and the main objectives of the process.

A well-defined charter will ensure the success of the next phase, service design. The charter lays the foundation for the process and is only changed under extreme conditions. It defines the primary goals of the SLM process, identifies in- and out-of-scope activities, and describes the roles and responsibilities of SLM staff and the CSFs of the process.

3.3.1 Typical contents

The following is a typical process charter table of contents.

3.3.1.1 Introduction

This section will set the stage for the audience by defining the next elements:

- **Service environment** High-level explanation of who the customers are, who the service providers are and what types of services are being provided
- **Service level management** As an ITSM best practice, what is the definition of the process and its goals
- **Objectives and audience** What we expect from this document and its benefits.

3.3.1.2 Process objectives

The process objectives are high-level goals that were developed as part of the CSFs. The process objectives defined here are refined and customized for this specific organization. This section will typically contain primary and secondary objectives. The following are the basic objectives of SLM:

- Define, document, agree, monitor, measure, report and review the level of IT services provided.
- Facilitate and improve the relationship and communication with the business and customers.
- Ensure that specific and measurable targets are developed for all IT services.
- Monitor and improve customer satisfaction with the quality of service delivered.
- Ensure that IT and the customers have a clear and unambiguous expectation of the level of service that will be delivered.
- Ensure that proactive measures to improve the levels of service delivered are implemented wherever it is cost-justifiable to do so.

3.3.1.3 CSFs and KPIs

The development of CSFs and KPIs is documented within the process charter. Some organizations define a standalone tool or document to manage the CSFs and KPIs, but it is recommended that for an individual process this can be done in the process charter.

Examples of CSFs and KPIs for service level management can be found in ITIL reference publications and the COBIT standard.

3.3.1.4 Process in scope and out of scope

The scope defines the areas of responsibility of SLM and defines many of the high-level activities. The following is a basic list of items in scope for SLM:

- Negotiation and agreement of the current requirements and targets by the owner of the service level agreement (SLA)
- Development and management of appropriate operational level agreements to ensure that targets are aligned with SLA targets
- Review of all underpinning supplier contracts and agreements with supplier management to ensure alignment with SLA targets
- Proactive prevention of service failures, reduction of service risks and improvement in the quality of service
- Reporting and management of all IT services.

The out-of-scope activities for the process are items that the organization needs to realize and that are not the responsibility of SLM. For example, SLM does not provide the services; rather, it ensures that the correct levels of service are being provided.

3.3.1.5 Process benefits

Here is our chance to show the business and other functions of ITSM how the organization can benefit from a well-designed SLM process. In this section we will illustrate the fact that SLM is not only a reporting function that monitors metrics. This list should be customized to the specific needs of the organization and should be written to satisfy the organization's objectives.

3.3.1.6 Process products

Some organizations call these outputs 'process deliverables' rather than 'process products'. Either way, they are the tangible outputs from the process. There are two types

- **Direct** Products under the responsibility of SLM (e.g. SLA, operational level agreement (OLA) and performance reports)
- **Indirect** Products with which SLM assists (e.g. service catalogue).

3.3.1.7 Communication plan

The communication plan will take the form of a table listing categories of stakeholder and the communication type. Keep in mind that this is not a project plan or a communication plan where you name individual stakeholders and you detail how you are planning to communicate with them; this takes a much higher-level approach.

3.3.1.8 Roles and responsibilities

In this section we will identify the roles that are required in order to undertake the process activities. They will be detailed in Chapter 6, but for the sake of the process charter we will provide a high-level definition for the service level manager and the three sub-processes of SLM:

■ Operations
■ Service reporting
■ Service relationship management.

Under each role, you should list two to five high-level responsibilities that will allow the audience to understand the position within the organization. The detail of the job description is different from one organization to another, and although ITIL suggests a standard definition for the service level manager, it does not mean that every service level manager adheres to the same policies and procedures – for the simple reason that every organizational goal is different.

3.3.1.9 Process cost estimate (operational versus capital)

When senior managers read a process charter, this is often the first chapter they read. They want to know: 'How much is this going to cost me?' Keep the estimate as simple and high-level as possible, and use the four Ps of service design to come up with realistic figures:

■ People – the SLM staff
■ Products – SLA reporting solution, continual service improvement (CSI) register
■ Processes – process consulting, time and effort to complete documentation

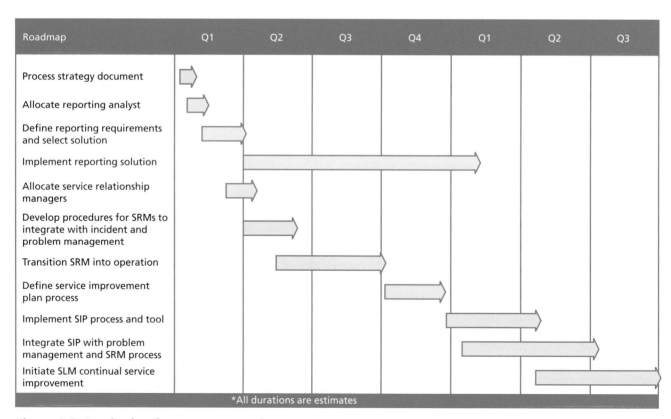

Figure 3.2 Service level assessment roadmap

- Partners – what vendors and service suppliers are you planning to outsource?

3.3.1.10 Process roadmap

The roadmap shown in Figure 3.2 is one of the most important deliverables of the envisioning exercise. It documents high-level action items and estimates the time it will take to complete them. The roadmap is a very useful tool when communicating with senior managers who prefer to visualize the recommendation rather than read a very detailed document.

3.3.1.11 Process risks

Do not confuse the process charter risks with risk management or the risk register. As you will remember, the charter is different from the other design documents. It is a high-level document and the 'bill of rights', so it is not intended to be changed frequently. For the audience this is still an educational tool and the process risk section continues to clarify different aspects of the process.

3.4 SUMMARY

They say that everything starts with a good plan. This chapter illustrates that even before planning you should establish your vision. A vision is defined as a description of an ideal future state of a matter; in our case it's the vision of an SLM process. As a result of this chapter, you should be able to form your vision, and trigger and accelerate your ability to achieve goals and resolutions that are within the scope of the SLM process.

SLM process
assessment based on
capability maturity

4

4 SLM process assessment based on capability maturity

We discover that the strategy for the service level management (SLM) process relies on the overall goals of the organization, and also on the governing principles that are established through activities such as envisioning workshops and critical success factor (CSF) development. In this chapter we take a step further by analysing our current state, defining precisely 'how much' and 'how well' we perform SLM activities compared with ITIL best practice.

This assessment (see Figure 4.1) will eventually link the strategic activities to the design activities by producing a roadmap and a list of tangible tasks that will be considered in the design phase.

4.1 SLM PROCESS ASSESSMENT OVERVIEW

The implementation of a formal SLM process can be time-consuming, expensive and sometimes organizationally exhausting. However, if approached correctly – with a baseline, a strategy and a well-formulated plan – it is likely to lead to a successful outcome.

So what do we do first? In the previous chapter we discussed the overall strategy of the process. We learned that there were multiple ways of strategizing the process and its relationship to the IT service management (ITSM) practice. However, your SLM service strategy activity has only just begun.

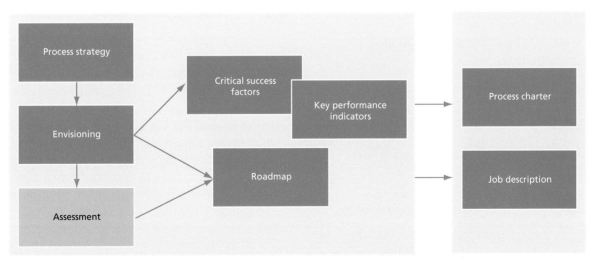

Figure 4.1 SLM strategy activities – assessment

Before any process implementation takes place, a baseline must be set, and our baseline will be the result of an assessment that will analyse the process and the people who interact with it. The assessment includes interviewing and sometimes observing IT staff regarding SLM activities, and collecting evidence, including documents and tools. This information is then compiled and compared with ITIL best practice.

These results will provide you with information enabling you to consider the following questions and make an assessment:

- How well do you perform SLM tasks?
- Does SLM integrate with other processes?
- Does SLM interface correctly with the customer?

Most importantly, the assessment will provide you with the areas that require improvements.

This chapter will introduce Capability Maturity Model Integration (CMMI), the process maturity framework, and will guide you through the steps to execute an effective assessment to complete your SLM strategy.

4.2 ITIL MATURITY ASSESSMENT OVERVIEW

The CMMI methodology was originally used to develop and refine an organization's software development process, but it is now being used more widely. CMMI was developed and promoted by the Software Engineering Institute (SEI) of Carnegie Mellon University. The model describes a five-level evolutionary path of increasingly organized and systematically mature processes.

ITIL Service Design includes a process maturity framework, which is aligned with CMMI, and makes reference to the same five levels of maturity:

- Level 1: Initial
- Level 2: Repeatable
- Level 3: Defined
- Level 4: Managed
- Level 5: Optimizing.

An assessment of the SLM process should cover the following areas:

- Vision and steering
- Process
- People
- Technology
- Culture.

The process maturity framework helps to characterize and understand the organization's current processes, and defines targets for improvement. It is important to understand that process maturity has both breadth (how widely it is applied in the organization) and depth (how complete the process is), which is why each level is assessed in the five dimensions listed above.

4.3 THE ASSESSMENT ACTIVITIES

This section will guide you through some of the activities that you can complete in order to better understand the maturity of your organization's SLM process (see Figure 4.2). The assessment will start with logistics preparation, allowing the lead assessor to plan for the execution of the assessment. The interviews are the primary activity of the assessment that will be documented. The roadmap should be treated as the main output of the assessment; while the documentation presents our current maturity level, the roadmap will tell us what actions are required to improve our process.

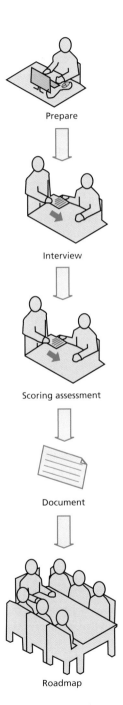

Prepare

Interview

Scoring assessment

Document

Roadmap

Figure 4.2 Assessment activities

4.3.1 Preparing for the process maturity assessment

The process maturity assessment is completed primarily through interviews and discussions with IT staff who are process stakeholders. Since the overall health of ITSM is being evaluated, the maturity assessments are performed against all ITIL processes and functions, rather than a single process. A process must be assessed as part of the entire model.

Before the actual assessment can begin, there are preparatory activities and issues to consider, as follows:

■ **Who executes the assessment?** The exercise can be either a self-assessment or conducted by an external entity. Whoever is assigned to execute the assessment must have a high level of ITIL expertise and an unbiased opinion.

■ **Who should be interviewed?** The short answer to this question is the primary process stakeholders. Keep in mind that you are interested in grasping the overall maturity of the process, and how its activities are being performed, so naturally seek those who carry out the activities. A common misconception is to interview the customer, who will assist in discovering the value perception of the process, which is one of the process's CSFs. Yet the customer can help with only one aspect of the process.

■ **Coordinate meetings** Attempt to complete all interviews in a reasonable time frame – for example, on the same day or over two days. This avoids the interviewee preparing answers by reviewing questions with those who were previously interviewed.

- **Two interviewers and one interviewee** Do not interview more than one person at a time. People tend to measure their answers in front of others, especially in front of their superiors. A one-on-one discussion can create a trusting atmosphere that will encourage honest answers and even generate volunteered information. We typically have two interviewers to ensure spontaneous discussion without the need to pause to take notes.
- **Interview method** The core of the assessment is a list of questions and the collection of answers. We suggest performing the interview as a discussion to expand beyond the questions. The useful information obtained will be compiled in the assessment.

Secrets of the trade

In many organizations with a low ITIL maturity level, you will find it difficult to identify a specific service level manager or IT staff member performing SLM activities, and this may be simply because no one has been assigned the role(s). The first step will be to find those that are the closest in duties to the service level manager, since you will not be able to rely on title. Then you should find out who owns the relationship with the customer, who request changes to services to align their business needs, and so on.

4.3.2 The interview

As part of the assessment, you will meet the stakeholders and ask them a range of questions. Every question should be asked during the interview or explored through general conversation. You are likely to have some mandatory questions that must be answered in a certain way in order to achieve a certain level of maturity. A subset of non-mandatory questions will also need to be answered in a required way to achieve each level of maturity.

4.3.3 Scoring the assessment

The interviewers should complete documentation (e.g. a table) for each interview and reconcile the answers immediately after each interview (especially when there are two interviewers involved). Record how each interviewee answers the questions, and don't forget to document any additional information collected while the interview is in session. Most of the recommendations will come from the discussion that the questions instigate, rather than from the answers themselves.

After all the interviews have been completed, evidence has been collected and observations have been made, the interviewers should review the answers and triangulate the final result for each question and the entire assessment within a master document.

Secrets of the trade

Never underestimate the importance of collecting evidence during the assessment. During one assessment, all of the interviewees stated there was an SLM charter established within the organization. While technically this was true, when the interviewers asked to see the charter and the assessors reviewed it, they found the charter to be poorly written, incomplete and stored in a location where limited access was available. There was a process charter, but it was so ineffective that the organization earned a 'zero' for this question. The assessors can and should overrule the interviewees when appropriate, based on their ITSM expertise and judgement.

When it is time to reconcile the final results, all of the interviewers/assessors should gather in private and discuss the results. For each level of maturity, the group should execute the following procedures:

- Read each question.
- Review the answers provided by the interviewees.
- Review any evidence collected.
- Discuss and triangulate the true answer that the organization deserves for the question.
- Repeat the procedure until all the questions for the level are completed.

Once all of the questions for the level have been reviewed and the final answers are set, it is time for the lead assessor to score the level.

This ITIL process maturity assessment is a compound model, resulting in a maturity level equivalent to the last minimum level reached. In order for an organization to reach a level, it must pass that level as well as all of the levels below it.

4.3.4 Documenting the assessment

Often, assessment results are accompanied by either an executive summary presentation or a full report. The process stakeholders will want to understand their maturity score completely, especially the levels and questions they failed. Documentation should be created for the assessment, describing the results, evidence and recommendations from the assessors, including detailed explanations of any gaps that were found.

Four suggested sections for the assessment document are:

- **Introduction** This describes the organization being assessed, the stakeholders and the main function. The introduction includes the processes and functions that are in scope and, just as importantly, those that are out of scope. It is also recommended to add to the introduction the overview and business drivers for the assessments, goals and intents, along with project summary statistics such as project duration, risks and milestones.
- **ITIL evaluation** This section provides the results, starting with overall observations and drilling down by element.
- **Remediation** For each gap that was uncovered in the evaluation section and set of actions, items are defined for its remediation.
- **Roadmap** This section suggests an approach to ordering and prioritizing the action items and remediation that were suggested.

Further details relating to the roadmap are set out in the following section.

4.3.5 Roadmap

The roadmap for improvement is where the assessors take all of the gaps, prioritize them, link gaps based on dependencies and make a recommendation for the organization's maturity level objective. The objective of the roadmap is to plan an implementation of activities that will raise the maturity level and, by doing so, naturally improve process effectiveness.

The first thing we need to do is to identify the gaps by reviewing the questions where the answers were 'no' within a level that failed. From there, we must determine which ones are quick fixes (so-called 'quick wins' or 'low hanging fruit', easily picked off) and which are longer-term fixes requiring more effort to complete. The duration estimates for the activities are not set in stone; the rule of thumb puts each activity into one of three categories:

- **Short term** These are initiatives that can be implemented within six to eight weeks and should have minimal operational impact, but would produce ITIL improvements that may be out of proportion to the required effort (e.g. the formal identification of currently active but unrecognized processes).
- **Medium term** These initiatives would be expected to deliver results between eight weeks and six months, and would require a greater amount of effort to achieve than the short-term initiatives (e.g. the adoption of new but prescribed working practices).
- **Long term** These are initiatives that would take longer than six months to implement and could be considered as a project with the amount of effort that is required (e.g. the implementation of new database structures).

You might realize that with a few quick changes you can raise the maturity level very rapidly. For example, if your organization has no SLM activities, which by definition means that its maturity level is zero, you could implement simple tools such as a process charter, communication plan with management, and discussion with the customer, and thereby vastly improve the process maturity.

When managers review assessment results, the roadmap is typically the section that they will spend time on. It gives a sense of the effort and cost entailed in the implementation and improvement of SLM. Discuss it with your peers and analyse your data correctly; find the gaps and separate the short-term fixes from the long term. Keep in mind that a successful roadmap will be converted into a project plan.

Secrets of the trade

There must be a target objective level of maturity for the organization. Not every organization must reach Maturity Level 5. The target level should align with the needs of the business and the customer. Because the Level-5 customer interface is usually critical to SLM and customer satisfaction, many organizations aim for a Level-5 maturity as the optimum level.

The example shown in Table 4.1 indicates that the maturity level is low, implying that there are no significant SLM activities. If we implement the short-term fixes, we can raise the maturity level to 3.0. Medium fixes will raise the maturity level to 4.0 and the long-term implementation activities will raise the maturity level to its optimum level, which is 5.0.

4.3.5.1 Roadmap example

Here is an example of a roadmap categorized by short-, medium- and long-term fixes.

Table 4.1 Assessment roadmap summary (example)

ITIL process	Current	Short	Medium	Long	Optimum
Service level management	2.0	3.0	4.0	5.0	5.0

Short-term improvement activities

- Set the scope of the SLM process by defining its benefits and creating a charter to identify the process owner, roles and responsibilities, staff training programme and communication plan with other processes.
- Set a mechanism to review service levels using a service level plan, supporting reports, a communications plan and a review period.
- Establish the foundation of a service level plan that will be reviewed on a monthly basis.
- Establish a procedure to communicate with the customer concerning service level agreement (SLA) compliance reports, new services and discussions regarding meeting business requirements with the existing service level, service improvement plans (SIPs) and customer satisfaction.

Medium-term improvement activities

- Define a process to establish ongoing communication with change management to ensure that changes of services, SLA targets and business impacts are understood and approved.
- Define procedures to establish ongoing communication with the service desk to ensure that service level objectives (SLOs)/targets are the same in both process tools (areas).
- Define a process to improve ongoing communications with management to provide trends in SLA breaches, service level trends, service requests and an overview of how achievements are measured against their targets.
- Identify underpinning contracts (UCs) and operational level agreements (OLAs) to support the SLAs, and establish a process to maintain and review those contracts.

- Expand the service improvement programme to include quality control activities, standards, procedures, advanced training for SLM personnel, setting targets and objectives for SLM, and using tools to improve SLM activities.

Long-term improvement activities

- Provide a mechanism that will automate SLM reporting for compliance reports, data mining, trending, operational and performance reports and escalation.
- Develop process documentation, including work instructions and activity monitoring.
- Standardize the following products and templates:
  - Service improvement plan
  - SLAs
  - Service catalogue.
- Have all the documents integrated and managed under the same rules, metrics and naming conventions.

For presentation purposes it is recommended to use a high-level diagram, showing the main milestones of the roadmap (see Figure 3.2). This tool is also included in the envisioning workshop discussed earlier. Make sure the results align with both the assessment and the envisioning exercise.

4.4 OUTPUTS OF THE ASSESSMENT

The assessment will bring to light your current maturity level compared with best practice. It will also provide you with an idea of how to approach remediation of those gaps, and the efforts required for implementation.

However, we are not ready to start our implementation project just yet. Remember that we are still at the strategy phase and there are still tasks ahead of us. Nevertheless, the assessment is a valuable source of information allowing us to complete the strategy tasks. As the next chapters indicate, we will be utilizing our SLM assessment results as an input to the following items:

- **Process charter** The charter is the high-level document defining the process. Its primary elements are the objectives and the scope of the project. The charter will also include other attributes, such as benefits, CSFs, deliverables and more. (For further information, see Chapter 3.)
- **Job description** This document focuses on the service level manager. It will define the service level manager's role and responsibilities and will describe the relationships with other processes and functions, including the customer, management and ITIL processes. It will also set out the knowledge, skills, attributes and qualifications required by the post holder.

Secrets of the trade

You will sometimes find the job description in the process charter, and at other times you will find it as an official human resources (HR) document. Either way, the charter and the job description form the cornerstone of the process. They provide the consent needed for the upcoming implementation of the process, activities and tools.

Make sure you work together with management on the documents to have them signed off and used in presentations and deliverables. Keep in mind that the assessment and its outputs are a key step towards successful process implementation.

4.5 SUMMARY

Before you begin to design the SLM process, it is important to know where the organization's capabilities are currently, as well as what capability gaps exist between current and future states. By conducting an SLM process capability assessment, pockets of best practice can be noted and used during the design phase to ensure that no one is recreating processes that already exist. This chapter described an assessment technique designed to help stakeholders strategize on what the SLM process should look like, where the most implementation effort will be needed, and how the process should map to the organization.

PART 2
Service design

Service structure

5

5 Service structure

After completing the service strategy phase, we should have a complete grasp of the objective of service level management (SLM) in our environment. We should have established an assessment and analysis of our organization and aligned ITIL best practice with our specific needs. We should have established our goals and developed our critical success factors (CSFs), and in our hands we should hold the process charter and job description for the service level manager. These components are the foundation for the process design work ahead.

The service design activities for a process are sometimes mistaken for process diagramming, modelling and work instructions. However, the design of SLM should include a service structure document, design of service levels and measurements, service level agreement (SLA) structure design, and much more (see Figure 5.1).

Although the service strategy deliverables are a good starting point, service level managers should begin the design work of the SLM process by defining and visualizing at a high level the service environment in a service structure document.

The service structure document will provide a consolidated vision of the entire service estate, including overall guiding principles, design objectives, high-level service descriptions, scope limitations and major assumptions. This will form the basis for a consistent development and implementation of future SLM products, including the SLA, service catalogue and service improvement plan (SIP).

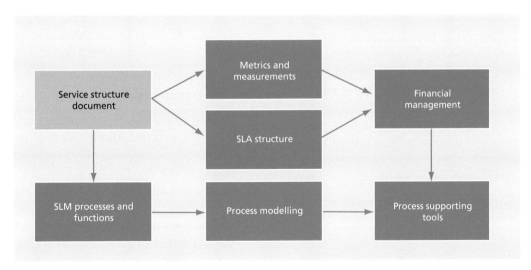

Figure 5.1 SLM service design activities

5.1 SERVICE STRUCTURE OVERVIEW

The service structure document describes, at a high level, the services offered by an organization and the services that are integrated to support business services. Most importantly, the document should consider customers who 'pay' for the services as well as the users who actually 'consume' these business services. The overall objective is to describe the relationships between the customer, the service provider and the services themselves.

The **service provider** is an organization that supplies services to one or more internal or external customers. The service provider might partner with one or more external suppliers to provide services to customers.

The **customer** is the person or group who pays for services and agrees to service level targets. The customer could represent multiple business units or a complete organization. It is important to distinguish between a customer and an end user (a person who uses the service on a day-to-day basis).

Ideally the service structure is developed as a prerequisite to service design activities, and this is why it is described in this first chapter in Part 2. However, practically speaking, ITIL practitioners will find themselves in organizations that have established SLAs, a service catalogue and services in production. For this scenario the development of the service structure may come as a continual service improvement (CSI) activity, aiming to advance the organization's maturity by making services consistent and clearly defined.

The type of customer structure, as described in the service structure document, will dictate the type of SLA and will have a significant impact on the SLM process design. For example, if the customer is represented by one entity, then we can design a single SLA that will cover a service provided to all customers; but if the service receivers are multiple lines of business with different needs, then we may need to have multiple SLAs that will be signed by each individual business unit. The degree to which the service provider will allow service customization per customer is important to decide and define in the service structure document.

One of the primary concerns for any service level manager is to define the boundaries of the environment for which they are responsible. There are several key questions they must ask when approaching SLM process design and creating the service structure:

- What are the guiding principles of service management?
- What are the services provided?
- Who are the customers?
- Who are the service providers?

The service structure should be a simple, executive summary answering these questions with clear, concise visual maps of the relationships. The service level manager should own this document and review/update it on an annual basis.

The major sections of the service structure document are described in detail in the following sections:

- **Guiding principles** These answer key questions about the organizational strategy and objectives for implementing service-based management.
- **Service provider** The service provider supports the services that are in scope, and defines who they are, what they are responsible for, interactions, work methods and structure.

■ **Customer** Description of the customers, attributes and structure.

■ **Services** A high-level view of the services that are ultimately in scope for SLM.

This list is not meant to be all-inclusive and, depending on your specific needs, you may find some sections obvious (e.g. the customer is the business for most enterprises) and others that may not be so but will be required (e.g. legal/commercial implications in the case of a commercial service provider with external clients with contracts for service). It should be considered important to sequence the document in a similar manner: you must understand who is delivering the services before you can understand to whom you are delivering services, and only then can you determine the structure of the services based on supplier and consumer defined at the highest level.

Those who benefit from the service structure will often be individuals who are new to the organization. The service structure also ensures long-term consistency in the definition of new services, changing services, or new service models and options being introduced. In the case of audiences who are new to the organization, they will neither want nor need an in-depth narrative on how services are organized and mapped together, but instead will be looking for a high-level understanding of the service environment. The service structure should be a starting point for education, reference and an input to the structure of SLAs and the service catalogue. Those practitioners who require a more detailed understanding can refer to the specific supporting documents.

Secrets of the trade

The service structure document is generally used differently by each organization. In fact you will find the document under different names: 'service environment description', 'organization structure' and others.

In one of my engagements, a service structure was developed and was owned by the project management office (PMO), which governed the ITIL processes. In this case, SLM became one of the primary contributors and editors, mostly because the process limited the influence and centralization of authority by the PMO. Eventually, as SLM matured as a process, it was apparent that the service structure was an essential element of the process, and it was agreed to transition the ownership of the document to SLM.

5.1.1 Guiding principles

The guiding principles of the service structure document may be gleaned from other service management strategy and planning documents, but may require some unique additions for the sake of this specific process. This section should capture key objectives, limitations, assumptions and requirements of the organization on the way that services are defined. These may be put into practice in terms of standards, policies, or other terms used by different organizations.

Consider the following topics when developing guiding principles:

■ **Service scope** At the highest level, is the intention to document the service in a granular (detailed) way? This decision will determine the level of reporting, cost analysis and charges.

- **Financial implications** Are there organizational limitations or requirements for how services can be defined within the organization? Does depreciation get handled at the cost-centre level or the corporate level? Are services revenue-generating? If so, how is the pricing strategy defined: does it map to service costs or market conditions?

- **Cost of accounting** With all service decisions – from metrics and reporting to cost and chargeback – there is a cost of reporting. If it is too granular, it may require a prohibitive cost to report on the data; if it is at too high a level, it may be meaningless to the users.

- **Service measurement and reporting** As you define services, can you report on them in a meaningful way? Are tools and processes in place to support the vision?

- **Budgets and funding** Does the organization plan to invest in developing a programme or in supporting efforts in a business in the usual manner?

- **How many services?** It is suggested to look at the entire estate of services from the start, even if only selected services will be fully implemented in the near term. This can help to ensure the above items are covered in a meaningful way and that service scope is neither too broad (too many services and options) nor too narrow (too few services, leaving little distinction).

- **Customer incentives** Consider behaviours that need to be changed or influenced through charging models, service design, etc., such as influencing employees to use more self-service tools rather than call the (costly) help desk with simple questions.

The guiding principles may not be exhaustive, but should be considered carefully and reviewed with a governance body for endorsement and agreement early in the process.

Secrets of the trade

On an engagement where I helped develop the service structure document, we discovered different approaches that were diametrically opposed. The technical teams wanted to define services in very granular terms that would produce reports on consumption, usage by department code, etc. However, corporate finance lacked the same level of granularity and required more detailed information to enable the chargeback process. It took a long time to identify the gap between the approaches, primarily because the guiding principles and assumptions were not defined in advance.

Eventually corporate finance prevailed, and services were defined at a level that not only allowed reporting, but also made more sense to the customer.

5.1.2 Service provider

The next section of the service structure document should describe the service provider at a high level. Once again, begin with the organizational chart and describe each of the major departments or groups. As a service level manager, you are expected to understand what the services in scope are and who the customers of the services are.

The example in Figure 5.2 is for an IT organization that has subscribed to, and is organized around, the ITIL service lifecycle. In this example, the IT service management (ITSM) group owns IT services as well as service portfolio management, IT service

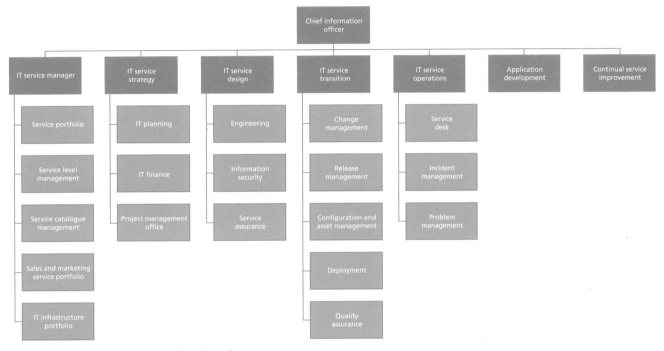

Figure 5.2 Sample IT organizational structure

catalogue management and SLM. The group is organized around the business, and the director of each department owns the IT services associated with that particular business unit. The director of the IT infrastructure portfolio owns the IT services that span all of the business units.

Finally, the last part of this sub-section should simply list the key external suppliers used to provide IT services and should describe the services provided at a high level. The objective is to provide the reader with a list of external suppliers and an idea of how these suppliers weave themselves into the IT business and support services for the company.

Significant suppliers such as managed services providers should be given special attention if they effectively deliver the service on your behalf to

your end customer. In this case, attention should also be given to demonstrating the governing processes and controls that your organization, as the supplier, has on your underpinning supplier.

5.1.3 Customer

The next section of the service structure document will describe the customer. This may or may not include an understanding of the customer's organization(s), structure and relationships with the service provider. In the case of an enterprise, this should be well understood and documented accordingly. In the case of an outsource engagement – especially for new or unknown future clients – profiles or target clients would be more appropriate to document. This latter scenario may require involvement from your organization's sales and/or marketing people to accurately capture the relevant information.

The objective of this section is to ensure that the reader clearly understands who the customers are (i.e. those who are paying for the services). It may also be helpful to the reader to understand something about what functions these customers fulfil for the business. A clear distinction through the explicit example of the customer versus the user should also be provided, so as to avoid confusion of these terms.

Using your company's or customer's organizational chart, describe each of the lines of business in a few sentences, name the IT stakeholders or liaison points (if any – these people may not yet be named or appointed). Furthermore, if it is available you may want to list the yearly revenue generated by each line of business and, finally, list the critical business functions for which each line of business is responsible.

If your organization is a service provider, you will also need to describe your external customers (other businesses or consumers) in broad terms. You do not need to name them all, especially if there are hundreds or thousands of them. It is more likely you can describe your customers in broader categories and summarize their importance to the business.

For example, let's assume our business is a typical manufacturing firm. The firm's organizational chart will likely describe the organization as having the following departments or groups:

- Corporate
- Production
- Distribution
- Sales and marketing.

As a service level manager, identifying your customers is extremely important. If you used the service structure to start implementing the SLM process, the customers will become your primary stakeholders and therefore additional effort on this section will eventually prove to be beneficial. Some services may deliver consistently across all of your customers, such as messaging (e.g. email and instant messaging), while others may be very specific and customized to a particular department (e.g. supply chain management applications).

5.1.4 Services

The service structure document will link the service provider and the customer by providing a basic understanding of the services in scope.

It is important to remember at this point that this document should stay at a high level, and providing the list of services in scope usually means listing the categories of services only. It is suggested that the entire landscape or estate of services is covered to ensure an inclusive model is created. However, limiting the descriptions to categories only may cause confusion later on. For example, do not refer to services merely as 'telecommunications', as that term is too broad and too vague; instead, ensure specific elements are described, such as internet access, LAN and WAN connectivity, phone services and others, and perhaps limit the scope by defining what is not in scope that may be perceived to be so, such as conferencing if this is done by another supplier.

'Service category' is a concept employed to simplify the view of the services model and align better with typical organizational boundaries. This may also be referred to as 'service towers' or 'lines of service' (LOSs). Typically, each service category is managed by a product or service manager. The benefit of this type of categorization is seen when we map the different services under the responsibility of one manager or one function. The categorization will eventually be imported into an SLA structure. The technique also helps to highlight the difference between discrete and unique services and service options.

In Table 5.1, a very simple model is created to demonstrate this concept of service categories. Rather than define hundreds of discrete services that would be complicated and likely to cause confusion to customers and users, a simplified model is employed to categorize such services. Within the service, further definition comes through the application of service options, as with desktop computing that includes desktop and laptop working as options, and with a laptop you get encryption as part of the service – it is bundled, not a completely separate service.

Secrets of the trade

Working with a customer to develop an initial service catalogue, the employees in IT all knew full well what was supported, what they did and what they did not do. Yet when it came time to answer the question, 'What are the services that you provide?', we were met with a combination of blank stares and widely ranging answers.

A number of very specific applications were named consistently. During a workshop we explored the idea that they did not deliver hundreds of services (one per application) but really delivered one single service category called 'managed applications', and the hundreds of specific applications were really instances of that service, not unique and specific services of themselves. This helped provide a lot of mental clarity and greatly reduced the confusion and complexity of the perceived service model.

The above is the type of confusion that the service structure aims to resolve. The organization must visualize the services it provides and have the ability to group and categorize them.

Table 5.1 Model to demonstrate the concept of service categories

	Service tower	Description and options
1	Managed application	Enterprise (HR, payroll), department (service category management)
2	Server services	For example, Windows, Linux, Solaris, Virtual Windows
3	Network	Internet, WAN, LAN, remote access
4	Service desk	Help desk, service request management, interactive voice response
5	Communication	Voice-over-internet protocol, conferencing, video
6	Desktop computing	Desktop, laptop, encryption, wireless

Service category definition is important to set the overall framework for the service catalogue and SLM at an early point in the process. It is the responsibility of ITSM, typically with business relationship management, to identify the most suitable combination of service categories. The customer's point of view must be considered at this stage to avoid pitfalls in developing services as they are provided, not as they are consumed.

When the service structure scope is widened to list the services, it is good practice to distinguish between business services and IT services. Thus we have the following:

■ **Business services** Services that the customer and end users access or utilize directly and that provide tangible business value. Business services are usually supported by IT services.

■ **IT services** Services that are not of direct value to customers but are instead used as building blocks for IT business services. IT services are usually considered back-office or IT infrastructure services.

■ **Operational services** In many organizations a third layer may be considered for the sake of organizational alignment or just the practicality of the way IT is delivered. This layer would be subsumed within IT services in a two-tier model.

The line between business services and IT services may blur in some organizations. The rule of thumb is that 'business service' is defined by the business. If IT provides a service to the business, but the business does not think of the service in any business context, then it is an IT service.

Figure 5.3 depicts the concept of a three-tier model. The layer at the top of the model represents the customer, who is consuming the

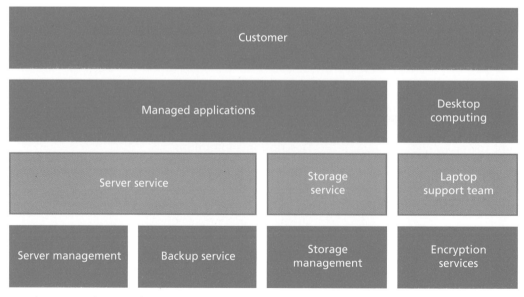

Figure 5.3 Business services and IT services

business services. The second layer represents the business services: managed applications and desktop computing – tangible services consumed directly by the end users. Supporting this layer are IT services: server and storage services that support applications, but provide no direct value to the business unless they are running an application. To further refine the model with operational services, an additional fourth layer can be added to demonstrate the deeper level of services provided within IT to enable IT services: for example, server management, backup services and encryption services. These are not consumed by the client, nor do they exist to support the business service directly; they are operational services required to deliver a server service.

If possible, attempt to build this list with existing service documentation and information, such as the service portfolio or service catalogue. If no service-related information is available, the list of services must be created from scratch in a workshop setting.

Secrets of the trade

Do not confuse the service structure with the service catalogue. The service catalogue is a more formalized document with information about all operational and chartered services. The service catalogue includes information about deliverables, prices, service levels, contact points, ordering and request procedures.

The service structure document defines the relationship between the customer and the service provider by describing them and visualizing their structures. The service structure also defines the services that are provided and remains at a high level just to allow an initial mapping to the service environment.

5.2 SUMMARY

The service structure is the first step in understanding how IT services are consumed and to whom they are provided. This will be critical later when SLAs are drafted. How can we define the SLA if the categories for the services are unknown? What if the mapping of IT services to business services is unclear? The service structure will be a very valuable document as service catalogue management and SLM are implemented, but it will also be useful in many other instances and for many other ITSM processes. This basic understanding of how services are provided and consumed has relevance at the service desk and within incident, problem, change, and configuration management, as well as other ITIL processes.

SLM functions and processes

6

6 SLM functions and processes

Although we initiated discussion of the design activities within the previous chapter (dealing with the service structure document), in actual fact the design of the process begins with the definitions of the processes and functions that are under the responsibility of service level management (SLM).

This chapter details the scope of SLM by laying out its processes and functions. We appreciate that organizations may define the scope of the process differently; however, this publication provides you with best practice, and also provides a model for you to strive for – an ideal SLM process.

6.1 SERVICE LEVEL MANAGEMENT – A HIGH-LEVEL PROCESS

The SLM process requires a high level of coordination and control. The process involves many different types of activity, which might create a complex and difficult environment to design, let alone to manage. Our process is responsible for tracking and reporting on the quality of the services, keeping a close business relationship with the customer, tracking the costs of services, and improving overall performance. Those activities are the ongoing tasks that are directly related to the services. Let's not forget also that SLM defines documents, and negotiates and agrees on the quality of services.

ITIL defines processes and functions that fall into the different lifecycle phases. SLM is a process within the service design lifecycle phase. In many organizations SLM possesses the elements of a function as it is a structured department owning

its resources. This department operates under different names: SLM, customer relationship management, global service quality management, and others.

Section 6.2 defines the three areas of focus that make up the SLM function. These areas will be the basis for our design and will provide the framework to guide us through the development of the sub-processes, roles and responsibilities. Section 6.3 considers an integrated SLM function based on five sub-processes, as illustrated in Figure 6.3.

6.2 SERVICE LEVEL MANAGEMENT – FUNCTIONAL AREAS

The SLM function, led by the service level manager, is responsible for carrying out the activities of the SLM process. The service level manager coordinates between the functional areas of focus and the various team members to ensure that all areas are striving towards the same goal.

Three important roles are defined for SLM: service level manager, reporting analyst and service relationship manager. Each requires different skill sets that will need to be coordinated and managed by the service level manager. The three functional areas associated with these roles (and described in the following sections) are:

■ **Service level management operations** The service level manager, as the owner of the service level agreement (SLA), leads the service review meetings and initiates service improvement tasks. The service level manager is responsible for coordinating the other two functional areas (below), and for staff training and quality control.

- **Service reporting** This functional area (performed primarily by a reporting analyst) provides reporting support to all service-related activities, and it includes the ownership of the report catalogue, communicating with data owners and preparing reports.
- **Service relationship management (SRM)** This functional area is responsible for developing the relationship with the customer and the service provider. SRM's main focus is on the service review meetings and the service improvement plan (SIP) process.

The service relationship manager and the reporting analyst are cast from different moulds. The service relationship manager's goal is to ensure a high level of customer satisfaction, aiming to manage customer perception by utilizing interpersonal skills and resourcefulness. The goal of the reporting analyst is to provide accurate and useful data that are presented in clear and structured reports. The reporting analyst is likely to be very analytical in their actions and will spend most of their time on data mining and report generation.

The service level manager has their work cut out. Apart from coordinating and monitoring the activities of the service relationship manager and the reporting analyst, the service level manager will need to reconcile the different priorities of their discipline.

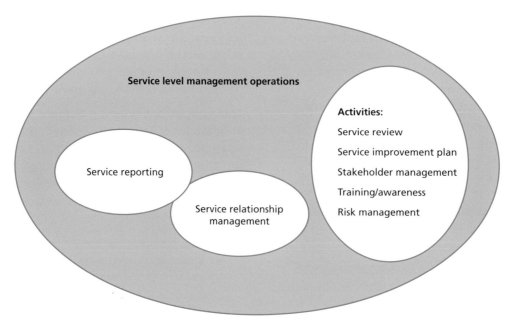

Figure 6.1 Service level management operations

Secrets of the trade

In some organizations the service level manager will fulfil all three roles, i.e. including those of the reporting analyst and the service relationship manager. The size of the organization and the scope of the responsibility of the SLM process will determine the SLM structure.

6.2.1 Service level management operations

The service level manager is directly responsible for the operations of the function, as shown in Figure 6.1. First and foremost this function is responsible for the execution of the SLM process activities, monitoring their effectiveness, and improving them when necessary. The process operation activities include stakeholder management and risk management, which are discussed in Chapter 19.

SLM operations is accountable for the overall health of the process and utilizes the ITIL lifecycle approach to categorize its areas of responsibility, which are set out below.

6.2.1.1 Process strategy

The service level manager will constantly reiterate and refine the related critical success factors (CSFs) to ensure that the SLM process is meeting the objectives of the organization.

The service level manager is also the focal point and the contact person who communicates with stakeholders to determine whether any changes have occurred in the overall strategy of the organization and to further determine whether these changes may impact the SLM process.

6.2.1.2 Process design

SLM operations is accountable for the ongoing business value and integrity of the process design across the functional and organizational boundaries. The design activities relate to:

- Processes, policies and procedures
- Process roles and responsibilities
- Key performance indicators (KPIs).

SLM operations will also ensure that, as part of the design process, integration is planned with external processes and functions such as incident management and the service desk.

6.2.1.3 Process implementation and transition

The service level manager will own, assure and approve the transition of the SLM service design into the live environment, as well as the implementation of its activities, processes and the recruiting of its personnel.

SLM operations is responsible for the implementation of tools to support the various process activities. The service level manager will lead the design of the SLA compliance reports and SIP.

6.2.1.4 Process execution and coordination

SLM operations is accountable for the execution of process activities. SLM operations is also responsible for measuring and reporting on process compliance across organizational silos.

The service level manager will also lead the following activities:

- Advocacy, representing the process and dealing with political issues
- Promoting a culture of process collaboration and integration

- Breaking down strong silo or functional mindsets
- Managing process exceptions
- Coordination between the functional areas of SLM
- Conflict resolution.

6.2.1.5 Continual process improvement

There are two categories for process improvements: reactive activities, which resolve local failures; and proactive activities that attempt to eliminate future failures. Below are some typical proactive activities that are carried out at regular intervals:

- Internal and external training
- New employee orientation
- Teambuilding exercises
- KPIs review
- Documentation review
- SLA audits.

6.2.2 Service reporting

Service reporting is responsible for producing and delivering reports of achievement and trends against service levels. Service reporting should agree on the format, content and frequency of reports with the customer. Bear in mind that these reporting activities will evolve as your customer's requirements and business requirements are refined or changed.

Traditionally, SLM was just a reporting process, responsible for tracking SLA results through monitoring and reporting. In today's practice, SLM's scope has expanded to also cover managing the relationship with the customer, negotiating terms and agreements, and tracking customer satisfaction. The reporting analyst's activities of data mining, report development and populations seem more of a constant burden or a necessary evil

for the service level manager. Therefore, when designing the process, make sure you define the function of service reporting and when possible allocate a separate resource for this role.

6.2.2.1 Service review reports

Service reporting's first priority is to prepare reports for the service review meetings, and to provide the reports in a timely and professional manner with accurate and meaningful data. The final reports should be approved by the service level manager. At the discretion of the service level manager, the reporting analyst may also be tasked with the presentation of the reports during the review meetings.

During a service review meeting, the service relationship manager and the customer may agree to modify the SLA compliance report results. In this case, service reporting is responsible for amending the reports and for generating a new and final report.

6.2.2.2 Data integrity and correct calculations

Some of the report information might be incorrect for various reasons:

- Corrupted data
- Wrong calculations
- Incorrect entries by operational staff.

Automation of the reporting process aims to eliminate the above issues, and the organization should strive to design its systems towards maximum automation of data flow. However, not all organizations own automated reporting systems and instead use the services of a reporting analyst as described above.

6.2.2.3 Report catalogue owner

The report catalogue maintains a list of reports and their definitions that have been discussed, analysed and agreed with the customer and the service provider. The reporting analyst will manage the report catalogue and ensure not only that it continually meets the changing needs of the business, but also that the reports that are developed reflect the specification of the catalogue. Much like the SLA, the reporting requirements must be negotiated between the parties and should include both scope and cost considerations.

6.2.2.4 Reporting solution contact person

Many organizations deploy a reporting software solution or an external reporting function, the sole responsibility of which is to generate performance reports. In this scenario, the SLM service reporting function will represent the reporting requirements of the process and will act as a liaison and as the main stakeholder interfacing with the external reporting function.

For a more detailed description of service reporting, refer to Chapter 15.

6.2.3 Service relationship management

In today's market the most efficient way to retain profitability is through customer loyalty and retention. The smarter companies now concentrate their attention on the most valuable customers and spend fewer resources on attracting new customers. To retain your customers you have to know them intimately, know what makes them happy and what their underlying business needs are. Service relationship management provides that role while working with the customer, building relationships with them and gaining their loyalty.

The service relationship manager is the everyday interface with the customer, including regular meetings to review service performance and/or assist with critical events and incidents. SRM will always be involved in any critical incidents that have a high impact on the customer. In such cases, the service relationship manager will participate in the incident management process and consistently communicate with the customer, providing the status of the incidents.

In a small organization with SLM, where the service level manager takes the role of the service relationship manager, this role becomes the focus of the service level manager's activities. In a larger-scale organization – specifically where the customer resides in different geographical locations – service relationship management is structured accordingly. In this case the global service relationship manager will interface with the service level manager and will coordinate the different service relationship managers per region (see Figure 6.2).

The structure of service relationship management can also be determined by the structure of the SLA. For example, if the SLA is categorized by services, we might want to designate a service relationship manager for each service. If different cultures and languages have a significant impact on service provision, we will allocate a service relationship manager on a regional basis.

For a detailed description of service relationship management, refer to Chapter 18.

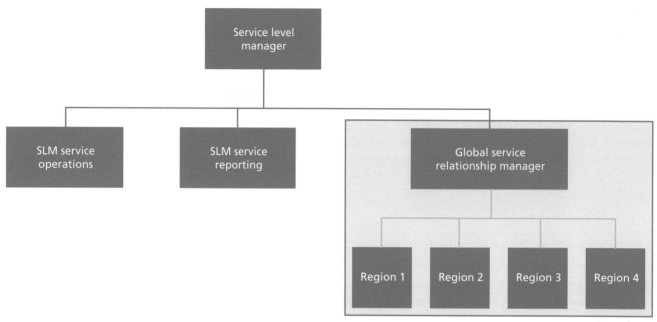

Figure 6.2 Service level management – function structure

6.2.3.1 Service review meeting and service improvement plan

Service review meetings are the pinnacle of service relationship management work. If the service review occurs on a weekly basis, the service relationship manager will prepare for the meeting throughout the week. The primary communication tool in SRM is the continual service improvement (CSI) register. The SRM functional area regularly updates the CSI register with new records or modifies existing records. This allows the service relationship manager to communicate efficiently with both the customer and the service provider.

6.2.3.2 Critical incidents

As part of the incident management process, the service relationship manager may be defined as one of the escalation levels in a hierarchical

approach known as management escalation. The types of event causing such escalation are often referred to as major incidents, critical incidents or 'Severity 1 or 2' incidents, and they are generally those that are highly visible to the customer when they occur.

The role of the service relationship manager in these cases is to interface with the customer throughout the lifecycle of the incident. The service relationship manager will provide status updates of the incident at regular intervals and will be available for the customer to call and discuss issues relevant to the incident.

Good practice in SRM is to define a root cause analysis (RCA) procedure as part of the critical incident process. In this case, after the incident has been resolved, the service relationship manager will review the documented RCA of the incident with the customer. The result of this discussion may initiate a SIP.

6.3 OVERALL INTEGRATED SLM PROCESS

To execute the process effectively, the three different functions must come together: SLM operations, service reporting and service relationship management. The structure of the function and the definition of the roles and responsibilities will depend on the amount of resources allocated for the process.

The three basic roles defined in the previous section are:

- Service level manager
- Reporting analyst
- Service relationship manager.

As part of the process implementation, as service level manager you will need to assign activities for each role and find the integration points between those activities. The result of this design will be an overall integrated SLM process, a primary input into process modelling, or any detailed design of the processes and procedures.

The design of the operational SLM process starts with the development and management of the SLA. The SLA is supported by three operational activities: monitoring and reporting, service review and SIPs.

In reality, SLA management is not considered to be an ongoing operational activity. The SLA is signed off and is not expected to be modified until its next audit – contrasting with the above three operational processes, which are ongoing cyclical activities that focus on daily service provision.

Continual process improvement is, as illustrated in Figure 6.3, a background process that is performed either at intervals or when triggered by an event. This process governs all the activities of the process and ensures their effectiveness.

6.3.1 SLA management

The SLA management sub-process focuses on the agreement itself and its conditions. The goal of this process is to define an agreement between the

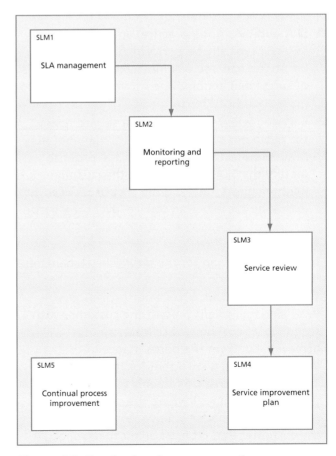

Figure 6.3 Service level management process

customer and the service provider, where the agreement will define the services and the quality of their provision.

The service level objectives (SLOs) defined in the SLA will be monitored and reported on. The process is subject to constant review; and such a review, regarding SLA structure and content, can be instigated by one or more of the following conditions:

- **End-of-service pilot SLA period ends** This period is normally the first period defined for the services to be provided against an initial SLA, and the SLA will generally be reviewed thereafter.
- **SLA audit** As good practice, an audit of the SLA will typically be performed on an annual basis. This exercise will most likely result in a list of suggested actions, one of which might be to make modifications to the SLA.
- **Service review** As a result of a service review, the customer or the service level manager may raise a request for change (RFC) in order to modify the SLA. For example, the customer might suggest lowering the cost of services in exchange for lowering service level compliance.

Secrets of the trade

It is not uncommon for the service level manager to suggest lowering the service level compliance threshold in certain circumstances. The service level manager might present the customer with scenarios where the service levels are not achievable and yet the performance of the service provided is sufficient for the business. This type of discussion can only take place in a positive environment where the service relationship manager builds a relationship with the customer that is based on mutual respect and mutual interest.

6.3.2 Monitoring and reporting service quality

Monitoring and reporting service quality is based directly and strictly on the conditions defined in the SLA. This activity is one of the three ongoing activities of the SLM process; the other two are the service review and SIP. The three activities are essentially integrated and coordinated throughout the SLA review period (typically a month). SLM reports on the SLA are presented and reviewed in the service review meeting. The service review meetings result in items to be improved that are processed through the SIP.

The monitoring and reporting sub-process is responsible for collecting data and generating calculations and reports to enable a review of service performance to take place constructively. The monitoring and reporting function owns the report catalogue and is a primary actor in defining the metrics and measurements under review.

6.3.3 Service review

The service review meeting is not just another regular meeting that is placed on the customer's and the service level manager's calendar. Service review meetings are essential to the process and are the main instruments used to build the relationship with the customer, review SLA results and follow up CSI register records related to degraded or disrupted services. There are specific inputs and outputs for the service review sub-process, along with a structured agenda to the meeting, and it cannot be stressed enough how important it is to design the sub-process as effectively and productively as possible.

6.3.4 Service improvement plan

The SIP process is designed for the service level manager to effectively use the CSI register to convey to the customer what is being completed regarding degraded or disrupted services. The CSI register is also used to communicate to the service provider the customer's expectations and prioritization of action items.

6.3.5 Continual process improvement

All aspects of SLM are subject to process improvement. Process improvements are not only performed at regular intervals; in fact, they can be triggered reactively by operational events or as a result of proactive measures. The improvement activities are considered to be a background process that is aimed at ensuring the effectiveness of the SLM process. Indeed, a high-level approach to continual process improvement – which is seen as part of the overall SLM process – should be taken into account in the early stages of SLM service design.

Greater detail regarding continual process improvement for SLM is given in Chapter 20.

6.4 SUMMARY

This chapter illustrates the high-level design of SLM. This structure is a direct result of the process strategy and its objectives.

The design of the process is made up of two major elements: areas of focus, and processes. We learned that SLM includes three areas of focus and five processes (if you include continual process improvement as a background process).

Table 6.1 presents the SLM sub-processes in a RACI (responsible, accountable, consulted and informed) format. The table links the areas of focus and the processes, and sets out the basis for the detailed design ahead of us.

Table 6.1 SLM sub-processes presented in a RACI format

Process step	SLM operations	Service relationship management	Service reporting
SLA management	R	A	I
Monitoring and reporting	C	C	A
Service review	R	A	C
Service improvement plan	R	A	I
Continual process improvement	A	I	I

Note: R = responsible for delivering the action; A = accountable for the action; C = consulted before the action; I = informed after the action.

Process modelling and documentation

7

7 Process modelling and documentation

This chapter provides practical guidance and a methodology that can be used to model the service level management (SLM) process. By the end, the reader will have the guidance that is necessary to model the SLM process and document the process in three related levels. As one might expect, the model will start with a high-level view of the process and finish with detailed work instructions.

7.1 PROCESS MODELLING THEORIES

Process modelling is the activity of analysing and designing the structure of business processes and the resources needed to implement them. An added benefit of process modelling is that processes may be evaluated and improved in the future.

Process models help visualize the process specification for both activity implementation and generating documentation, with the eventual purpose of relating to procedures and work instructions. This allows processes to be more effectively implemented and consistently executed across an organization. The models promote productivity and serve as a reference.

There are typically three distinctive levels to process modelling. We will define the levels here and later demonstrate their use in documenting the SLM process:

- **Process** This is the Level 1 modelling that provides a high-level fundamental understanding of the process. It defines a process as a set of larger components, their relationships and their interfaces to other processes, functions or organizations. A process's Level 1 model is typically documented on a single page.
- **Procedures** This is the Level 2 modelling that provides documentation of the various activities, decisions and events, as well as the detailed interfaces of the process. This level of the model will be referenced the most by process users. The Level 2 process flows must be clear, and easy to follow; they are often spread across multiple pages.
- **Work instructions** This is the Level 3 modelling that includes step-by-step instructions for the process's end users. Unlike Levels 1 and 2, work instructions are usually developed as a series of documents providing a narrative, templates and other tools for the end user. Some organizations elect not to create work instructions for all processes.

7.2 SERVICE LEVEL MANAGEMENT – MODELLING AND DOCUMENTATION

7.2.1 Process modelling guidelines

Process modelling takes time and focus. Very few people in this world actually enjoy process modelling, and few people have the skills, background and detail orientation required for effective process modelling, especially when it comes to work instructions. Many organizations will elect to outsource this task to a consultant or a contractor.

7.2.1.1 Tools

There are many tools based on the unified modelling language (UML) and business process modelling (BPM) frameworks that can be used for process modelling. Microsoft's Visio is a well-used tool for process modelling; in particular, Visio 2007 includes a process modelling template that can be used for SLM process modelling.

7.2.1.2 Modelling notation

There are many different modelling symbols and standards available today. Some of these standards (such as the business process modelling notation, or BPMN) are very good and quite popular. The notations used within this chapter are a hybrid of several best practices and techniques collected over a decade.

7.2.1.3 Documentation conventions

Keep the Level 1 process model limited to one page. Often, organizations will print Level 1 on a plotter, frame the process and place it where it can be easily referenced by the SLM team. Level 2 models can span multiple pages and are usually stored in a binder along with the Level 3 work instructions.

If at all possible, keep the process flows online, and avoid multiple locations and copies, which can generate inconsistencies. Visio can be used to create active web pages that link Visio diagrams together and can also reference work instructions, templates, other online tools and process deliverables.

7.2.1.4 Verification and acceptance

Each process model at Levels 1 and 2 should be signed off as accepted and complete by the appropriate responsible stakeholders. Identifying

Secrets of the trade

In order to help readers differentiate one IT service management (ITSM) process flow from another, we recommend each process be assigned a unique colour within the Level 1 and 2 diagrams. Otherwise, the family of ITSM process modelling diagrams can run together and be hard to follow. For service level management, we are assigning the process a lighter tint.

Each process, procedure and work-level instruction must be given a unique identity (ID) number or code. We recommend a letter code be used to represent service level management in order to give the reader an additional visual clue.

We are going to assign service level management a process code of 'SLM'. Each process component within the Level 1 process model will have an ID starting with SLM1, then SLM2, etc. Each Level 2 procedure will follow this hierarchy – for example, the procedures that fall under SLM1 will be numbered SLM1.1, SLM1.2, SLM1.3, and so on.

these stakeholders before the modelling begins is essential. Processes are living documents that can and should change with the needs of the business and the structure of the IT organization.

7.2.1.5 The final product

When the modelling is completed, there will be several layers of documentation. These must all be maintained electronically, but they can also be printed and posted on a wall. Many organizations make large poster plots and frame the Level 1 process framework or even the Level 2 process flows.

7.2.2 Collecting data

You will be in one of two situations when it comes to collecting data for modelling the process:

- The process does not exist currently and can be designed to meet requirements.
- The process exists already and needs to be documented, optimized and standardized.

Secrets of the trade

Numerous consulting firms offer off-the-shelf, generic ITIL process models and documentation that anyone can purchase. Other firms offer generic ITIL processes, but they customize and train organizations to use the processes as part of a service. Either of these options is viable if the funding is available.

Be sure to examine the consulting firm's sample processes before buying, to ensure that the correct level of detail is available as well as a process model documentation format being one that your organization can use. We have seen a whole range of product qualities on offer, yet some firms offer processes only in non-editable Adobe PDF format.

Most importantly, keep in mind that off-the-shelf processes will not work for the majority of IT organizations. Customization is typically required to meld the ITIL process model to a business, culture, organizational structure and the rest of the IT operation.

If the process does not exist at all, then the modelling will be a simpler task. The process model can be created based on ITIL best practice. Source material can be purchased or created by a process modelling expert. However, even if the process is new, it should never be created in a vacuum; collaboration and agreement must be fostered with all of the process stakeholders.

If at least some form of process associated with SLM already exists, performing a work study observation session will help the process modeller understand what activities are being performed. Using your assessment of the maturity of the SLM process as a guide (see Chapter 4), interview the people who execute the process to get a sense of which activities take place, who executes the activities, which templates or tools are used, where the process interfaces with the business or another ITSM process, and what strengths and weaknesses exist in the process today.

Some interview questions we recommend during the interview are:

- What is your view of SLM today?
  If the interviewee does not understand ITSM or SLM, ensure there is a component of education at the beginning of the interview. If the interviewee is not familiar with ITIL's vernacular, try to map their vocabulary onto ITIL's terms during the interview.
- Could you please describe your role and responsibility as they pertain to SLM?
- Can you kindly describe what you do on a typical day when you are focused on SLM?
  Probe deeper about whom that person works with, get sample deliverables and reports, and ask whether you can be present to observe future meetings or conversations. Ask about time, effort and the cycles the interviewee has available to complete each major activity. Try to gauge the effectiveness of each activity.

As the interview progresses, the interviewer should begin to form a mental picture of the process flow being described. The interviewee may point towards others who can help to further describe the existing process. The interview and observation process then repeats until the interviewer believes that they have built up a complete picture of what takes place.

7.3 LEVEL 1 – THE PROCESS FRAMEWORK

In order to model the SLM process, we need a framework or a blueprint to follow. At Level 1, an organization needs to agree on the major components of the process, how these components map together and what are the major process interfaces with other ITSM processes or functions.

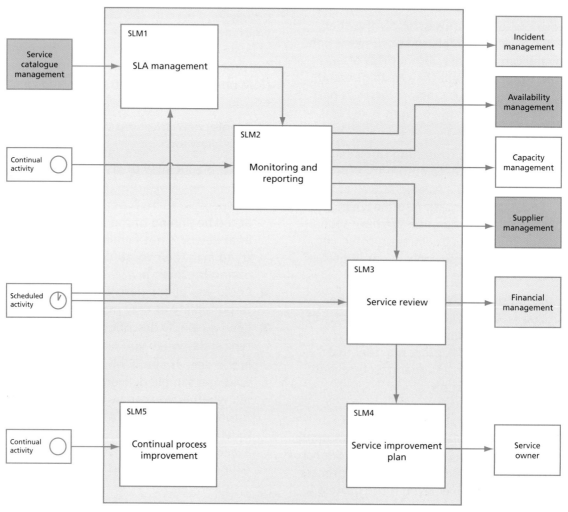

Figure 7.1 SLM process framework for Level 1 with external interfaces

If we begin with the ITIL framework, the process's components are well defined already. This is a good place to start, but by no means where Level 1 must end up. If an organization needs to change the process components, leave one out or split the process in a different way, this is completely appropriate.

The SLM process components are defined as:

- SLM1: service level agreement (SLA) management
- SLM2: monitoring and reporting
- SLM3: service review
- SLM4: service improvement plan (SIP)
- SLM5: continual process improvement.

If we map these components as part of the SLM process along with their major interfaces, the result may look something like Figure 6.3.

Next, the process modeller must consider what interfaces or integrations should be added to the Level 1 process framework. This is where the other ITIL processes need to be considered, as well as other IT and business functions. A process component may be triggered by a scheduled or continual activity. For example, service reviews are usually conducted with customers or the business on a monthly basis, while monitoring and reporting on SLA achievement is a continual (often automated) process.

Figure 7.1 adds the major inputs and outputs of the process. Once again, these components of the Level 1 framework will often vary widely between organizations, depending on what processes or functions are in place to support SLM. Notice that all of the other processes referenced here also have a particular tint assigned to them.

The process modeller must ensure the Level 1 diagram is clear, concise and aesthetically pleasing. There is no need to have every process interface or integration referenced at Level 1 – only the major or most important interfaces need be modelled. Try to make the process flow look logical, and adjust the order and spacing of the process components until the diagram reaches an acceptable level of clarity and conciseness.

Once the process modeller believes the Level 1 process model is ready for review, they should present it to a group of process stakeholders. Generally there are not a lot of comments or disagreements when Level 1 is discussed and agreed upon. There might be some issues with the inputs and outputs, but these can usually be addressed quite easily. Do not let the process interfaces become too complex or the diagram might lose its visual appeal.

7.4 LEVEL 2 – PROCESS FLOWS

Once Level 1 has been agreed, a Level 2 process flow must be created for each process component defined at Level 1. Continuing with the example framework, there are five flows that must be created for (SLM1 to SLM5). In this section, SLM3, service review, will be used as the example.

Process flow modelling has two phases. Firstly, create or document the process on a flexible medium. Before the process is formally sketched out, it will go through numerous iterations. A whiteboard or a blank wall covered in poster paper often works well, combined with coloured marker pens and sticky notes as other favourite modelling tools in the physical world.

Secondly, once the process flow seems complete, it is time to commit the flow to an electronic medium. This task can be time-consuming and tedious, but it is necessary in order to ensure that the process is in a format that can be easily shared across the organization.

Secrets of the trade

Besides Microsoft Visio, there are numerous other process modelling software packages available in the marketplace. These packages are designed to make the modelling process simpler and less time-consuming through automated drawing techniques. Despite its idiosyncrasies, Microsoft Visio remains the most popular process modelling tool in use.

When process flows are created, they often evolve over time as the modeller begins to find clarity and simplicity in the diagram. As in Level 1, how the diagram looks is important. If a process flow is too complicated or difficult to follow, the reader is not likely to take the time to analyse and understand it. Dividing complex flows over multiple pages is almost always necessary. Do not try to cram a process onto a single page.

The following four steps are recommended.

7.4.1 Step 1 – process flow creation for Level 2

7.4.1.1 Preparations

Using Level 1 as a guide, the modeller now dives into each of the process components. If this is a new process flow for the organization, it should be largely based on best practice that has been adapted to fit the organization. If the process exists within the organization today, the interview and observation notes should be melded with best practice in order to create the target process.

The SLM process must also be practical – especially when it comes to the resources required to execute the process. As the modeller is creating the process, consider available or approved headcount and the level of effort required to perform a task or create a deliverable.

7.4.1.2 List major activities

Select a Level 1 process framework component and begin listing the major activities that should take place within the process. As the list takes shape, reorder the tasks and begin to create an outline with primary tasks and subtasks.

Drawing on the ITIL framework for SLM, and specifically for service review as our example, the primary activities within SLM3 are:

- Planning for service review
- Preparing for a service review meeting
- Conducting a service review meeting
- Post-service review activities.

Now try to dig deeper into each of these four primary activities such that the process flow provides complete guidance to the reader. Building on this list, a more detailed set of activities for the first two primary activities (above) within SLM3 can be set out as follows:

- Planning for service review
  - Create the meeting's agenda
  - Submit special requirements
  - Schedule the meeting and invite attendees
- Preparing for a service review meeting
  - Prepare service reports
  - Examine service performance deficiencies

- Calculate penalties
- Prepare root cause analyses for major incidents
- Consolidate the service improvement plan
- Acquire the change schedule
- Compile final presentation.

Certainly, stakeholders could argue for additional activities, the combining of activities or even the reordering of some activities. This is only an example and could be modified in numerous ways to better fit a number of different IT organizations and businesses.

7.4.1.3 Build an initial flow

Now is the time when the pen-and-paper exercise comes to an end and the modeller moves to a larger medium such as a whiteboard or a poster board. Try to secure a large space to work in over a period of days, where materials can remain in place undisturbed. Coloured sticky notes are an excellent tool for representing activities and decision points in the process flow.

7.4.1.4 Review the flow and collect early feedback

As the flow takes shape, invite a larger audience to view the flow and provide initial feedback. Ensure any external interfaces with other processes are discussed, as well as any deliverables or products that the process will require. For example, understanding what reports availability and capacity management can provide for a given service is critical to the success of the process.

7.4.2 Step 2 – process flow diagramming for Level 2

Once the process flow has been refined on the whiteboard and initially agreed to by a small group of stakeholders, it is now time to commit the process flow to electronic media.

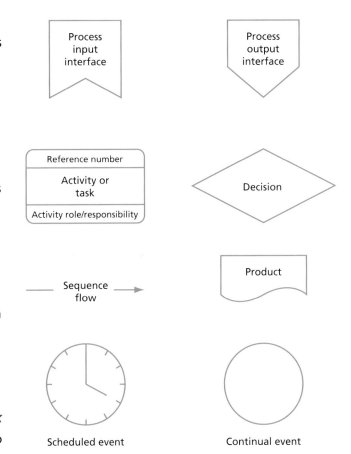

Figure 7.2 Process flow diagram components

The diagramming standard used within this chapter is a hybrid created from several standards and some best practices picked up during the last decade. It is a favourite of this author, but is by no means the only way to model a process flow.

Figure 7.2 is a guide to the different process modelling shapes that will be used within this chapter when creating the Level 2 process flows. The description for each shape is as follows:

- **Process input interface** This is the process activity or output that triggers the process flow to begin.
- **Process output interface** Once a process flow is completed or must be continued on another page, this symbol indicates the coded activity number, activity name and allotted colour of the process that follows.
- **Activity or task** This is the primary shape used within most process flows. It lists three pieces of information. At the top of the box is the activity number code, in the middle of the box is the name of the activity, and at the bottom is the role that is assigned responsibility for the activity's execution.

- **Decision** A decision will only follow an activity symbol and contain a question. Decisions are not given a coded number but are instead associated with the previous process activity. Each decision has one process sequence flow into the decision and two or more coming out to the decision.
- **Sequence flow** Directional indicators for the process flow.
- **Product** A report, completed form or other deliverable that is produced and/or consumed by a process.
- **Scheduled event** A process input that triggers an activity that is scheduled once or on a recurring basis.
- **Continual event** A process input that triggers an activity that is continually taking place.

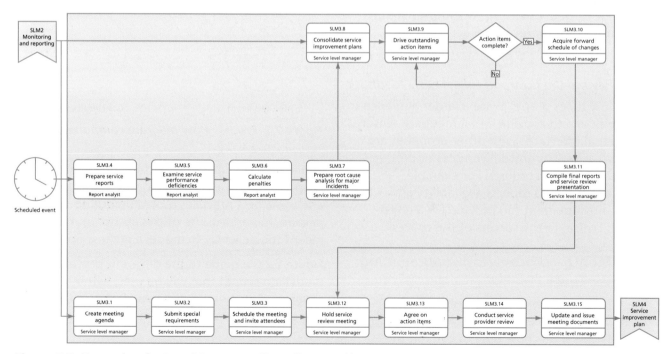

Figure 7.3 Example of a Level 2 process flow diagram (for SLM3)

Processes modelled at Level 2 are often broken up across multiple pages at logical points. The example used in this chapter, which represents about 20% of one process component, is shown in Figure 7.3.

The process is read left to right, with the process inputs or triggers on the left side of the diagram and the outputs to the right. For this process flow, there are parallel activities that are triggered at the same time. Each activity has a unique ID number, which will be referred to when the Level 3 work instructions are created (see section 7.5).

After viewing the process flow and reading a few paragraphs describing the flow at a high level, you should have a very clear idea about how the process works. If not, then the process probably needs to be simplified or divided up further.

You would then continue creating process flow models until the entire Level 1 framework components are mapped at Level 2. Be prepared for it to take approximately one week's effort (40 hours) per process flow to complete this task.

7.4.3 Step 3 – document the process flows for Level 2

As in Level 1, there must be a documented narrative that accompanies the Level 2 process flows. Many organizations choose to expand the Level 1 documentation to include Level 2 at this point. Otherwise, a lot of the information provided within the Level 1 document will be repeated within Level 2.

The following table of contents could be used to create the Level 2 process flow documentation:

- Introduction
  - Purpose and scope
  - Document layout and descriptions of sections
  - References and related documents
- Process overview and description
  - ITSM philosophy
  - Purpose and scope of SLM
  - Process goals and objectives
  - Process benefits to the organization (IT and the business)
- Level 1: Process framework diagram
  - Sub-process descriptions (one paragraph per sub-process)
    - SLM1: SLA management
    - SLM2: Monitoring and reporting
    - SLM3: Service review
    - SLM4: Service improvement plan
    - SLM5: Continual process improvement
  - Major interfaces with other ITSM processes
  - Process stakeholders, roles and responsibilities
- Level 2: Process flow diagrams
  - SLM1: SLA management
    - Process diagram(s) for Level 2
    - Initiation criteria
    - Process inputs
    - Reference data sources (e.g. tools, systems, or functions)
    - Process description – each process activity described at a high level
    - RACI (responsible, accountable, consulted and informed) chart
    - Exit criteria
    - Process outputs

(Note: Repeat the sub-sections above for SLM2 through to SLM5.)

- Process tools and systems
- Process governance and continual process improvement
  - Governance
  - Auditing
  - Metrics
  - Reporting.

At Level 2, the documentation is meant to relate to each sub-process, but not for each activity or decision made. For example, consider the process flow example that was provided for SLM3 (Figure 7.3), where the documentation for SLM3 should relate to the entire process flow.

With regard to the example of a RACI matrix in Table 7.1, the matrix would be expanded such that there is a row for each activity within the SLM3 sub-process (creating 15 rows in total – see Figure 7.3).

This documentation will take time and considerable effort to produce (probably two to three weeks of solid effort after the diagrams are finished), but it will become an extremely valuable reference – and especially for those learning the process for the first time.

7.4.4 Step 4 – review, revision and agreement

Now that the Level 1 and Level 2 process flows are documented electronically, it is time to share them with a wider audience for comments, questions and corrections. The review process is iterative and usually begins via an email distribution to the process stakeholders.

7.5 LEVEL 3 – WORK INSTRUCTIONS

Now that the Level 2 process flow has been completed and agreed, it is time to describe the details behind each of the process activities and decisions. A work instruction (WI) should be created for each numbered activity. If a decision follows a particular activity, the decision criteria are described as well.

A WI contains much more detail than a process flow (Level 2) and is only created if very detailed instructions are needed. The intent of the WI is to be used as a reference: it will provide guidance and consistency when resources perform specific quality-related tasks within a department.

Table 7.1 Example of a RACI matrix for SLM3, service review

Activity	Responsible	Accountable	Consulted	Informed
SLM3.1 Create agenda	Service level manager	IT service manager	Customer or business rep	Meeting attendees
SLM3.2 Submit special requirements	Customer or business rep	IT service manager	Service level manager	IT service owner
SLM3.3 Schedule meeting and invite attendees	Service level manager	IT service manager	Customer or business rep	Meeting attendees
SLM3.4 Prepare service reports	Service level manager	IT service manager	IT service reporting manager	IT service owner

The structure of the WI document should be developed to meet the needs of the process at hand. The WI elements suggested below are based on best practice and meet the requirements for a comprehensive WI document:

- **Initiation criteria** The prerequisite activities that must be completed before the current activity can be initiated
- **Inputs** The list of mandatory and optional inputs for the activity
- **Outputs** The list of deliverables or products that are generated by the activity
- **Procedure** The detailed series of steps taken to accomplish an activity
- **Exit criteria** The conditions under which the activity can be confirmed as having been completed.

Continuing with the SLM process example in Figure 7.3, we can see that there are 15 Level 3 WIs required for process component SLM3.

Consider the audience who will be reading and following the WIs as they are being written. The WIs written for a frontline service desk employee are going to have a very different tone and structure from those written for SLM. A service desk resource will need to be informed in detail about how to use the telephone and incident management systems, how to escalate or assign an incident to a backline group, etc. These are very technical tasks. In contrast, SLM personnel will need to know how and where to collect performance reports, analyse these reports, research performance abnormalities, and be prepared to explain service performance in non-technical terms to a business audience.

7.6 SUMMARY

Process modelling can be tedious and time-consuming, but it is required in order to ensure that the process design is well understood, agreed and documented as a reference for those who will execute the process.

The key to clear, concise process modelling is breaking the process down into levels or layers of detail. If an organization starts with the big picture (Level 1, process framework), then defines the process sub-components (Level 2, procedural flows) and lastly builds the detail behind each process activity and decision point (Level 3, work instructions), the process modelling effort will be more effective. As with any large effort, breaking the work down into manageable pieces and ensuring there are checkpoints along the way will ensure success and acceptance.

Structure of service level agreements

8

8 Structure of service level agreements

Service level agreements (SLAs), being one of the service level management (SLM) essentials, require special examination. Lack of experience in defining the structure of the SLA may result in the failure of SLM itself, and possibly the failure of service provision.

This chapter addresses the structure of the SLA and describes in detail its elements (see Figure 8.1). Note that processes and activities that are related to the SLA, such as metrics, negotiations and reporting, are addressed in other chapters.

By the end of this chapter you should be able to develop an SLA that will fit the specific needs of your organization. The structure of the SLA will then provide a platform that only needs to be populated with content.

8.1 SERVICE LEVEL AGREEMENT OVERVIEW

The SLA is a principal instrument for SLM to monitor, measure and report the levels of service that were agreed with the customer, with the aim of continual service improvement (CSI).

Definition: service level agreement

A service level agreement is an agreement between an IT service provider and a customer. It describes the IT service, documents service level targets, and specifies the responsibilities of the IT service provider and the customer. A single agreement may cover multiple IT services or multiple customers (ITIL Glossary).

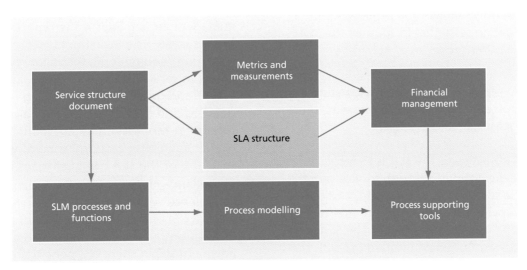

Figure 8.1 SLM design activity map – SLA structure

There are many different approaches and associated templates for creating an SLA – so many, in fact, that it is often difficult and confusing for an organization to select a suitable one. Moreover, many of the prescribed approaches regard the SLA as the end result, and not a means to an end. As such, you can end up with an appealing document that sits in the bottom drawer of your desk.

Without the focus on CSI, which can only be achieved through a practical SLA, SLA management disintegrates into an insufferable quarrel over a document that has no resemblance to the services it is meant to measure and improve.

Secrets of the trade

The service level agreement (SLA) is one of the most common items in an IT service management (ITSM) framework. Most companies that have not adopted ITIL assume that if they implement an SLA they are ITIL-compliant. Some companies focus on the SLA to the point where they establish SLA management rather than SLM, ignoring not only many of the processes and functions that are essential to support the SLA but also the other processes of SLM.

The SLA is an important tool and requires analysis and planning regarding its structure and content – but, as this publication suggests, there is more to SLM than just the SLA.

The primary objective of the SLA is to set reasonable expectations, through service targets, regarding the services being provided, and grant the service provider the ability to monitor, measure and report on agreed service levels. The SLA is documented, negotiated and signed off with the customer by the service level manager. Internal functions and processes ensure that the service targets are reflected in service provision, as well as being monitored and reported as agreed.

In this chapter we present a practical SLA structure that guarantees the execution of CSI activities and facilitates effective SLA management. Our approach to SLAs, which is based on tried-and-tested best practice, allows you to address the challenges of building and managing a practical SLA by prescribing a structure that will help you with the following:

- **Navigation** The SLA contains a great deal of information relating to stakeholders and services. The SLA should be user friendly and designed in such a way that information can be easily found and understood.
- **Scalability** The structure of the SLA should facilitate modifications, additions and deletions of services and service metrics without significant changes to the structure and content of the document. See section 14.5.4 on SLA audit for further details.
- **Reporting** One of the most important SLA management activities is the reporting of service levels. The SLA should incorporate reporting requirements that allow both quick access to service status – e.g. by using RAG (red, amber and green) status reporting – and detailed drill-down root cause analysis reporting. Moreover, the SLA metric structure, explained in later sections, should reflect the structure of the SLA compliance report.
- **Compliance management** Demonstrating compliance with service targets is crucial to effective SLM and the managing of customer perceptions and expectations. This can be pertinent when there are penalties and/or bonuses associated with SLA compliance.

Note that the process for developing service metrics and measurements, which will be included in the SLA, is handled separately in Chapter 9.

It is good practice to perform a pilot period for the SLA. The pilot SLA allows a new SLA to be reviewed within an agreed time period to evaluate whether the conditions and targets specified within the SLA best reflect the needs of both the customer and the service provider.

Secrets of the trade

While working on different projects and developing this chapter, I spoke to many experts in the field to collect opinions and approaches. As we went through the different SLA structures laid out before us, we documented the advantages and disadvantages of each. This chapter presents a solution to many of the setbacks and attempts to cover all the needs and scenarios of SLM.

You may find yourself working with an existing SLA simply because it is the legacy document. If this document is defective, the situation will cause a chain reaction that will negatively impact other activities you are responsible for. In this case, you should go back to the first chapter of this publication and implement the service strategy of the process, work on the design and prove to your stakeholders (mainly senior managers and customers) via a business case that a new structure of SLA is required to improve service delivery.

8.2 REFINING THE SLA STRUCTURE

Although this chapter prescribes a common SLA structure that can be applied to most service organizations, you still need to refine the structure when considering the following SLA design prerequisites:

- **Customer-based vs service-based SLA** A customer-based SLA is an agreement that covers all the services for one customer. A service-based SLA is an agreement that covers one service for multiple customers. This publication very much recommends the customer-based SLA, which allows greater control and flexibility for maintenance and improvements.
- **Service catalogue** In a well-established and mature ITSM environment, the service catalogue provides the single source of information on all chartered and agreed-to services with the customer. In such an environment all services required for the SLA can be found in the service catalogue. If a service catalogue is available, then the structure of the SLA should be borrowed from the service catalogue as shown in Figure 8.2.

If a service catalogue is not available, you are well advised to spend time creating common service definitions and avoid the pitfalls of creating an SLA structure that already exists for similar services offered to different customers. It is not uncommon for account managers to commit the service organization to widely differing service measurements and targets for what are basically identical services.

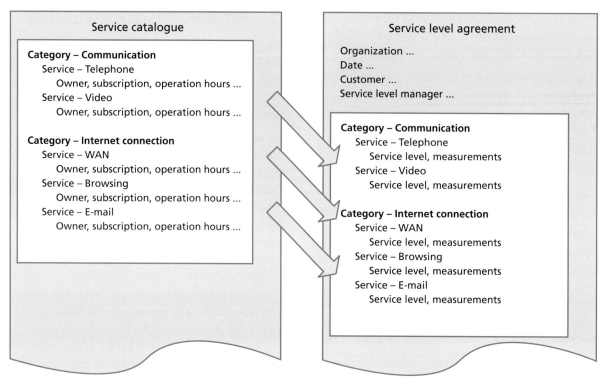

Figure 8.2 Service catalogue parallel to SLA

8.2.1 Service structure document

The service structure document forms the basis for the SLA. Factors such as the structure of the customer base as well as the services being offered will certainly influence the SLA structure design.

For example, if you discover that the customer is being represented as a single entity, it may be possible to incorporate all services into a single SLA. Equally, if you have a limited service offering to multiple customers, it may be possible to create a master SLA that requires minimal change when deployed to each new customer. Alternatively, if you have multiple customers consuming multiple services, or customers that require an organizational or geographical mix of services, you may require a more complex SLA structure, such as a multi-tier SLA, to cater for the multitude of possible service offerings.

8.2.2 Outsourcing engagement versus enterprise

In an outsourcing engagement, the SLA is often included as a schedule to a commercial contract. In this case the agreed service measurements, metrics and targets are contractually binding and can have a significant impact on the overall contract. It is not uncommon for a service contract to specify provisions for cancelling the contract in the event of continued service level breaches. In this case the desire to establish a simplified and standard SLA is secondary to meeting the specific contractual requirements of the customer.

In an enterprise engagement, the SLA is an internal document that reflects the service targets of internal customers. As such, the SLA structure can be more informal and the focus can be on a simplified and standard SLA structure.

8.3   THE SLA STRUCTURE

The SLA structure proposed in this chapter aims to balance two often competing interests, namely flexible and reusable SLAs versus customer requirements.

Many SLAs we have encountered attempt to capture all possible variations of customer requirements and expectations into a single monolithic document, resulting in an SLA structure that is disorganized, difficult to understand and impossible to manage. Alternatively, where SLA owners have attempted to standardize and simplify the SLA structure, this often results in limited abilities to capture changes and customization that are justifiably required by the business.

By separating the service definitions from the service measurements, we are able to present an SLA structure that is both uncomplicated and easy to manage, yet capable of supporting a broad range of customization. Two distinct parts are established in the SLA, and they are detailed in sections 8.3.1 and 8.3.2 respectively below. The two parts are:

- **SLA definitions document** The first part of the SLA, in textual format, provides general information regarding the agreement and details the scope of services.

- **Service objectives table** The second part of the SLA, in table format, lists the services and their associated service level targets.

The advantage of this two-part structure is that it allows you to keep the basic elements of all the services (in the SLA definitions part) while providing the flexibility to meet customer expectations (in the service objectives table).

Another advantage is that after initial SLA negotiations and approval, it is straightforward to maintain the service objectives table without the need to modify the underpinning SLA definitions. After all, the most important information regarding the SLA is the list of service level objectives (SLOs) and their respective targets.

Secrets of the trade

During different opportunities for speaking about the SLA structure, I was frequently asked 'What are the critical components of an SLA?' or 'What are the components that must be included in every SLA?'

This chapter provides a simplified SLA structure and details its components. However, it is important to learn the theory behind the development of the SLA. There are four essential components to a good SLA: service description, targets, calculations and penalty/reward. The theme that runs through these four components tells the story of the relationship between the service provider and the customer. What are the services that you provide? What are the targets for those services? How do you measure them? And what are the consequences of good or poor service provision?

At the operational level the service objectives table provides a reference document for implementing service level monitoring and reporting. For example, the SLA compliance report can be designed to mirror the list in the service objective table, and the agenda of the service review meeting may be ordered by the list indicated in the service objective table.

8.3.1 SLA definitions document

The SLA definitions document describes the common and global elements of SLM between the service provider and customer. It acts as a reference document, providing intrinsic detail of service level monitoring, calculation methods and reporting requirements.

The document is composed of two main sections. The first section provides general agreements and information that applies to all services and that addresses the common elements of the agreement. The second section provides an overview of services, service measurements, SLA tracking periods and detailed calculation definitions.

By separating the common features of service level monitoring from customer-specific SLOs and targets, we greatly reduce the complexities of managing multiple SLAs. The SLA definitions document holds fixed information common to all the SLAs – for example, charts of working hours, metric calculation algorithms and SLA exception tables.

The required content of the SLA definitions document is set out in more detail below. Note that it is not recommended that every type of SLA should necessarily contain all the content listed. It is suggested that you consider the proposed content when designing an SLA structure and templates, incorporating only content that is relevant and appropriate to your customer needs.

Before we expand on the SLA definitions document, consider the following two guidelines:

- **Variables** Attempt to document the variables of the service itself. Avoid specifying elements that are dependent on the customer type and usage of the service.
- **Simple language** There is no need for the agreement to be written in legal terminology. Plain language aids common understanding and will lessen the risk of the customers misinterpreting the SLA. It is also recommended that the SLA contains a glossary defining any terms and providing clarity for any areas of ambiguity.

8.3.1.1 Section 1 – general agreements

The general agreements section is used to define component services at a very high level, and to document the expectations of both sides.

- **Description of the agreement** Brief description of the contents of the SLA, including an introduction to the organization/business and the objective of the agreement.
- **Version reference number** Each SLA version is assigned a unique identification number for audit control purposes and is copied as a configuration item in the configuration management database.
- **Owner** This entry identifies who is responsible for the SLA document. Typically the service level manager is responsible for the SLA, but it is imperative to assign an owner as a contact person in case of changes and for review purposes.
- **Customer** This describes the person and/or organization that is purchasing the products/services defined in this SLA. The entry must clearly identify the resource or function that is authorized to sign the agreement and ultimately review its performance.

- **Service provider** The service provider is a single entity identified for the customer as carrying out operational activities. Note that the service level manager should not be identified as the service provider; the service level manager is responsible for monitoring and reporting on the quality of services, while the service provider is responsible for the provision of the services.
- **SLA period** This is the effective period of the SLA, not the effective period of the services. The SLA period is tied to the contract between the service provider and the customer, and can be renewed or retired at the end of the period. Services listed in the SLA may specify effective periods or dates that identify transition periods for service level measurement.
- **Pilot SLA period** The pilot SLA period is a time when service levels are monitored and reported to verify customer expectations and service baselines. At the end of this period, the SLA is reviewed through the SLA audit process and, if necessary, adjusted and finalized. The entry should also define how adjustments to the SLA are managed at the end of the pilot SLA period. Note that the pilot SLA period can be set up for each service level measurement and is not necessarily for the entire SLA. In this case, additional attributes will be defined for each SLO.
- **Service review** This entry gives a short description of the service review process by answering critical questions such as:
  - Who is included in these meetings?
  - What is the agenda?
  - What are the responsibilities of the parties?
  - When are these meetings?
  - What is the timing?

- **Service level credits** It is good practice to incorporate service level penalties and/or bonuses into the SLA. Service level credits or bonuses may be defined as an earn-back mechanism on incurred service level penalties. Service level credits are an excellent instrument for both motivating and influencing service provision. For further information on penalty calculations, see Chapter 10.
- **Service level reporting** Service level reporting is an important and ongoing function of SLA management. Reports for SLA compliance, service credits and underpinning operational data need to be defined and agreed. In this section the stakeholders will agree on the reporting requirements, including:
  - Report format or platform
  - Interval – weekly, monthly etc.
  - Report receivers
  - Report content.

8.3.1.2 Section 2 – service definitions

- **Service name and description** In non-technical language, provide the name and a high-level description of the key business functions, deliverables and all relevant information necessary to describe the service and its scale, impact and priority for the business.

  The service name is the service category or service tower, where instances of service names can be, for example, 'email', 'internet', 'WAN', 'LAN' or 'voice'. The service level description will be structured in groups of service categories, and for each service we identify service measurements.
- **SLA tracking periods** This entry outlines the periods in which SLA measurements are tracked for compliance purposes. This is particularly

important where service provision crosses time zones and national boundaries where business hours and public holidays differ. It is also good practice to have a tiered structure and define SLA tracking period options. For example, SLA tracking may be tailored in accordance with the criticality of customer sites or services. Table 8.1 provides an example of tracking periods.

Table 8.1 Example of SLA tracking periods

Tier	Site type	Working hours
1	Very critical site	24×7
2	Critical site	24×7 excluding public holidays
3	Premium site	7 a.m.–6 p.m. Monday–Friday
4	Basic site	9 a.m.–5 p.m. Monday–Friday

Secrets of the trade

Defining working hours is one of the most complicated tasks. We recommend that it is completed at the service design stage and documented in the service catalogue. However, it is not uncommon for the service level manager to define this as part of the SLA deployment work. In this case, we advise spending time with the service provider and with operations to study workloads and analyse the cost of support hours. Many times you will find that the cost of providing 24×7 support is not much more than 9–5 support, allowing you to increase customer satisfaction without having to spend significantly more than the 9–5 support costs.

- **Service maintenance** Services require maintenance from time to time for repairs, upgrades and preventive measures. Although you should attempt to perform maintenance activities without interrupting service provision, and services should be designed for continuous availability of service, the SLA should define provisions for:
  - **Planned downtime** The planned downtime is a scheduled time for service providers to work on service maintenance. This time requires unavailability of the service.
  - **Unplanned downtime** This is time that cannot be predicted or planned. Unplanned downtime is usually allowed after the customer has been notified and approval has been given in writing. It is generally agreed that the time will be deducted from the SLA performance calculation as service unavailability.

- **SLA exceptions** The service provider will do its best to provide services as defined in the SLA. However, we should anticipate exceptions that are outside the control of the service provider. Those exceptions will be defined and agreed with the customer in this entry. Table 8.2 gives examples that might appear in an exception list. The exceptions are often referred to as 'SLA clock stoppers'.

- **Service measurements** A list of service measurements should be included in the service description (see, for example, Table 8.3). The service measurements will be converted into SLOs once service level targets are assigned to them. Note that the SLOs and the service level targets are defined in the service objectives table.

- **Metric definitions** Each metric definition provides a detailed description of how a service measurement is implemented. The purpose of creating a metric definition is to involve technical functions in the definition of service levels and ensure that metrics are measurable and reportable. Table 8.4 outlines a recommended template for specifying a service metric.

Table 8.2 Examples of exception codes

Exception type	Description
Phone delay	An attempt was made to contact the customer for information, but was unsuccessful because the customer was unavailable. You do not have the information needed from the customer to continue incident resolution.
End user delay	The end user has requested that work be performed at a later time.
Customer delay	The customer has requested that work be performed at a later time or the engineer cannot perform an action as a direct result of a customer. For instance, a patch might be needed on a customer system and incidents related to the problem cannot be resolved until the customer applies the patch.
Awaiting parts	Infrastructure configuration items are not in storage, which prevents the restoration of the service.
Vendor delay	Work being performed by a vendor prevents an engineer from working on the customer's problem.

Table 8.3 Example of service and service measurement hierarchy

Service	Service measurement
Network availability	Percentage of time that the network is available
	Time to respond to network availability incidents
	Time to resolve network availability incidents
Video services	Videoconferencing network availability
	Successful videoconferencing start-ups
	Time to respond to video services incidents
	Web conferencing network availability

■ **Data sources and tools** When designing service levels and their calculations, you have to keep in mind the data availability and quality that will be required to support the calculation. This will require your meeting with the operational teams to obtain technical information including data mapping and data integrity.

We have now concluded our description of the SLA definitions document within the SLA. Remember that the objective of the document is to provide all the information for tracking and monitoring the relevant services. This is not the service catalogue; you do not have to provide all information regarding the services, but only information that is relevant to the customer and the performance of the services.

Secrets of the trade

In a previous project I took part in an emergency service review meeting. The customer called the main ITIL process owners and other operational managers, including the service desk, to analyse why service levels for 'time to respond' were at 65%, when they should be at 98% for many of the service levels. This SLA contained severe penalty clauses that created tension and mistrust between the sides. The customer more than anything wanted to know 'why?'.

The service provider gathered resources on that day to analyse the data. The result of the analysis indicated that, in many incidents, engineers were deployed on site to resolve the incidents but were stopped at the building's security desk because they did not carry adequate access authorization. This issue led to many service level breaches.

A service improvement plan was defined immediately in the CSI register, composed of two action items. The first was to provide the engineers with access passes to the customer's sites. The second action item was the addition of an exception code to the incident management system allowing an SLA clock stop in such scenarios. The impact of the implementation of the foregoing was immediate, and the following SLA report was clear of breaches.

Table 8.4 Metric definitions template

Attribute	Description
Name	Unique name for the service metric
Description	Brief description from a customer's point of view of what the metric is measuring
Unit	The unit of measurement being returned by the metric, e.g. percentage or hours
Time periods	The different time periods for which this metric is able to calculate, e.g. hourly, daily, weekly, monthly, quarterly or yearly
Measurement dimensions	The different measurement dimensions for which this metric is able to calculate, e.g. region → country → city → site
Tracking periods	Timeslots that apply to the metric, e.g. business hours, 24×7, excluding public holidays
Targets and parameters	The required service level targets and (optional) parameters that can be specified for the metric
Measurement	Detailed description of how the measurement is undertaken, including definitions of measurement components and any constraints
Calculation	The mathematical formula used to calculate the result
Data sources	Detailed description of data elements needed to calculate the measurement
Methodology	Detailed description of how data are to be collected for measurement purposes

Table 8.5 Example of a basic service objectives table for a WAN service

SLA reference	Service level objectives	Compliance level (%)
2.1	End-to-end WAN availability (very critical sites)	99.80
2.2	End-to-end WAN availability (critical sites)	99.60
2.3	End-to-end WAN availability (premium sites)	99.60
2.4	Timely notification of excessive network utilization	99.80
2.5	Timely notification of network under-utilization	99.50
2.6	Round-trip transit delay of WAN core services below target threshold	99.80

8.3.2 Service objectives table

The service objectives table specifies the customer's objective for service level targets, presenting the compliance level for each service. Whereas the SLA definitions document within the SLA specifies general agreements, service definitions and detailed metric definitions, the list of SLOs specifies only compliance levels as agreed with the customer. After the SLA is signed, the service objectives table is used at an operational level to measure and report service level compliance.

SLOs are specific measurable characteristics of the service mapped to a service level target. For example, videoconferencing may have two SLOs with their corresponding service level targets.

What attributes should be specified for SLOs? Table 8.5 shows an example containing a basic set of attributes. The service, an SLO identity, an SLO name and the service level target are considered the minimum set of data to include in the service objectives table entry. Note that an SLA may specify multiple service level targets (e.g. minimum target and expected target).

It is recommended that attributes used to configure SLOs are consistent across all SLOs specified for the customer. There are three main options for defining SLOs:

■ **Basic SLO definitions** In this option the SLO uses the service level target, with all additional definitions and conditions defined explicitly in the SLA definition document. The advantage of this option is that it has a light structure and is simple to navigate and easy to understand. The disadvantage is that this option will require the user to look up the definition for the services when questions are raised.

■ **Comprehensive SLO definitions** In this option each SLO defines all of the attributes specified in the SLA definitions document. Put another way, the SLA definitions document acts as a data dictionary for SLO definitions. This option is very useful in complex SLA situations.

■ **Customized SLO definitions** Many service level managers customize their SLO definitions by striking a balance between the two alternatives (basic and comprehensive) shown above. In this option the SLA definitions document gives all the possible entries and each SLO defines those attributes that are applicable to meet customer requirements. This is a very common approach in the industry because it gives the flexibility to modify the SLO on an ongoing basis while knowing that all information is documented in the SLA definitions document (see, for example, Table 8.6).

Customized SLO definitions are often desirable as it may not be practical or feasible to apply all SLA definitions to an SLO implementation.

8.4 CRITICAL SERVICE LEVELS VERSUS KEY PERFORMANCE INDICATORS

When designing the SLA structure, we consider two types of SLO:

■ **Critical service levels** The SLOs are specific and measurable characteristics of the SLA, such as availability and response time. They are the critical measurements of the service and are subject to financial penalties in the event of a service performance breach.

■ **Key performance indicators (KPIs)** The SLOs are the early-warning indicators for operational issues and permit corrective actions to be implemented. KPIs are not subject to service level credits or penalties but serve as an indicator of delivery performance and measure the performance of the service provider to the customer. Typically, the KPI will monitor elements of the service that are of interest to the customer but are not critical for the operation of the business. They form the base for performance reporting requirements.

Critical service levels and KPIs should be clearly distinguished in the SLA definitions document and in the list of SLOs. Since their management is undertaken differently and they are approached differently, it is good practice to separate them within both the SLA definitions document and the service objectives table.

Table 8.6 Expanded service level objectives for a WAN service (see Table 8.5 for the list of service level objectives and compliance levels)

SLA reference	Penalty (%)	Working hours	Planned downtime	Unplanned downtime	Exception (Y/N)
2.1	2.00	24×7	Fri 8–10 p.m.	N	N
2.2	1.50	24×7	Fri 8–10 p.m.	N	N
2.3	1.00	7 a.m. to 6 p.m..	Fri 8–10 p.m.	Y	N
2.4	1.00	N/A	N/A	N/A	N
2.5	1.00	N/A	N/A	N/A	N
2.6	1.00	N/A	N/A	N/A	N

8.5 SUMMARY

The structure of the SLA will determine much of the success of SLM. The two-part SLA illustrated in this chapter ensures the simplification and standardization that are key elements for the ongoing management of the SLA.

In later chapters we discuss different approaches for improving the SLA, using elements such as pilot period, SLA audits and CSI. Those elements are based on the assumptions that the SLA is structured according to a design founded on analysis and an alignment with technical and business requirements.

Metrics development and the 'solution sets' technique

9

9 Metrics development and the 'solution sets' technique

In this chapter you will learn about measuring services through the use of service metrics. We will start by considering current approaches to measuring service quality, from a customer's point of view, and present a set of service metric types that capture the main quality aspects of an IT service.

We will then apply these service metric types within a three-step development process that will guide you through the process of developing service metrics to measure service quality, based on both technical capabilities and customer needs. At the end of the process you will be in a position to offer your customer some options of service levels that reflect, and balance, your technical and organizational constraints with the budgetary and business constraints of your customers.

We will close the chapter by providing you with some practical guidelines on metric development, including guidance for optimizing metric design and deployment through the use of 'solution sets', an adept approach to service metric management.

9.1 SERVICE MEASUREMENT OVERVIEW

In previous chapters we developed the strategy and processes of our organization and started the design of the service level agreement (SLA) by analysing the service delivery environment and

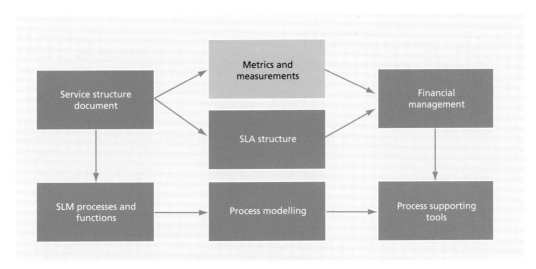

Figure 9.1 SLM design activity map – metrics and measurement

identifying processes and procedures that support the overall service level management (SLM) process. These activities proved excellent inputs into the development of the SLA structure.

Although in our description of service level maintenance in this publication we have completed the SLA structure, we are not yet ready to negotiate the SLA with the customer. First, we must gather the requirements for service measurement, agree calculation methods and define service level targets with supporting business cases. In other words, we need to design and implement the underpinning service metrics (see Figure 9.1).

The development of service metrics for service measurement purposes is the analytical part of the SLM process. It requires us to analyse the service being offered (or proposed) and to work together with stakeholders to create a list of service metrics that are capable of monitoring and reporting the customer's desired quality of service against quantifiable service level targets.

When negotiating with the customer, you should be prepared to present, with the relevant detail, the service levels and service targets, including their calculations and metric collection methods. By doing so, you will establish your reputation as a professional and trusted adviser – two characteristics that will grant you rapid and smooth SLA negotiation and sign-off.

Secrets of the trade

Many of the service levels listed in SLAs may give you a feeling of déjà vu. The figure 99.99% seems to take a dominant place on the sheet. I have been in meetings where it was explained to the customer: 'We will do our best to provide you with the highest level of service – but according to ITIL it is not a good practice to set 100% targets and so we have set them at 99.99% across the board.' And I am sitting there thinking, 'There are so many things wrong with that statement, on so many levels.'

In real terms a downtime of 99.99% implies a permissible outage of:

- Less than 9 seconds in a 24-hour period
- Less than 5 minutes in a 30-day month
- Less than 53 minutes in a 365-day year.

Be prepared to maintain extremely reliable and robust systems, processes and procedures to accommodate such a high service level!

In mid-2009, I took part in a process improvement project where I was an adviser to one of the most professional service level managers I have ever worked with. We did not see eye to eye on some of the basic concepts of SLM. For example, he was a lot firmer with the customer than I would recommend. However, he always prepared his presentations and whatever came out of his mouth was based on data that he worked hard to collect and analyse. It was common to find him reworking data at 10 p.m. in his office.

One of the deliverables we worked on was the SLA annual review. When this particular service level manager accepted his position, he inherited legacy processes and SLAs. This review was a good opportunity to improve core assets of the process, including service targets. The work that we did to prepare the material included process documentation, calculation of different service targets, and options based on different cost models.

What the service level manager achieved through this work was customer respect and buy-in. There were barely any negotiations involved in the process; the customer was clear on the service levels and their options, which resulted in the completion of the SLA review in a matter of days, with high customer satisfaction.

Service measurement is as much an art as a science. It may prove difficult at first but the results are, over time, worth the effort. Moreover, rigorous documentation provides valuable ongoing reference material. Keep in mind, though, that service measurement is not an end in itself. The end result is an efficient monitoring and reporting activity that will improve the actual and perceived quality of service to the customer. As such, do not be afraid of trial and error, making adjustments to the service metrics as needed.

Although service measurement from a customer's perspective is the stated goal, the cost of implementing any proposed service metrics measurement must also be considered, as must the costs associated with meeting increased service level targets. This may sound too high-level or even obvious, but in this chapter we will illustrate how the balance between customer satisfaction and cost takes a very practical stance.

9.2 SERVICE METRICS OVERVIEW

There are many theories and methodologies regarding service metrics. Continual service improvement (CSI) defines three types of metrics for the organization to support CSI activities:

- **Service metrics** Metrics associated with measuring the quality of the service being delivered to the customer
- **Process metrics** Metrics associated with measuring service management processes, often derived from proven best practice (e.g. ITIL or COBIT)
- **Technology metrics** Metrics associated with measuring the underlying technical components that comprise the customer services (e.g. processor performance, disk usage, database utilization).

SLM focuses on service metrics. Unfortunately, the distinction between metric types has not always been clear cut, and in many cases process metrics and technology metrics have become part of SLA measurements. This obscurity surrounding the metric types stems from practical considerations as well as more philosophical beliefs regarding the scope and meaning of 'IT service'.

The practical considerations are often associated with technical limitations or availability of automated monitoring tools to capture the customer's view of a service. For instance, the desire to measure the end-to-end response time of a business application across a LAN/WAN connection is no trivial undertaking. Without the appropriate 'tooling', it may not be possible to implement this desired service metric.

Despite significant advances in available monitoring tools, too often we still see a focus on components and component management, rather than the management of customer services. How many IT service providers proudly present a colourful dashboard with a plethora of measurements from systems, applications and databases? Always keep in mind the goal of service metrics, which is the measurement of service quality from the customer's experience. Measurements like database utilization rarely correlate directly with customer experience or satisfaction level.

The contention surrounding the many different interpretations and views of 'IT services', combined with the latest vogue in service management, may result in service metrics that include anything from 'the percentage of undetected firewall attacks' to 'the percentage of patients who do not require a follow-up doctor's appointment'. The approach adopted in this publication does not subscribe to any particular philosophy or latest fad in service management; neither does it prescribe any absolute view on service processes. Rather, it draws on a number of well-established service measurement approaches to derive a common framework, based on service metric types, for the development of service metrics.

The ultimate goal of service metrics design is to arrive at a list of service metrics that translates into an SLA in a manner where service quality can be measured and reported as required by your customer, within practical and cost limitations. To this end we prescribe a number of metric types that can be applied to any service definition, yet provide a uniform SLA structure.

9.2.1 Service measurement approaches

One of the biggest challenges in SLM is defining metrics that truly measure the quality of services from a customer's point of view. In the past, metrics have focused primarily on monitoring infrastructure component availability and overall system performance, such as the availability and performance of databases and network components. However, as IT service management (ITSM) matures we are starting to see a positive move towards a business-centric, service-oriented approach, where the service metrics are defined in terms of service availability, performance, reliability and functionality for customers and end users. Within this context, the extent to which IT services are intertwined with business processes or service management processes does not prevent us from defining a set of service metric types that can be applied to a wide range of IT services.

Adopting a standard set of service metric types facilitates reuse of metrics across services, and the ability to compare like with like when reviewing multiple SLAs or comparing service quality measurements across multiple services. The service metric types presented in this chapter are drawn from a number of prevailing and widely used service measurement approaches – in particular, the 'end-to-end service management' and the 'availability management' service quality measurement approaches.

The former of these two approaches focuses on service quality measures for availability, performance and support. The latter approach focuses on quality measures for availability, reliability and maintainability. Although the two approaches are similar in measuring availability, the latter approach omits performance measures and extends the focus of availability to include overall reliability of the service (i.e. time between disruptions). Finally, the support measures of the end-to-end approach focus on the quality of support on a per-service disruption basis, whereas the maintainability measure considers the overall effectiveness of restoring the service to normal, based on all recorded disruptions.

Keep in mind, though, that the philosophical discussions of what is the superior approach for service measurement will continue to resonate in our industry but, truth be told, there is no single best approach. This is mainly because both IT service providers and IT customers are increasingly looking to exploit improved service management capabilities in today's complex and ever-changing business and IT environments.

The service metric types set out below do not prescribe any particular measurement method or technology but, rather, represent service quality measurements that align with user perceptions of service quality. So before designing and implementing your service metrics you should understand the different measurement methods and technologies available to you.

9.2.2 Service metric types

When you purchase an internet connection for your home, you expect certain levels of service quality from your chosen service provider. You may want to have guaranteed access during the day, but will accept occasional maintenance periods at night. You may want a fast download rate, but are not too concerned about the upload rate. In the case of a service disruption, you would expect a quick response to your query and a quick resolution. And, finally, you expect a certain level of stability in the service, i.e. you would not expect service disruptions to occur on a regular basis or to last for excessive time periods. These same service quality measurements are expected by a business

unit that receives IT services from its IT department and the same is expected by a customer who pays for IT services.

Let's break down the foregoing example. The measurements that we can derive from our customer perspective on service quality are service availability, service performance, service support and service stability. As a customer your main concern is that the service is available to be used; secondly, you want adequate performance levels; and, thirdly, if the service is not available or does not perform adequately, you want a quick response to your incident and quick recovery of the service; you also expect a level of consistency and stability in the overall service provision.

This breakdown of desired service measurements provides us with the following service metric types (with their outline definitions):

- **Service availability** Ability of a service to perform its agreed function when required, and to measure the end users' ability to access the service at a given point in time
- **Service performance** Ability of a service to perform to an agreed level that the end user deems acceptable. There is often a grey area between performance and availability – i.e. at what level of diminished performance is the service deemed to be unavailable?
- **Time to respond** As part of service support, time-to-respond metrics measure the time it takes the support function to respond to a service failure or a query submitted by an end user
- **Time to resolve** As part of service support, the time-to-resolve metric measures the time it takes the support function to resolve a service disruption and restore normal service operation

- **Reliability** As part of service stability, a measure of how long a service can perform its agreed function without interruption. Both mean time between service incidents (MTBSI) and mean time between failures (MTBF) can be used to measure reliability
- **Maintainability** As part of service stability, an overall measure of the time required to restore the service to normal working after a disruption. Mean time to restore service (MTRS) is used to measure maintainability.

The first two metric types, service availability and service performance, go hand in hand with ITIL's elements of service value creation, namely utility and warranty. ITIL defines 'utility' in terms of what services the customer receives, and 'warranty' in terms of how services are delivered. These two metric types underpin service value creation by safeguarding the utility and warranty elements of service provision.

The time-to-respond metric type aims to reassure the end user that their issue is being worked on and to provide them with the comfort that they are being taken care of. This is an interesting measurement since it relies mainly on human emotion and illustrates how we monitor the 'customer experience' part of the service. The definition of response time can be controversial. In some cases it can mean as little as a phone call or an email reply. In other cases it might mean the time it takes the technician to appear on site.

Equally, the definition of 'time to resolve' can be an area of contention. This metric does not measure the support function's ability to provide a solution for the event or fix the problem. It measures the service from the user experience aspect, which means how long before the customer can use the service again. An incident

record in a customer support system typically includes many time stamps: time logged, time assigned, time resolved, time notified, time closed – and possibly many more. The challenge is to allocate a time stamp that truly represents the customer's view of the world and not just time stamps associated with internal support processes.

The last two metric types in the above list (namely reliability and maintainability), although apparently not of immediate concern to the customer, represent important measurements regarding the perceived quality of the service being provided. A service that is reliable and maintainable increases the customer's confidence in the service provider and is essential for continued first-rate customer relationship management.

The metric types suggested above are not set in stone and you are not restricted to their exclusive use. They do, however, focus on the overall service experience of the customer and provide a framework for standardizing service quality measurements across SLAs. The following section incorporates these metric types in a prescribed process for creating metric definitions.

9.3 SERVICE LEVEL PACKAGES AND SERVICE DIFFERENTIATION

In the previous section we were able to list a set of service metric types that capture the quality of service provision as experienced and desired by the customer. In this section we will apply these metric types to develop service differentiation using service level packages (SLPs) that are typically generated in service strategy, for inclusion in both the service catalogue and the customer's SLA.

ITIL includes the concept of the SLP. The SLP provides a definite level of utility or warranty and is associated with a set of service levels and pricing policies. The primary goal of the SLP is to support different levels of service demand and different market segments. Further information can be found in the demand management documentation (see particularly section 9.5.1.3).

SLM utilizes SLPs and provides different service levels to come up with service differentiation. The process of metric development, illustrated in this chapter, ensures accurate compilation of those service targets.

The primary responsibility of SLM is to ensure that the required levels of service, as expressed and expected by the customer, are aligned with both the technical and organizational capabilities of the service provider, and that the resulting service level measurements are technically feasible, financially justifiable and capable of monitoring and reporting the service provision from a customer's experience.

Moreover, a customer-focused or service-driven IT organization will present the customer with a selection of service level options, allowing the customer to align service level expectations with financial constraints and budgetary realities. Table 9.1 provides an example of a service differentiation for an IT service. Concise and clear, it provides the customer with the option to select an appropriate service level based on cost and needs.

Although the resulting service differentiation may seem straightforward and trivial (an important feature of a customer-focused approach), do not underestimate the level of technical and organizational detail required to derive the tangible figures. Developing the underpinning service metrics together with their associated calculations, monitoring requirements and technical and organizational capabilities is anything but trivial or straightforward. Combine this with the necessity to align internal capabilities with customer

Table 9.1 Example of service differentiation

Service level package	Gold	Silver	Bronze
Service metric			
Service availability	99.99%	98.00%	95.00%
Service performance	1% packet loss	2.5% packet loss	5% packet loss
Time to respond	24×7 support	9 a.m.–5 p.m. support	9 a.m.–5 p.m. support
	Response in 10 minutes	Response in 30 minutes	Response in 60 minutes
Time to resolve	30 minutes	4 hours	8 hours
Reliability	MTBF = 30 days	MTBF = 15 days	MTBF = 7 days
Maintainability	MTRS = 15 minutes	MTRS = 120 minutes	MTRS = 240 minutes
Service costs	$100,000	$75,000	$50,000

requirements and you will quickly appreciate the level of professionalism, skill and tenacity required to set up such a measurement system.

9.4 SERVICE METRIC DEFINITION

Before going on to the development process, it is important to keep in mind that at the core of service differentiation are well-defined and practical service metrics. By collaborating with the appropriate service management processes and functions, and using the list of recommended service metric types, you will develop a set of metric definitions that are capable (when implemented) of measuring the quality of service provision as experienced by the customer.

Table 9.2 outlines the attributes that comprise a service metric definition (based on the template given in Table 8.4 in Chapter 8). Each metric definition provides a detailed analysis and breakdown of all facets of service level monitoring, starting at the top, from the customer's required service levels, right down to the tools and processes needed to perform the metric calculations.

Although the customer will select SLPs based on an analysis of the service metric definitions against customer service target expectations and service provision capabilities, the details of each service metric should be clearly documented and included in the customer's SLA – for further information see Chapter 8. Typically, the customer will expect the details of metric implementation and management to be part of the contractual agreement for service provision and monitoring.

9.5 THE DEVELOPMENT PROCESS

The actual process of developing the service differentiation, and associated service metrics, is performed top-down, starting with a clear understanding of the service at hand (along with customer expectations for measuring service quality), followed by a breakdown of the service into actual quantifiable performance measurements. The final step in the process analyses the financial and technical constraints to arrive at a set of service targets. The three steps to metric development prescribed in this chapter can be summarized as follows (note that although the process is presented as a sequence of steps, in practice a more iterative approach is required):

- **Analyse and map service elements** We start by gathering information about a service, including underlying business requirements and customer expectations. Working together with service portfolio management, service catalogue management and other service management processes and functions is vital in this step. It provides a breakdown of service elements requiring service level measurements.

- **Quantify service targets and service level requirements** During this step of the process, the 'service availability' and 'service performance' metric types (described in section 9.2.2) are scrutinized and specified in detail as tangible service targets against the service elements. A detailed analysis of the technical environment, including available monitoring tools, and agreement with the customer regarding measurement methods and calculations are documented in the service metric definitions.

Table 9.2 Attributes of a service metric definition

Attribute	Description
Service element	Description of the service element being measured
Name	Unique name for the service metric
Description	Brief description from a customer's point of view of what the metric is measuring
Unit	The unit being returned by the metric, e.g. percentage or hours
Time periods	The different time periods that this metric is able to calculate for, e.g. hourly, daily, weekly, monthly, quarterly or yearly
Dimensions	The different measurement dimensions this metric is able to calculate for, e.g. region → country → city → site
Timeslots	Timeslots that apply to the metric, e.g. business hours, 24×7, excluding public holidays
Targets and parameters	The required service level targets and (optional) parameters that can be specified for the metric. Targets and parameters are used to create SLPs
Measurement	Detailed description of how the measurement is undertaken, including definitions of measurement components and any constraints
Calculation	The mathematical formula used for calculating the result
Data sources	Detailed description of data elements needed to calculate the measurement
Methodology	Detailed description of how data are to be collected for measurement purposes
Tools	List of tools to be used for this metric
Dependencies	Identify supporting systems/processes/functions required to provide service and/or metric(s)
Relationships	If this metric is used as a basis for further calculation(s), list those here
User counts	If users are affected and end-user downtime is to be derived/calculated
Audit	Description of whether the metric is to be retained for a particular duration and/or for historical purposes
Escalation	Process to be followed if the metric fails or continues to fail for an agreed period

■ **Quantify service constraints** In the final step, constraints on measurements are investigated and agreed with the customer. Although the stated service targets through the second bullet point are the customer's desired service levels, technical and financial constraints (e.g. resource requirements, technical capability and budget) may dictate limitations on service provision, the end result being a set of service targets acceptable to the customer.

The process enables the development of service metrics that measure service achievement against end-user-focused service level targets within agreed technical and financial constraints. The resulting service targets can be recorded in the customer's SLA and the service catalogue.

The following sections provide you with the necessary detail to complete each step in the process. Each process step is described as follows:

■ **Objective** The primary goal of the step that you are trying to achieve
■ **Inputs** The items you will need to collect before initiating the activities. This also includes the processes and functions that will support you in the activities
■ **Activities** What you need to do and how you need to do it
■ **Outputs** The required deliverables of the step.

Step-specific considerations are also provided with each step.

9.5.1 Step 1 – Analyse and map service elements

Service metrics measure the quality of service provision from a customer's perspective. However, in order to implement meaningful and realistic quality measures, service metrics must be aligned with service usage, customer expectations and technical constraints. In this first step we lay out the relevant information in a structured manner, identifying service elements based on usage and quality requirements.

9.5.1.1 Objective

The objective of Step 1 is to analyse service usage and service quality requirements in order to derive one or more service elements that can be measured, calculated and reported within the customer's SLA. This should include an initial statement regarding the service metric types listed under section 9.2.2.

9.5.1.2 Inputs

To accomplish a comprehensive understanding of the service and the customer's requirements, you will need to collaborate with external processes that hold information about the service, including account management, service management, financial management, and operations management. Inputs typically will include:

■ Service specifications
■ Service catalogue
■ Customer requirements.

9.5.1.3 Activities

Your activity here is to undertake an analysis and compilation of external data. In a mature organization, demand management, IT financial management and service catalogue management develop documents that describe the services in terms of value, business need and cost. Your job is to derive service elements that align with usage patterns, customer expectations and the ability to implement quality measures.

9.5.1.4 Outputs

The result of this activity is a set of service specifications described in business terms, with associated high-level statements regarding service quality measures. You will notice that the definitions are still vague in terms of service quality measures, and in some cases even ambiguous. However, each service element allows service targets to be quantified within the SLA.

9.5.1.5 Organizational considerations

The metric development process is complex and dependent on your organization's structure and maturity. Many tasks in this step are actually outside the scope of SLM. However, you will find yourself facing gaps in the available information, compelling you to spend time delving into and analysing the service, going back and forth between the customer and operations to create an ideal mapping of service measurement requirements.

The two extreme scenarios identified here can be grouped into high- and low-maturity environments. Which one your organization falls into will determine your level of involvement:

■ **High maturity** Organizations that possess a high level of IT service management maturity follow the ITIL lifecycle model, which impacts the SLM process greatly. Service portfolio management, as part of service strategy, defines, analyses, approves and charters new or existing services. The service portfolio utilizes demand management and financial management to examine the services and ensure that decision-making processes are based on accurate data and planning confidence. Decisions regarding services are passed to service design, where service catalogue management documents the services, clearly defining each service by working with stakeholders.

■ **Low maturity** In organizations that are typically smaller in size or have yet to fully adopt best practice such as ITIL or project management, the process of developing the service measurements is significantly different. The resource responsible for monitoring the service levels may be the service level manager – or a delivery manager, who usually also owns the SLAs. This resource performs activities associated with service strategy and service design, including examining the services from the customer perspective, managing stakeholders and identifying requirements.

If you are working in the first type of environment, the process of developing the metric definitions discussed in this chapter (specifically the analysis and mapping of the service) occurs in the overall ITIL service lifecycle development. If you find yourself working in the second type of environment, the process of metric development requires you to carry out a far wider set of activities, including the service specifications, service catalogue and quality measurements. It is outside the scope of this chapter to prescribe a detailed process for developing a service catalogue.

9.5.1.6 Analysing services

When analysing services, keep in mind that the information you collect and map must be sufficient to identify service measurements that are quantifiable and aligned with customer usage patterns. In other words, you will have to perform adequate analysis to enable the implementation of practical service level targets.

To help you gather the information needed for your analysis, here are the types of questions that should be answered during the analysis process:

■ What business need does the service fulfil?
■ What type of availability does the customer require?
■ What is the impact or cost of loss of service?
■ What measurement dimensions should be applied?
■ Does the measurement need to be calculated for different time periods?
■ How long can the customer survive without the service?
■ How much does the customer expect to pay for the level of service they are requesting?
■ What are the different user profiles (e.g. executives, sales staff, administrators etc.) for the service?
■ What are the anticipated peak usage periods of the service?
■ What is the expected maximum usage?

The preferred format of this activity is an examination of existing documents that are produced by the service strategy and service design processes. However, as explained above, you might discover that you are missing information, which requires you to meet with the business and service design functions to complete this step.

You must start with a high-level understanding of the service. See the example box which gives a service description for a videoconferencing service.

9.5.1.7 Mapping service elements
Mapping the initial SLPs represents the breakdown of the core service package into service quality requirements based on customer usage patterns. The objective of this mapping exercise is to set the stage for quantifying the service measurements.

Example

The organization has experienced increased interest in a videoconferencing service in line with what other enterprises are utilizing, with the aim of lowering travelling expenses, making real-time decisions via collaboration, increasing productivity, enhancing collaboration and shortening time-to-market cycles.

The service will be provided via two options:

■ **Personal-based service** This provides a personal high-definition videoconferencing experience and is targeted to support executives and board members
■ **Room-based service** For general videoconferencing use by all staff.

The business requires videoconferencing to be working five days a week since it does not anticipate using the facility at weekends. However, since the different sites are located internationally (within different time zones) and work closely, the personal-based service is required to be available 24×7, while the room-based service can be provided during working hours only. Working hours will be based on GMT.

The peak usage of the service is during senior management calls on Monday mornings, sales call on Wednesday afternoons and quarterly progress meetings.

First, we need to establish the number of SLPs. In the videoconferencing example, there are two packages (personal-based and room-based) dependent on three different user profiles (sales managers, executives and general staff) – see Table 9.3.

The mapping identifies the subservices and their usage. Note that not all services can be broken down into smaller sets of services; nevertheless, their description and usage must be clearly documented through the identification of user profiles.

Once we have identified the service packages that make up the overall service, we map out the three elements of the service – availability, performance and support – and describe their requirements in textual format, as shown in Table 9.4.

9.5.2 Step 2 – Quantify service targets and service level requirements

In Step 2 of the development process, we work with the operational teams to understand how the service is being provided from an operational and technical standpoint. The result is a set of service metric definitions, based on the service metric types given in section 9.2.2. The metric definitions allow us to have an intelligent discussion regarding the customer's expected service targets and to document the desired service targets utilizing service level requirements (SLRs).

9.5.2.1 Objective

The objective of this step is twofold: firstly to create detailed service metric definitions for the service level packages; and, secondly, to document the customer's expressed service targets. Note that this is not the final service target assigned to the service; those figures will have to be reviewed by operations and refined to include any provisioning or technical constraints.

9.5.2.2 Inputs

The inputs for this activity are the service elements documented in Step 1. Other inputs include:

■ Technical documentation and capabilities
■ SLR customer requirements for service targets.

9.5.2.3 Activities

With a clear understanding of customer requirements and business needs, including a basic understanding of service quality measurements,

Table 9.3 Service mapping (videoconferencing example)

Element	Description	User profile
Personal-based	A personal webcam-based videoconferencing facility that enables mobility	Sales managers, executives
Room-based	Stationary cameras and monitors for dedicated conference rooms	General staff

Table 9.4 Service quality measurements (videoconferencing example)

Element	Availability	Performance	Support
Personal-based	24 (hours) × 5 (days a week)	High performance	Phone support 24×5
Room-based	Working hours	Medium performance	On-site support 24×5

we need to go back to the operations and study the service carefully from the technical side. A detailed analysis of the technical environment and underpinning monitoring tools and processes is used to create the metric definitions. Finally, the customer provides input in regard to expected service targets.

9.5.2.4 Outputs

The result of this step is a set of detailed service metric definitions, including service targets, for each service element. Note that the service targets defined here are only temporary and present the desired or ideal situation from the customer's perspective.

9.5.2.5 Defining service level objectives

This step requires you to work with the technical groups, operations, application management and service management process owners to derive the ideal way to measure the user experience of the service. Measurements are expressed in terms of service level objectives (SLOs).

Continuing with the videoconferencing example, we will take one SLP, namely the room-based service, and define it in terms of service availability, service performance and support metric types. Table 9.5 shows a number of SLOs associated with each of the measurements:

Each SLO subsequently needs to be fully specified and agreed with both the customer and internal functions charged with implementing and maintaining the metrics. The customer will be interested in the calculation method (business logic) underlying the service metric, in the granularity of measurements (e.g. time periods, organizational hierarchy or geographical dimensions), in the details used in the measurements and, in some cases, in the tools and methods of service monitoring.

Internal functional groupings, such as technical teams, process managers and reporting teams, are responsible for implementing and maintaining the metrics. They provide important input regarding the technical and financial feasibility of service

Table 9.5 Service measurements (for room-based videoconferencing)

Measurement	Service level objective	Description
Availability	Application availability	The ability of the service to be utilized when required
Performance	Packet loss	Measures the performance of the network in terms of data packets passing across the network that fail to reach their destination
	Jitter	A factor in the assessment of network performance, jitter is a measure of the variability over time of the packet latency across a network
	Latency	Latency measures the delay caused by communication between processors and memory modules over the network in a parallel system
Support	Time to respond	The time it takes the support team to respond to an incident
	Time to resolve	The time it takes to resolve the incident

measurements. You should not underestimate the importance of buy-in from internal teams, including commitments to implement and maintain monitoring data for measurement purposes. Table 9.6 provides an example of a metric definition.

At this point you have come a long way, analysing the service, understanding customer expectations, identifying SLPs and finally coming up with a list of SLOs (metrics) that measure the level of service provision. Now comes the tricky part: we have to come up with service targets with actual numerical levels.

9.5.2.6 Defining service level targets

One of the most important roles of SLM is communication between the service provider and the customer. Without SLM the service provider

will be asking the customer 'How much "network jitter" can you handle?' or 'What is the application availability you expect?' You can imagine the negative energy that can emerge from those types of meeting.

Here is where the value of SLM becomes apparent. The service level manager's role in this activity is to translate technical language to business language, working with the customers to convert their requirements into actual service metric targets – and all done through the SLR document. For example, as a service level manager you will need to explain to the customer that in order to measure the availability of the service, you will have to monitor the application and 'ping' it on a five-

Table 9.6 Example of a service metric definition

Attribute	Description
Name	Latency
Description	Any of several kinds of delay typically incurred in processing network data. A so-called 'low latency' network connection is one that generally experiences short delay times, while a 'high latency' connection generally suffers from long delays.
Unit	Milliseconds (ms)
Time periods	Monthly
Dimensions	Low latency: < 150 ms
	Average latency: < 400 ms
	High latency: > 400 ms
Measurement	Determining the time it takes a given network packet to travel from source to destination and back, the so-called 'round-trip' time
Data sources	Oracle database receives data dumps from ping tests and the Traceroute monitoring tool
Tools	Ping tests, Traceroute

minute interval; or for you to derive thresholds for service performance, you will need to know how many hours of downtime are acceptable.

It is important to establish the SLRs at this point in order to capture the true business needs for the new service – indeed, the SLRs should be an integral part of the process. Doing this will allow you to edit your SLRs with an outline of potential service targets so that, instead of approaching the document with a blank page asking 'What would you like?', you establish a starting point for a productive conversation.

This is a crucial point in the discussion with the customer. The customer calculates cost and business impact regarding unavailability events. And that's why the unavailability must be in a business context and is often expressed as the cost of the service as impacted by unavailability. For example, what does it cost an enterprise for every web sale lost due to the failure of the hosting server? However, there are intangible costs too, and these are a bit more difficult to calculate. For example, if your website is not responding well your competition is just a click away.

The service may be defined as critical, e.g. when the business loses money due to service unavailability. In the videoconferencing example we have been using, the customer may indicate that the service is not critical, although the personal-based videoconferencing assists in sales efforts and therefore cannot tolerate more than an hour of downtime a month. On the other hand, in a case of unavailability of the room-based service, the business can fall back on audio/phone conferencing as 'Plan B', and therefore can tolerate approximately three hours of downtime.

Example

After talking to the customer and working with operations, we conclude that the tolerance for unavailability of the subservices for the videoconferencing service is one hour per month for the personal-based service and three hours per month for the room-based service. How does that translate into percentage of availability?

Maximum permissible unavailability/downtime as a percentage of working hours can be calculated using the following formula:

$u = (t/w) \times 100$

where u equals the percentage of tolerated unavailability/downtime, t equates to the tolerated unavailability in working hours for the specified period, and w equates to working hours in the period.

In a 30-day month we have a total of 2,592,000 seconds. In one hour we have 3,600 seconds. Thus, using the above formula we can calculate that

$u = (3600/2592000) \times 100 = 0.14$ (to 2 dp) This indicates that we are permitted a maximum of 0.14% unavailability, which requires us to provide 99.86% availability for the personal-based service.

The room-based service can tolerate three hours of unavailability. Using the same formula, but this time with three hours (10,800 seconds) for the value of t, we have:

$u = (10800/2592000) \times 100 = 0.42$ (to 2 dp)

The above calculation indicates that we allow for 0.42% unavailability, requiring us to provide 99.58% availability for the room-based service. Notice that the above calculations are based on a 30-day month, which includes weekends, whereas our service is being provided for five days a week. This will have us change our calculations to those where *w* is based on a 21-day month (1,814,400 seconds).

Therefore our calculation for one hour in 21 days, is:

$u = (3600/1814400) \times 100 = 0.19$

which indicates that we allow for 0.19% unavailability, requiring us to provide 99.81% availability for the personal-based service for a five-day week. Similarly:

$u = (10800/1814400) \times 100 = 0.60$ which indicates that we allow for 0.6% unavailability, equivalent to 99.4% availability, for the room-based service for a five-day week.

Extending the formula above to calculate availability for the period directly gives:

Availability target = $100 - [(t/w) \times 100]$

In the example nearby, we take you through an analysis of one metrics service level related to our videoconferencing example. We demonstrate how to arrive at service targets that reflect the customer's expectations and the ability of the operations function to provide the service. One set of results (for availability of the room-based service over a five-day week) is reflected in the example service targets for room-based videoconferencing shown in Table 9.7.

9.5.3 Step 3 – Quantify service constraints

In the first iteration of the development process, you will by now have a clear specification of service elements, a detailed set of service metric definitions, and documented customer expectations for service targets. However, your work is not done yet. Up until this point you should view the customer's expectations more as desires and aspirations rather than agreed requirements. You still need to take into an account the operational constraints of delivering the services to the desired service levels.

Table 9.7 Example of service level targets (for room-based videoconferencing)

Metric type	Service level objective	Service level targets
Availability	Application availability	99.4%
Performance	Packet loss	1%
	Jitter	50 ms
	Latency	150 ms
Support	Time to respond	10 minutes
	Time to resolve (high priority)	30 minutes
	Time to resolve (low priority)	8 hours

9.5.3.1 Objective

The objective of this step is to identify any constraints on the customer's expectations, and to develop SLPs that represent practical and achievable service targets, and which provide the customer with flexible options for either increasing or decreasing service levels in line with the customer's needs and financial constraints.

9.5.3.2 Inputs

To complete this step successfully, you will require the customer-specified service targets as documented in the relevant SLRs, combined with inputs from IT financial management, account management and operations management.

9.5.3.3 Activities

You will need to work closely with operations and analyse their abilities, in conjunction with their constraints, regarding the service being provided. Generally, there are three aspects of service provision that should be addressed:

- **Service utilization** The infrastructure that supports the service must meet the need of the business. Can it deliver the utility of the service? Can it handle the number of concurrent users? Is the network reliable to uphold peak usage? Is it resilient enough to deliver the consistent and repeated demand?
- **Workload analysis** This is relevant mostly to service support, where workload analysis determines whether or not there are enough staff to provide the required service, including first and second lines of support who can handle incidents and service requests.
- **Service maintenance** All IT components supporting the service should be subject to planned maintenance time. The requirement

for planned downtime clearly influences the level of availability that can be delivered for an IT service, particularly those that have stringent availability requirements. In some cases (for instance, where continuous operation is required), unavailable time may not be acceptable to the business and all maintenance activity will need to be performed without impacting the availability of the service.

9.5.3.4 Outputs

Along with service differentiation, and through joint effort with operations, the output from the foregoing activities will comprise updated service specifications and metric definitions. Additional information will include work hours, support times and maintenance schedules.

9.5.3.5 Complete service level packages

Most of the activities in this step are the responsibility of the operations function, including the service owner, but they also involve financial managers and other design functions. SLM assists in facilitating and coordinating these activities, acting as an agent of the customer and presenting their requirements regarding the service. SLM also helps operations to come up with reasonable service targets according to its abilities.

The options provided by service differentiation will be presented to the customer, allowing them to choose different levels of service according to their needs and their financial budget. From an operations perspective, those options support an essential concept in service management, which is finding the balance between cost and providing a suitable quality of service. An example of service differentiation was given earlier in Table 9.1.

It is inevitable that this activity with operations will uncover gaps between the customer expectations and the service provider's capability. Your job as the service level manager is not to come back to the business and say, 'Sorry we can't do it.' Your responsibility is to find ways to negotiate between the sides and close those gaps and/or offer alternative approaches, metrics or reports.

In an outsourcing engagement, the service level manager provides costing options for the customer and makes clear that, to reach the level of service they want, specific costs will apply.

The service level manager works with the customer and with operations to negotiate a solution to fill the gap. In our example here, one solution might be to assist with developing a business case for additional funds for operations so as to enable them to meet the business needs.

9.6 METRICS GUIDELINES

This section augments the development process with a number of general guidelines regarding metrics development. Pay close attention to them, because they have been compiled by those who have experienced the difficulties of defining metrics and have the battle scars to show for it. Benefit from their mistakes.

9.6.1 Metrics matter

The most important tip that I can give is to continually improve your metrics. Most organizations suffer from a lack of quality metrics and consequently suffer from an inability to measure and control services. The statement 'If it ain't broke, don't fix it' clashes immensely with the philosophy of ITIL and, unfortunately, many managers subscribe to this motto. Organizations that depend on technical metrics for service measurement are in dire need of transformation. Do not give in to the 'It's not me, it's the organizational culture' mentality. This is the time to take the initiative, create a business case, present to senior management the benefits of investing resources in a metrics-development-and-improvement project, and get to work.

9.6.2 Keep it simple

If you happen to find yourself in the privileged position of leading a project to develop metrics for service measurement, make sure you keep it as simple as possible – from the measurement definition to the calculation, from the monitoring tools to data collection, all the way to defining the exception codes. Make sure the metrics are easy to understand, easy to monitor and easy to maintain. Technical tools for monitoring and reporting are key areas that will benefit from uncomplicated definitions of metrics. Furthermore, a customer review will go much more smoothly if the metrics exclude complicated mathematical, legal and technical terminology.

9.6.3 Less is more

Define the minimum number of metrics that measure the performance of the service. If, during service analysis, you determine that one metric can measure service quality from the customer's point of view, stop there – there is no need for additional metrics. A long list of service metrics results in more management overhead, more monitoring, more tools, more data processing, more reports and longer reviews, and all of this for little or no additional value to the customer.

9.6.4 Pilot the SLA

It is highly recommended for SLM to define a pilot period, i.e. a trial period, to test the SLA, including the service targets, before committing to the target. For example, the service provider may deliver 95% availability for a specific service within the customer's budget constraints and current technical capabilities. Reviewing this result with the customer may reveal that the customer is not impacted by not reaching the 99.85% level and that the currently achieved service level of 95% is acceptable to both parties. This will result in the amendment of the service target for the service at the end of the pilot period, after which there will be agreement and sign-off by both sides.

9.6.5 Act on results

The output of each metrics calculation is a numeric figure that is intended to present useful information. If the result presents an underachievement of the service target, an action item must be specified based on the value achieved. But the reported result must be clear and unambiguous for this to be possible.

A meaningful metric result will allow quick determination of who owns the action item and quick categorization of the service interruption. An example of a meaningful result from a metric would be '70% of Severity 3 conferencing incidents are resolved within 4 hours'.

9.7 SOLUTION SETS

9.7.1 Why solution sets?

The management of service metrics is a complicated task. Even after the completion of metrics design, there is still a lot of work ahead.

In complex service delivery environments, large volumes of metrics can create chaos and difficulties in managing the effective measurement of services. The 'solution sets' technique provides the flexibility and standardization that is essential for metrics management, allowing more effective management of changes, scalability and service improvements.

9.7.2 What is a 'solution set'?

The basic idea behind so-called 'solution sets' is to develop reusable metrics based on common business logic. Solution sets standardize the design and implementation of metrics, calculations and reporting options.

For example, a time-to-resolve (TTR) metric essentially measures the duration of resolving service-affecting incidents. This type of metric is usually expressed as a percentage, as in '97% of incidents were resolved within 5 hours'. To improve our understanding of the service performance, you may want to apply this metric to different incident severities, different resolution times or different service elements, such as '97% of Severity 2 incidents were resolved within 5 hours, during business hours.'

Using the solution-set approach, the metric is designed to cater for multiple deployments by specifying variable parameters that change the measurement context of the metrics. Although the metric now supports multiple measurement requirements, the technical implementation, including underpinning data sources and business logic, remains the same. This allows simpler management of the metrics and its specifications.

Let's examine the following examples of TTR measurement requirements:

- 90% of Severity 1 network incidents must be resolved within four hours
- No less than 95% of Severity 2 priority voice issues must be responded to within eight hours during working hours
- WAN Severity 1 incidents must be resolved in less than one hour on 99% of occasions during all hours, excluding weekends, public holidays and planned maintenance downtimes.

The above measurements would have been discussed with operations and agreed with the customer. The reporting function will have reviewed the calculations and reporting requirements and approved the metrics for development. However, a closer analysis shows that the business logic, and data requirements, of the measurements are identical. We could develop and, subsequently, manage three separate metric definitions, or we could adopt a solution-set approach to simplify the implementation and ongoing management of the metrics.

Let's reorganize the above metrics according to the solution-set approach. To accomplish that, we need to do three things:

1 Define a common global metric for all three metrics that normalizes its structure and business logic

2 Define metric parameters to act as variables for configuring the metric to meet different measurement requirements

3 Assign values to the parameters.

For the TTR metric, we could define the following common measurement and metric parameters: <SERVICE_TARGET> % of severity <SEVERITY> incidents for <SERVICE_TYPE> services must be resolved within <DURATION> hours during <WORKING_HOURS> working hours. By assigning values to the metric definition, we can implement the three required TTR measurements using the one metric implementation and definition (see Table 9.8).

Table 9.8 Example of TTR measurements

Service target	Severity	Service type	Duration	Working hours
90% (90% of Severity 1 incidents for network services must be resolved within 4 hours during 24×7 working hours)	1	Network	4	24×7
95% (95% of Severity 2 incidents for voice services must be resolved within 8 hours during normal (9 to 5) working hours)	2	Voice	8	9 a.m. to 5 p.m.
99% (99% of Severity 1 incidents for WAN services must be resolved within 1 hour during 24×7 working hours)	1	WAN	1	24×7

Table 9.8 clearly illustrates the advantage of adopting solution sets for service metrics. Comparing the initial list of metrics with the solution-set format, it is easy to see the benefits of this structure. The management of the metrics and their respective parameters and values are essential for standardization and will promote a common language across the process and functions interacting with the metrics.

9.7.3 Modelling solution sets

To assemble all your service metrics into solution sets, you will need a project to collect all service measurements, categorize them and examine both their commonalities and their discrepancies. This project should conclude with an awareness campaign that will provide primary stakeholders – such as reporting functions, monitoring processes, account managers and customers – with a knowledge of solution sets and their capabilities.

The metrics development process, discussed earlier in this chapter, is an excellent opportunity to start working with solution sets. The solution-set approach will provide you with an ongoing structure to continually improve existing metrics or develop new ones.

There are a few steps that assist in defining solution sets:

■ **Collection and identification** Firstly we need to collect and understand the complete set of service measurements and SLPs that need to be addressed. Regardless of whether you are in the midst of developing new metrics or improving existing metrics, they should all be identified.

■ **Categorization** It is impossible to initiate this task without the confidence that all metrics are identified. Categorizing the metrics is the most important task in the solution-set modelling process. This determines the various solution sets that will apply.

Each category represents a set of metrics that can easily be managed as one group (see Table 9.9). A fine balance should be struck between having too many categories (which ultimately defeats the purpose of the solution-set method) and not enough categories (creating overloaded and complicated solution sets).

Note that some metrics cannot be categorized and will be documented as 'specific metrics' – these are metrics that are unique and cannot be grouped. The 'first-line resolution' measurement is an example of a specific metric – e.g. '70% of low-priority calls must be resolved by first-level support'.

■ **Parameter definition** The categorization activity will reveal the parameters that require definition (see again Table 9.9). For each parameter we must define the following:

● **Data type** Date, integer, time interval or character

● **Data source** The value populating the parameter might be selected from a database. For example, SITE_TYPE may be a value stored in a column in a table

● **Possible values** It is a good proactive approach to allow a restricted set of values (also called 'list of values'). For example, the SEVERITY parameter may allow integer values such as 1, 2, 3, 4 or 5, or character values such as 'Severity 1', 'Severity 2', 'Severity 3', 'Severity 4' or 'Severity 5'.

When modelling solution sets, make sure that you consider the organization's specific needs and, more importantly, customize the solution sets to your needs. The purpose of the solution-set

Table 9.9 Example of metric categories

Category	Global metric	Parameters
TTR (3 parameters)	TARGET % of incidents must be ACTION_TYPE within DURATION hours	TARGET – service level, percentage format
		ACTION_TYPE – 'Resolved' or 'Responded to'
		DURATION – Time interval HH:MM:SS
TTR (4 parameters)	TARGET % of SEVERITY incidents must be ACTION_TYPE within DURATION hours	TARGET – service level, percentage format
		SEVERITY – 1, 2, 3, 4 or 5
		ACTION_TYPE – 'Resolved' or 'Responded to'
		DURATION – Time interval HH:MM:SS
Service availability (2 parameters)	SERVICE availability must exceed TARGET % monthly	SERVICE – Service name being measured (WAN, LAN)
		TARGET – service level, percentage format
Service availability (3 parameters)	SERVICE availability for SITE_TYPE must exceed TARGET % monthly	SERVICE – Service name being measured (WAN, LAN)
		SITE_TYPE – 'Critical' or 'Premium'
		TARGET – service level, percentage format

approach is to simplify the implementation and maintenance of metrics, thus enhancing your ability to communicate standardized measurements to other processes, functions and, ultimately, customers.

9.8 SUMMARY

We've covered a lot of ground! After completing this chapter you should understand how to analyse a service based on business requirements, describe them in operational terms, develop applicable metrics and state targets to measure the performance of the service in a meaningful way for the business customer – and, most significantly, from the customer's perspective.

Financial management for SLM

10 Financial management for SLM

Although the service level manager is not expected to act as the financial manager, the former must possess specific financial skills that are relevant to service level management (SLM). In today's advanced environment we are expected to align quality of services to cost. Provision of services and related expenditure must be transparent and compiled into monetary figures.

This chapter will guide you through all the financial activities necessary to operate advanced SLM. If your organization charges for services, you must first build a cost model to understand the expenses of the service, and the charging method you choose must correspond to the culture and needs of the business.

Service level penalties are a touchy subject and before you introduce them to your organization you must have a complete understanding of the concept and how it will affect your service providers and customers. To implement service level penalties correctly you should consider penalty earn-back and bonuses, which will be detailed in this chapter.

10.1 FINANCIAL MANAGEMENT AND IT SERVICE MANAGEMENT

As part of the IT service management (ITSM) framework, financial management provides other processes with a platform for decision-making, particularly in the service strategy and service design phases. Financial management quantifies, in financial terms, the value of services and assets in the ITSM environment.

Organizations that have obtained high ITSM maturity by adopting practices such as ITIL understand and control factors of supply and demand to provide services cost-effectively while maximizing visibility into related cost structures. When performing an ITIL maturity assessment, one of the earliest indications of a low-maturity service management environment is a lack of financial management.

Financial management within an SLM context seeks to drive down the cost of service while improving its provision. SLM works closely with financial management and benefits greatly from the operational decision-making data that financial management aggregates, refines and distributes.

The cliché 'it all comes down to money' fits well with SLM objectives. SLM ensures quality service delivery, customer satisfaction and cost-effective service provision. For instance, in an outsourcing engagement it is possible to provide services for financial profit. In this case, if the services we provide do not meet the customer's expectation we might lose money or the contract will be terminated. Moreover, if we overspend on service delivery, our profit margin will decline, possibly resulting in a net loss rather than a gain.

SLM must see the services through the eyes of the company's financial controller. The measurements included in the service level agreement (SLA) must take account of financial data, as illustrated in Chapter 9 – the level of service is provided relative to the ability to pay for it.

Financial management assists SLM in every activity of its lifecycle, from the initial value creation to the measurement, development and prioritizing of activities related to the continual service improvement (CSI) register. However, there are two activities of financial management that sometimes fall within the scope of SLM:

- **Chargeback** Recovering revenue to a master budget from users or customers for services consumed on a group account – in simple words, a system where the customer is charged by the service provider for the services provided
- **Penalties** Also known as 'credits', which are paid back to the customer in the event of an SLA breach. The service provider may later on recover funds that were lost due to penalties via earn-back, subsequent to improvement of services. Under the topic of penalties and earn-back, we also find bonuses granted to the service providers as a result of excellent achievements.

Neither chargeback nor penalties can be executed without transparency of service cost. Financial management, with the assistance of service catalogue management and SLM, should develop a cost model for each service, which details and calculates the total cost of ownership of the service. Therefore you can initiate appropriate financial activities by implementing the cost model, allowing deployment of chargeback and penalties effectively and efficiently.

10.2 COST MODELLING

The textbook definition of 'cost model' is 'a set of mathematical equations that converts resource data into cost data'.

In order to calculate the costs of providing services, it is necessary to design and build a framework – a cost model – in which all costs can be recorded and then allocated or apportioned to specific customers or other activities. Such a cost model can be developed to show, for example, the cost of each service, the cost for each customer or the cost for each location.

Although the development of a cost model for services is under the scope of financial management, it is common for the service level manager to be heavily involved in the process, mainly because SLM is familiar firstly with the services and secondly with the service owners. Moreover, in many organizations where SLM possesses a high level of authority in parallel to weak financial management practice, the development of the cost model will be executed and led by the service level manager.

Regardless of who is responsible for the cost-modelling project, it is important to be familiar with the process. The following are the main activities of cost modelling:

- **Define the goal** The first requirement is to understand why you are modelling the cost of the service. Will you utilize the model for chargeback purposes or is it required for a business case to justify a purchase of a service? The purpose of the cost model will help dictate the structure and the attributes of the cost model.
- **Identify services** A common mistake in cost modelling is to prioritize the services to be modelled and model them one by one, while not considering them as a whole. We must visualize the complete list of services that are in scope so that we can determine the model structure that fits all, while allowing minimum customization in the future.

■ **Select model** Select the type of cost model that will be utilized for this exercise and the cost categories to be included. In this phase you will also need to determine the major model structure breakdowns: capital versus expenses, or initial versus ongoing, etc.

■ **Identify cost drivers** Define a list of underlying costs for the services, such as labour, server systems, telephony facilities and more. This list is ultimately a breakdown of the cost categories identified in the 'select model' phase.

■ **Populate model data** Once the stage is set, it is time to work with the operations and service owners to obtain the costs for each cost driver. The completion of that work must result in service-owner sign-off of the cost model.

■ **Operate the model** The operation of the model means the utilization of the data that were captured during the development process. During this period, documentation of disparities must be generated that will allow adjustments to the model to be made as part of the optimization process (see next bullet point).

■ **Optimize the model** It is virtually impossible to achieve a perfect model the first time round. The optimization process suggests execution of improvement measures based on information documented while operating the model.

The procedure suggested for developing the cost model is based on good and proven practices. Notice that the process is aligned perfectly with the ITIL lifecycle approach, as illustrated in Figure 10.1.

Secrets of the trade

Although ideally the financial manager will lead the cost-modelling project with collaboration from the service level manager and service catalogue manager, it is rarely done that way. Modelling the cost of the service is typically done as an ad-hoc activity to underpin a larger objective, such as justifying the purchase of a service or chargeback, or to uncover unnecessary spending.

In a previous cost-modelling project that I was asked to supervise, I realized that there were some internal politics that needed to be addressed. The service level manager was convinced that the project should be handled by the SLM function, given the fact that the cost model will enable the chargeback associated with SLM. The service level manager alienated other IT managers, who should have been identified as primary stakeholders to the process.

The project was well under way when I was brought in. In an attempt to defuse the negative tension, I persuaded the service level manager to allow the project to take a step back and define the goal of the cost modelling. I also noticed that the stakeholder identification activity was missing. The service level manager agreed to adhere to the proposed process – which revealed significant gaps, including missing cost drivers.

Initiating the project by defining a clear goal and identifying stakeholders created an exposure to the project within the organization, which generated the support that was much needed from the rest of the management group.

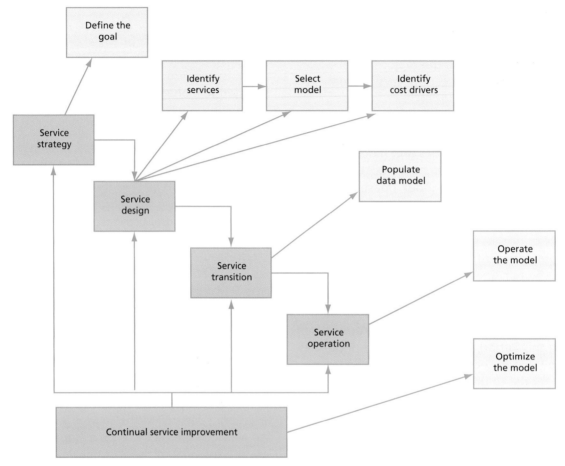

Figure 10.1 Cost-modelling process aligned with the ITIL lifecycle approach

It is virtually impossible to achieve a flawless cost model from the outset; it should be viewed as a starting point for an improvement process aiming at a stable and reliable model. This process suggests activities, such as optimizing the model, to put you in a position to allow ongoing iterations to continually improve the model.

If the cost model is to be utilized for chargeback, it is strongly recommended to go through multiple cycles to optimize the model. 'Notional charging' can be introduced, which is where the customer is informed of what the charge would be for the service used, although no actual funds are transferred. Notional charging can help set the expectation of upcoming costs, while allowing time for cost figures to be validated until they can be trusted and approved for actual charging.

10.3 CHARGEBACK

10.3.1 Chargeback overview

The ultimate goal of ITSM regarding chargeback is to create, on the one hand, a platform to run a cost-effective IT department and, on the other, a cost-conscious culture, increasing accountability for IT consumption. 'You pay for what you use' needs to be instilled into the organization because, as customers will tell you: 'Without chargeback, there's no reason not to be wasteful.'

The basic definition of chargeback is the recovering of revenue to a master budget from users and customers for services consumed on a group account. Take the example of a parent at home, who must provide their children with 'basic necessities' such as mobile phones. Your monthly bill is $200, arising from Daniel ($75), David ($60) and Naomi ($65). Charging back from your children will mean going to each one of them, showing them the invoice from the mobile phone company and collecting the money used in order to reimburse your budget. (Many parents might, of course, apply notional charging here – but you get the idea.)

10.3.2 Chargeback and service level management

In an ideal service management environment the financial logic is straightforward. The customer consumes services from the service provider. If the services are provided as agreed, the customer pays the full amount. If services are lacking, the service provider is penalized or the customer pays less via a rebate. The interface process with the customer determines whether the services were provided at the levels agreed with SLM via an SLA.

Thus chargeback is typically under the responsibility of SLM. Although you will find some organizations that will position chargeback under financial management, we strongly suggest that financial management should provide the data and support the process but allow SLM to make the ultimate operational decisions regarding charging back and penalties that are affected by the service levels achieved.

10.3.3 Chargeback methods

There are different methods to calculate chargeback for services. There is no single correct answer; the method should be based on the specific needs of the organization and its objectives. The fundamental decision on chargeback is to choose among three main approaches:

- **Partial cost recovery** The IT function seeks to recover some of its costs, essentially topping up services that are partially funded under its own budget with additional funds from customers.
- **Zero-sum game** Whatever total costs the IT function spends, 100% of these costs are charged back to the internal business units as a cost to them. This method is very common among enterprises that provide the services internally and are not inclined to make a profit from the consumers.
- **Profit-oriented pricing** Here, a profit margin is added to the total cost of the service. This method is utilized by external service providers and organizations that run their operations like a business, allowing their IT department to make a profit on their services for future expenses.

Once the basic purpose of charging back is established, there are numerous methods to choose from. Aligned with the ITIL service lifecycle, the following are chargeback methods:

- **Notional charging** Charges are calculated and customers are informed of the charge, but no money is actually transferred. This method is used as an interlocution to initiate the process before actual funds are transferred.

Secrets of the trade

On a project where my team was asked to establish a chargeback mechanism for an enterprise to recover IT costs, we worked to develop a cost model and initiate the charging back of funds on a tight schedule. This was the first time that IT was planning to charge back the business for a specific service. Most IT costs were covered under the IT organization's budget, which was approved annually by the business.

The IT function wanted to transition from a cost centre to a chargeback model, and it saw the introduction of a new and valuable service as a good way to start. However, because this new service was optional, organizations had to subscribe and agree to a per-user fee. This approach backfired and led to very slow adoption of what was expected to be a popular service. IT eventually had to change its plan, deploy its services globally and return to its traditional method of covering costs.

In hindsight, the use of notional charging, where charges are calculated and presented to customers but no money is actually charged, would have been a good way to introduce the company to chargeback as a concept. Over time, all IT services could have been presented using notional charging, with a plan announced to transition to actual charging by a certain date.

- **Tiered subscription** This method involves varying levels of warranty and/or utility offered for a service or service bundle, all of which have been priced with the appropriate chargeback models applied. The subscriptions are most commonly referred to as 'gold', 'silver' and 'bronze' levels of service.

- **Metered usage** Also known as measured resource use (MRU), this method is based on measured consumption of IT resources and involves a more mature financial environment and operational capability, where demand modelling is incorporated with utility computing capabilities to provide confidence in the capture of real-time usage.

- **Direct plus** This is a more simplistic model where those costs that can be attributed directly to a service are charged accordingly, with some percentage of indirect costs shared amongst all.

- **Fixed or user cost** The most simplistic of chargeback models, this approach takes the actual cost and divides it by an agreed denominator such as number of users. Although this is a common practice in the IT industry, it generates resistance and frustration among consumers due to the inherent unfairness of the method.

Studies, including Gartner's publication from May 2005 ('Selecting a chargeback method depends on the business unit and IT service'; available online via http://my.gartner.com/portal), show that MRU will emerge as the favoured chargeback method. It provides an optimal solution for measuring the actual usage of resources. MRU can help organizations discover which user, business unit or application is the heaviest user of the service.

When I was asked to develop a gap analysis for a service desk function, I concluded that a fixed chargeback method was unfair for the business units and must be changed immediately to the tiered or metered method of charging, especially due to the fact that data were available to establish more accurate chargeback. My proposal was rejected. It was explained to me that the business units were very happy with the support with which they were provided and they believed that the cost for the service was insignificant.

This is a great lesson for every ITIL consultant – namely that expert knowledge and experience is not enough, and you must take into account your customer's culture and attitudes when making recommendations.

10.4 FINANCIAL INCENTIVES AND PENALTIES

In addition to cost modelling and charging of IT services, it is common – and indeed recommended – to implement financial incentives and penalties to safeguard and improve the quality of service provision. Whereas the responsibility for cost modelling and charging activities is shared by financial management and SLM, financial incentives and penalties are best positioned within SLM alone.

The ongoing provision of services, and in particular the safeguarding of service levels, is documented within the SLA. Achieved levels of service are monitored, measured and reviewed on a regular basis, and a typical SLA will also specify clauses for corrective action, even the possible termination of services, if agreed service level targets are regularly breached. Financial incentives and penalties can be harnessed to influence behaviour, avoid corrective action and increase the customer's confidence and sense of control.

However, you should not underestimate the impact of financial incentives and penalties on organizational culture, human behaviour or customer–supplier relationships. Although financial incentives and penalties can have a very positive and energizing effect all round, applied inappropriately (either intentionally or by chance) they can diminish service commitment, compromise integrity and severely damage relationships.

Financial incentives and penalties should not be used as a 'big stick' to continually hit the service provider with and thereby effectively discourage a service ethos. The level of incentives and penalties should be aimed at motivating and influencing operational behaviour, not triggering a legal battle at the contract management level.

In one outsourcing project I worked on, the service level penalties were so punitive that senior management and legal staff were required at each monthly service level review. Needless to say, the entire focus of the meetings was on disputing service level penalties rather than maintaining and improving service provision.

Effective financial incentives and penalties require objective and well-defined measurement if they are to be unambiguous, quantifiable and even-handed. The metrics – service level objectives (SLOs) and key performance indicators (KPIs) – specified in the SLA provide outstanding measurement 'handles' for linking financial incentives and penalties with the provision of service.

We will now consider three approaches of financial incentives and penalties that can be seamlessly incorporated into a customer's SLA. These are:

- **Service level penalties** An incentive to safeguard service provision by applying financial penalties on the service provider when agreed service level targets are not met
- **Penalty earn-back** An incentive to improve service provision by allowing the service provider to recoup financial penalties incurred for failure to meet agreed service level targets
- **Bonus payments** An incentive to both safeguard and improve service provision by rewarding the service provider with financial bonuses if agreed service level targets are exceeded.

At first glance, the bonus payments approach seems to encapsulate the incentive both to safeguard service provision and to encourage service improvements. However, bonuses should be used with caution and are most fraught with danger when it comes to unintended consequences. Short-term risk-taking within the financial sector has nearly become synonymous with financial bonuses, and although service providers are unlikely to share the lofty bonuses awarded to bankers, the underlying principles and potential negative forces are always lurking in the background.

Secrets of the trade

A common financial incentive is to award bonus payments for handling customer calls. One particular emergency services organization was horrified to find that the service provider had initiated a plethora of 'ghost calls' to cash in bonus payments paid for exceeding call-handling service levels.

These three approaches are described next, and we finish the section with a list of guidelines to follow in relation to financial incentives and penalties.

10.4.1 Service level penalties overview

Service level penalties, often also referred to as service credits, are designed as an incentive for service providers to safeguard service levels from breaching agreed service level targets or, where service level targets have already been breached, from further deteriorating service provision. As a service level manager you should do your upmost to avoid incurring service level penalties.

Sourcing services are based on the risk transfer concept. The customer is transferring the risk of providing the services, including allocation of resources, ongoing operations and much more. This transfer of risk, when done with an external service provider, costs money. On the other hand, it must be understood that when the services are not available the customer becomes unproductive and hence loses money. If this is to be expected by both the customer and the service provider, the penalties cease to be punishment and become a simple execution of the risk transfer. If the service provider causes loss of money, the service provider is responsible for reimbursing those funds via penalties. For that reason the term 'credits', rather than 'penalties', is preferred by many.

The topic of service level penalties is often a very sensitive one. Unlike service chargeback, which is an agreed and predictable amount to be paid by the customer, service level penalties are subject to stringent measurement, accurate calculation and reliable reporting, as well as negotiation, customer and service provider relationship, and service level manager discretion and judgement.

The somewhat volatile nature of service level penalties can result in the stated aim of safeguarding service levels being missed, and instead lead to a troubled relationship between customer and service provider, resulting in poor service provision.

Secrets of the trade

The quality of service, which more or less determines the allocation of service level penalties, is dictated just as much (or often more) by perception as it is by the hard reality of measurement. The punitive nature of service level penalties affords a certain amount of empathy that can be used to reduce service level penalties if a high level of trust is established.

In the role of service level manager for a major financial institution I was able to cancel out incurred penalties by ensuring ad-hoc service requests were carried out in a timely manner, even though we were contractually not obliged to do so. This created a high level of trust and allowed the operational team to address service provision issues without incurring penalties.

It is often said that perception equals reality. Although it is important to ensure actual service level targets are met, you should not underestimate the power of perception. Although my network manager called it 'smoke and mirrors', it saved a lot of money.

10.4.2 Service level penalties – methods

The objective is to create a financial incentive and penalty that will safeguard the quality of service, and not damage the relationship or result in underhand and misleading service level reporting. The guidelines listed at the end of this section should be a help in this regard.

There are two common methods for implementing service level penalties:

- The risk pool method
- The sliding-scale method.

In both methods the SLA would typically include a clause that stipulates that if the service provider fails to deliver the promised levels of service, it will issue a credit for that month's fee. Funds are paid by the service provider, or deducted from the customer's invoice, when services are not provided according to the agreed level.

Secrets of the trade

The transfer of funds arising from penalties can be paid directly to the customer or deducted from the customer's invoice. Although the penalties practice is becoming common, the preferred way of actually transferring the funds has not generally been determined. Crediting the customer invoice can simplify the process, but it can also hold up the issuing of the invoice until negotiation over the credit is complete.

In a large outsourcing engagement, service level penalties were implemented after many reviews. The decision concerning the transfer of funds was to include an attribution in a particular month's invoice for the next invoice to include that month's credit. For example, if January carried penalties of $10,000, these would be credited on the February invoice. This process allowed the service provider to submit the monthly invoice on time yet allowed the negotiations over penalties to continue throughout the following month.

10.4.2.1 The risk pool method

The risk pool method places in a monetary pool a percentage of the monthly invoice amount 'at risk' if the service provider does not meet service level targets. The total at-risk pool is allocated, as a percentage, across predefined service towers within the SLA, where each service tower represents a grouping of related SLOs and KPIs (metrics).

Within a service tower, the allocated pool of service level penalties is subsequently allocated to the metrics defined within the tower, where the total allocation of penalties within the pool is 100%. For example, the LAN tower may have four service levels: two of them could be 'availability' of devices and two of them could be 'time to resolve'. You may choose to give more importance to the availability metrics by allocating 30% to each (total of 60%), and then allocating 20% to each of the 'time to resolve' metrics (total of 40%).

There are three variables to consider for the calculations associated with the risk pool method:

- **At-risk amount** The percentage of the monthly invoice amount that is subject to service level penalties

- **Service tower pool allocation** The percentage of the total service level penalties allocated to the service tower

- **Service level allocation** The percentage of the service level penalties allocated to the metrics within the service tower.

In the example shown in Figure 10.2, the at-risk amount is 15% of the monthly invoice amount, and the service tower pool allocation is across three service towers, with the service tower pool allocation further allocated across various metrics within the tower.

Based on the total pool of service level penalties and the allocation of the total pool across service towers and metrics, it is possible to determine the percentage of the invoice amount that each metric will incur if service level penalties are incurred for not meeting agreed service level targets. Thus for the three service levels shown for the WAN service tower in Figure 10.2, the percentage of invoice amount as shown in Table 10.1 applies.

Thus (from the first row of Table 10.1), if WAN availability fails its service level target in a month where the total invoice amount is $100,000, then the metric will incur a financial penalty of 1.5% of

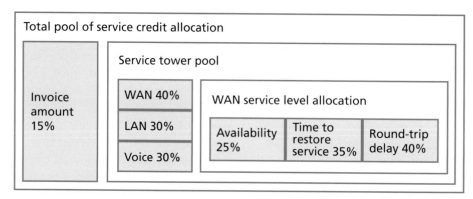

Figure 10.2 Example of service tower pool allocation

Table 10.1 Invoice percentages pooled for the WAN service tower example

Service level allocation	Invoice amount (%)*
Availability 25%	15% × 40% × 25% = 1.50%
Time to restore service 35%	15% × 40% × 35% = 2.10%
Round-trip delay 40%	15% × 40% × 40% = 2.40%
Total allocation 100%	Total WAN pool = 6.00%

*See Figure 10.2 for the source of the figures in these calculations.

$100,000, i.e. $1,500. And from the last row of Table 10.1, WAN services can incur total penalties equal to 6% of the monthly invoice amount.

The advantage of this method is that it is easy to implement and calculate, and penalties are weighted both on the service tower and on the service levels within each tower. Also, the total incurred service penalties are capped to the total pool allocation, which makes it easy to change the overall penalty level without modifying the underlying weightings.

The disadvantage to the method is that there are no incentives to safeguard service levels once a breach has occurred. The sliding-scale method provides an example of a progressive service level penalty calculation with incentives to address service provision issues beyond the initial breach.

10.4.2.2 The sliding-scale method

The key element of the risk pool method is that each service level may incur service penalties based on a percentage of the monthly invoice amount if the service level target is breached. In contrast, the sliding-scale method demonstrates how to maintain the incentive to safeguard service levels after the service level target has been breached.

In the sliding-scale method, each service level defines two service level targets: the expected target and the minimum target. When the achieved service level falls below the expected target, a service level penalty is incurred. However, the penalty increases as the achieved service level falls further towards the minimum target. When the achieved service level reaches or falls below the minimum target, then the maximum service level penalty is incurred, which is 100% of the penalty for the metric.

Consider an example where the achieved service level for the tracking period is 96.4%. It therefore stands 1.6 percentage points below the expected target of 98% in the 'window' of 3.0 percentage points between expected and minimum service levels. Thus the penalty level would be 1.6/3.0 × 100%, i.e. 53.33% (to 2 decimal places).

Note that the example provided does not indicate how service credits are assigned to each service level; it merely provides an example of how the incentive to safeguard service levels can be maintained after the initial breach of the service level target.

10.4.3 Penalty earn-back

Although service level penalties are an excellent method of safeguarding service quality by linking financial penalties to service level targets, penalty earn-back provides the additional incentive to improve services by allowing the service provider to earn back the incurred penalty charges.

A penalty earn-back facility allows the service provider to reduce the amount of incurred penalties for poor past performance by providing enhanced, or a more stable and consistent, service provision in the future or across the service measurement period.

Examples of penalty earn-back methods include:

- **Direct earn-back** Penalty earn-back is calculated and applied directly to each tracking period, where service level penalties have been incurred in a previous tracking period and where earn-back is based on predefined conditions being met.

  Table 10.2 shows an example of direct earn-back during a four-month period of January to April. In the month of February $12,600 of service penalties are incurred for failing the minimum service level target. However, in the following two months of March and April the achieved service level exceeds (or meets) the expected service level target and, as such, half ($6,300) of the service penalties is earned back in the month of April.

- **Deferred earn-back** An alternative approach is to base service credit earn-backs on an annual evaluation of overall service level performance (for instance, at the end of the contract year). Table 10.3 shows an example of deferred earn-back. The yearly average achieved service level is greater than the expected service level target of 98%. It is also apparent that February, August and October were the three months that incurred the greatest amount of service penalties and are thus subject to earn-back (totalling $70,000).

  In general, with deferred earn-back methods the balance of service level penalties, after any such earn-back, is paid at the end of the contract year.

The methods for implementing earn-backs for service level penalties can be designed in a multitude of ways. However, regardless of the method chosen, you should ensure that the formula is easy to understand (you should not

Table 10.2 Example of direct earn-back

Category	January	February	March	April
Expected target	98%	98%	98%	98%
Minimum target	95%	95%	95%	95%
Achieved target	96%	94%	98%	99%
Penalties	0	$12,600	0	0
Earn-back	0	0	0	$6,300

Table 10.3 Example of deferred earn-back

Category	Three worst performing months			Yearly average	Earn-back
	February	August	October		
Expected target	98%	98%	98%	98%	
Minimum target	95%	95%	95%	95%	
Achieved target	94%	93%	92%	98.2%	
Penalties	$12,000	$25,000	$33,000		
Earn-back					$70,000

need a PhD in mathematics) and acts as an incentive to improve service levels based on past performance.

Secrets of the trade

Make sure that the earn-back method you implement is realistic and achievable, either within a relatively short time frame (not more than four months) or within the current SLA review period (usually yearly or half-yearly). Service providers will become despondent about service improvement initiatives if the benefits and rewards are perceived as unattainable.

10.4.4 Bonus payments

Attaching bonus payments to service level targets is another way of providing an incentive for improved service delivery. Bonus payments are a less common method than service level penalties or associated penalty earn-back formulas for incentivizing service providers. This is probably in line with the more common view that preventing service level breaches is more important than exceeding agreed service level targets.

After all, a key objective of service level targets is to align the cost of service provision with business needs. Encouraging the service provider to constantly exceed agreed service level targets will only be effective if improved service levels are cost-neutral, if they improve business outcomes or if the promised bonus at least exceeds any (potential) increase in delivery costs.

Service providers should also guard against the unintended consequences of providing increased service levels in the pursuit of bonus payments. Service levels that are consistently higher than the agreed service level targets soon become the new norm. Then the hard-fought-for bonus can quickly turn into negative customer perception when service levels move closer to agreed service level targets.

Regardless of the potential downsides to bonus payments, there may well be good reasons to link bonus payments to service level targets. If this is the case then, as with service level penalties and penalty earn-back, you should consider the guidelines listed below when choosing a bonus payment method.

Secrets of the trade

A justification I have often heard for implementing service level penalties is the need for the IT service provider to share the 'pain' experienced by the business as a result of IT service failures. Although, at face value, this may seem a reasonable argument for employing service level penalties, it should also follow that the IT service provider shares the gains where business success is attributed to IT services.

Linking service level measurement to business outcomes is a major undertaking that exposes the impact of IT on business outcomes. If IT service providers are to feel the pain, then they should definitely look forward to some gain.

10.4.5 Guidelines for financial penalties

Financial incentives and penalties are a powerful means of safeguarding ongoing service provision and encouraging service improvement. However, like any instrument of potential great good, they can also be a destructive force that pushes the customer–service provider relationship to the brink.

The following list provides guidelines for the design and implementation of financial incentives and penalties in the customer's SLA:

- Must not be too complicated (i.e. you shouldn't need to be a mathematician to understand the calculations)
  - Best to have penalties defined per SLO; don't try to do fancy combinations of events
  - Avoid complex formulas
- Should be designed as a constructive criticism (to motivate and focus efforts) rather than to drive the supplier to despair

- Cap the service credits
- Allow for earn-backs
- Consider bonuses (careful with this one, for it could lead to short-term risk-taking or dodgy data-gathering. We all like a bonus!)
- Must not lead to a point where the provider has reached the limit on credits and thinks: 'Slow down support, as we can't get any more penalties'
  - Use credit accelerator techniques (e.g. repeat failure multiplier)
  - Add contractual provisions for taking more serious action if penalties are continually incurred
  - Apply a finer level of granularity on penalties, but do not cap per measurement unit or SLO
- Must be set on selected services rather than all of them
  - Critical service levels versus KPIs
  - Apply only on service levels that significantly impact the business.
- Penalty charges must be allied to the cost of delivering the services and how much the business is losing if the service fails.
- There should always be a review process. Although automating the calculation helps, the service level manager together with the customer should negotiate and agree on the actual amount during service review meetings.
- Define a pilot SLA period. Penalties should not start from day one of service provision. Afford the service a settling-in period, with a formal review for commencement of incentives.

10.5 SUMMARY

The service level manager is not the financial manager; however, there are some financial skills that are required for SLM. The service level manager ensures that services are provided as agreed, but also that services are provided at an adequate cost level and that charging for services is according to a calculation method that suits the organization.

SLM needs to fully understand the consequences of poor service delivery. Service level penalties are a sensitive topic that must be executed with a well-defined design and intent. Direct or deferred penalties, earn-back mechanisms and bonus payments are all possible methods that you could use to introduce appropriate incentives within SLM.

Support tools for SLM

11

11 Support tools for SLM

It is not a coincidence that this chapter is the last of Part 2 on service design. Once we have the process established, then we can start considering the tools and solutions to support the process and functions of the organization. The technology should always support the process and not the other way around.

In this chapter we will outline the basic activities of selecting the support tools suitable for your organizational needs by documenting the functional requirements of the basic support tools that are typically deployed by service level management (SLM).

Note that the process of purchasing a software solution is very difficult. Many service level managers are required to provide a business case and a solid return on investment (ROI) before any acquisition can be considered. The procurement process details are out of scope for this chapter; however, the purchasing process will include the functional requirements document, which is the main focus of this chapter.

11.1 FUNCTIONAL REQUIREMENTS DOCUMENT

The objective of this chapter is to provide you with an overview of the functional requirements for tools and solutions that support the activities of the SLM process. Before diving into the development process for these requirements, let's examine the overall structure of such a document.

The functional requirements document captures the intended behaviour of the system and is sometimes referred to as the software requirements specification. This document is a complete description of the behaviour of the system to be implemented. It includes a set of use cases that describes all the interactions the users will have with the software. In addition, the document contains non-functional requirements that impose constraints on the design, such as performance requirements, quality standards and/ or design constraints.

Most companies will specify their functional requirements for vendors using the request for proposal (RFP). There are many ways to collect and compile the functional requirements and in the next section we propose the use-case method, which is a simple method to implement and is very effective.

11.1.1 Functional requirements via the use case method

We recommend the use-case method as a framework on which to develop our functional requirements.

Use cases have become a popular way to express software requirements because they are very practical. A use case bridges the gap between user needs and system functionality by directly stating the user's intention and the system response for each step in a particular interaction (see Figure 11.1).

Use cases were introduced as part of an object-oriented development methodology by Ivar Jacobson in *Object-Oriented Software Engineering*

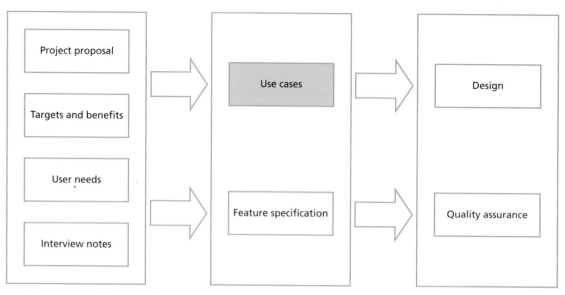

Figure 11.1 Use case within a software requirements specification

(ACM Press, 1992), but more recently they have been extended into a general technique for defining functional requirements. A use case defines a set of interactions between the actors – in our case the end users – and the solution under consideration. The actor is defined in the user profile section when the categorization occurs.

Generally, use-case steps are written in an easy-to-understand process orientation. The use-case development is completed by engaging the users who will validate the process and its activities. Note that the development of the use-case process is not documented in the functional requirements document; only its results are published within the document. Table 11.1 contains a number of example use cases for a service level agreement (SLA) system.

An effective use case is largely a sequence of interactions between the user and the solution, written in natural language that is easy to

understand. Remember that in order for a use case to be successful, it must be well planned and include the stakeholder's (mainly the user's) identification and their requirements.

11.2 CHOOSING APPROPRIATE TOOLS

The volume and complexity of activities will determine the types of tools required to support the SLM process. In small organizations the use of spreadsheets and Microsoft® Word will be sufficient to meet the needs of SLM. In larger organizations where the service structure is complex, there is a need for a robust solution to allow consistency and control over the process.

Technology has progressed greatly and there are many software solutions companies competing for market share. How would you make the right decision to select the tool that will fit your SLM

Table 11.1 Example of steps for analysing an SLA compliance report

User intention	System response	Comments
Login to dashboard	The initial screen subsequent to login is a dashboard providing four different views: SLA report, open incidents, financial report, closed incidents by site	The specific requirements for dashboards and reports are detailed in the report catalogue
Filter SLA breaches	The system will filter out all those SLAs within compliance, presenting only those that are in warning or breached	Warning levels are thresholds that are defined within the SLA
Drill down	By clicking on the SLA result, the system will drill down to a more detailed report	The drill-downs per SLA are defined in the report catalogue

needs and meet your business requirements? What are the steps in such a process?

We will focus on four areas that may require you to develop or purchase a solution to support the activities of SLM:

■ **Metrics management** The development of metrics, key performance indicators (KPIs) and service levels can grow into complex calculations that require a solution to manage.

■ **Performance reports** Performance monitoring, data-gathering and compilation procedures are time-consuming tasks that greatly benefit from automated systems.

■ **Service improvement plan (SIP)** The SIP outlines the improvements to be made, their priorities, owners and estimated completion time.

■ **Cost management** There is the need for visibility regarding underlying service cost drivers so that a solution can be utilized that enables cost modelling.

Keep in mind that SLM is a process which incorporates activities that essentially need to be integrated and, by the same token, the tools that underpin these activities must be integrated as well. Remember to consider the integration between the tools on both the process side and the technical side.

There is a common thread through the solutions that support SLM and a link that should be transparent in the overall solution requirements. The metrics and measurements are derived from the service list. The measurements will be utilized by the SLA and the SLA compliance report. The review of the SLA compliance report produces a set of action items that are addressed by the SIP. Figure 11.2 depicts the high-level relationship between the SLM systems.

The remaining sections consider the four main SLM tools in more detail, providing you with an overview of the primary functional requirements.

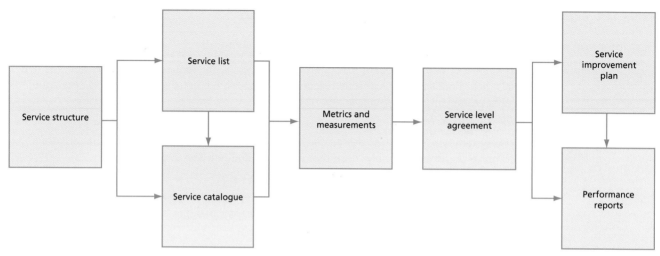

Figure 11.2 Linking between SLM elements

Table 11.2 List of primary requirements for a metrics management solution

Requirement	Description
Visual interface	The structure of the metrics management must reflect the service structure of the organization (see Chapter 5). A graphical user interface will allow easy access and navigation through the metrics.
Design capabilities	The solution must provide a platform to support the design calculation of the metrics. The design of the measurements is laid out much like a process, and it is diagrammed step by step (see Figure 11.3). Each step is accompanied by documentation explaining the designer's intent.
Open code	The calculation is imported from the diagram into a code, allowing minimum manual modification. However, the solution must be flexible to allow the developer further coding.
Metric definition	A metric such as 'Incidents must be resolved within %variable% hours' will be linked to a calculation.
Solution sets	The categorization of metrics and their management use different numbers of variables (see Chapter 9).
Integration with reporting	Data produced through the calculations and the output results become the source for the performance reports.

11.3   METRICS MANAGEMENT SOLUTION

11.3.1 Overview

The metrics management solution is a collection of available metrics. It consists of the metrics, measurements and calculations for the services. The metrics management solution supports the activities of developing, modifying and managing the metrics in a structured fashion.

Ideally the metrics management solution is integrated with the performance reporting solution; but even in a case where it stands alone, the metric definitions must be available for the reporting solution to be utilized.

Table 11.2 lists the primary requirements for a metrics management solution, but it is not all-inclusive. When developing the use case, consider this list along with the user requirements.

11.3.2 Guidelines and recommendations

11.3.2.1 Prerequisite design

Do not confuse the deployment of the metrics management solution with your design work. The design activities for the implementation of SLM, which this publication provides, include the documentation of process activities, SLA structure and the overall structure of the SLM function. The solution that manages your metrics is focused on performance measurements only and not on the overall design of the process.

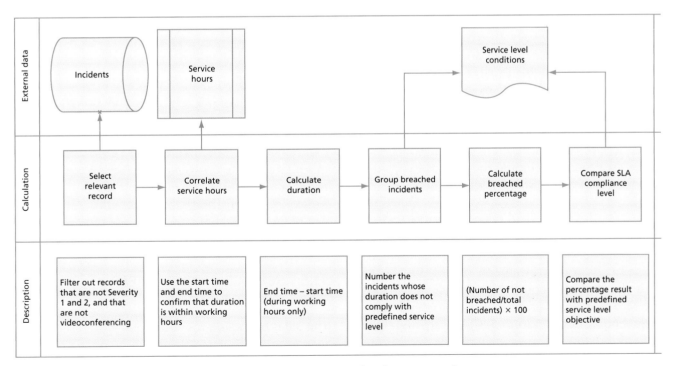

Figure 11.3 Videoconferencing example – Severity 1 and 2 time to resolve

11.3.2.2 Metrics and reporting

One of the most common pitfalls in the implementation of a metrics management solution is the compromise on the implementation of a performance reporting solution, neglecting the management of metrics that underpin the reports. If you decide to purchase a solution that fulfils both your reporting requirements and your metrics requirements, assess your metrics management requirements individually and make sure that the solution can satisfy these requirements.

11.4 PERFORMANCE REPORTS SOLUTION

11.4.1 Overview

The performance reports solution is considered by many to be the main tool to support SLM activities.

The primary report generated by the reporting solution is the SLA compliance report. This report will provide RAG (red, amber and green) results for each service level objective (SLO). The complete set of reports and dashboards are detailed in Part 4 (on service operation) and specifically in Chapter 15.

Table 11.3 is a list of primary requirements for a performance reports solution, but it is not all-inclusive. When developing the use case, consider this list along with the user requirements.

11.4.2 Guidelines and recommendations

11.4.2.1 The Excel addiction

Some habits are hard to break, but the Excel habit is the hardest of them all. Many reporting analysts are Microsoft Excel wizards and perform all their reporting duties using spreadsheet functionalities. One of the goals of this publication is to promote thinking outside the box for ITIL practitioners. The adoption of an automated reporting tool will allow you to spend more time on activities that you never had time for before, such as improving your procedures, paying better attention to your customers, and overall performance in best-practice activities.

11.4.2.2 The integrity of your data source

Those who have any type of experience with implementation of the SLM reporting solution will confess to ongoing nightmares and anxiety disorder symptoms, all as a result of the data sources encountered. Your reports are only as good as your data, and the number-one risk on the reporting project plan comes from the data sources.

Do not be blinded by the attractive interface of the solution and the data adaptor agents of the solution. If your data sources are not accessible or lack basic integrity, there is much work to be done before selecting the correct tool.

11.4.2.3 Stakeholder management

The reporting analyst is not the only stakeholder in the reporting environment. One of your main stakeholders is the customer. In the case of an external service provider, the SLM reports take a much larger role. Customer satisfaction tends to rise when a login to the reporting solution is provided. The customer feels that information is not hidden from them and they view the service provider more as a partner than an external vendor.

11.5 SERVICE IMPROVEMENT PLAN SOLUTION

The SIP is becoming more popular within service management practices, and rightly so. The primary objective is to create a continual service

Table 11.3 List of primary requirements for a performance reports solution

Requirement	Description
User access	Users should be able to access the reports via a thin layer such as a web browser. The login will manage access permissions to user groups such as reporting analyst, SLM staff, customer and operations.
Dashboard	For each user group a default dashboard is set up, presenting different reports in the same view.
Report configuration	The users will be able to change basic report configurations, such as sorting, filtering and time duration.
Reports navigation	There is easy-to-use navigation from one report to another, including drill-downs, saved reports, recently used reports and importation of reports into different formats.
Service review preparation	Analysis of a predefined list of reports, the creation of reports for presentation, root cause analysis reports and SIP alignment.
SLA adjudication	Modification of the SLA results process, including the approval process with the customer; modification of data source and recalculation of results; modification of high-level SLA results.
Customized view	Each use will be given a default view according to its user group. Within that, the users will be able to customize their view by saving reports, creating a mailing list and modifying dashboards.
Export	The user will be able to export the reports in different formats – Excel, Word, images. This feature includes sending reports via email.
Report catalogue	The reporting analyst will utilize the solution as the report catalogue, managing the reports by title, description and target audience.
Data refresh	The updating of the data source underpinning the reports will be refreshed according to the nature of the reports. Some reports, such as open ticket status, may need refreshing every 15 minutes, while the SLA compliance report requires only a daily refresh.
Metrics management	In cases where the metrics management solution is a separate solution, the design of the reporting solution must include tight integration between the systems to allow the reporting solution to base its calculations on the measurements in the metrics management solution.
Alerting	The solution will enable the reporting analyst to establish thresholds for the SLOs and generate automatic alerts when the threshold is reached.
Admin requirements	Owing to the high importance of the availability of the system and the integrity of the data, the solution must provide the administration function with the ability of data processing, especially for the main data links that create the data bottleneck: data source link, calculation and report generation.

improvement (CSI) register of improvement opportunities to track projects that are related to the improvement of services.

Table 11.4 is a list of primary requirements for a CSI register solution, but it is not all-inclusive. When developing the use case, consider this list along with the user requirements.

11.5.1 Guidelines and recommendations

11.5.1.1 The intimidation factor

The SIP process is fairly new and has only recently been introduced to some organizations. Many other organizations are comfortable doing what they always have done, following operational processes such as incident management and problem management, tracking services through performance reports. Managers tend to say: 'If it works, why change it?'

The SIP process has been proven to promote communication among the customer, SLM and operations, and it also adds the structure of service improvement that is missing in many organizations.

11.5.1.2 KISS (keep it simple, stupid)

When designing the CSI register solution, the scope of its attributes must be well defined, avoiding any attempt to include excessive and often unnecessary information. Simplicity is a virtue.

Table 11.4 Primary requirements for a CSI register solution

Requirement	Description
CSI register population	The potential CSI register records for review are generated from three sources: SLA compliance reports, the incident management system and manual entries. The first two should be automatically generated utilizing 'pull' or 'push' data. The manual entries should be handled via the solution interface.
CSI register review	The CSI register owner reviews the register on an ongoing basis, including access permissions to user groups. The viewing of CSI register content will allow record sorting by priority, category and outstanding action items.
Select and filter	The CSI register owner will have permission to filter out records for later review, as well as to change content and add comments.
Prioritization	During service review meetings and ongoing communication with customers and operations, the prioritization is subject to change. The other attribute related to this action is the completion date.
Alerting	The solution will enable the CSI register owner to establish thresholds for records and generate automatic alerts when the threshold is reached.
Reporting	The reporting work is done through collaboration with the SLM reporting function and typically includes: outstanding open records, closed by priority, and closed by category.

Table 11.5 Primary requirements for a cost management solution

Requirement	Description
Cost model design	The cost model will allow development of the cost model structure, including its categories and cost drivers. The solution will allow changes to the structure and content.
Cost allocation and population	Population of the cost model will be performed by connecting to financial systems and automatically collecting the data, allowing for manually entered data also. The solution will include editing features to permit the user to overwrite information supported by log files.
Budgeting and planning	A clear view is provided of the budget versus actual position, and the configuration of a process to manage future gaps.
Charging	The solution will support different charging methods and invoice the business units according to their service consumption.
Penalties	The solution will support the measurement of penalties for which the service provider is responsible in the event of SLA breaches. The solution will also support the ongoing process of determining the final figure for the penalty following negotiations between the customer and the service provider.
Earn-backs	The service provider may earn back penalties after providing a high level of service provision. The solution must be able to calculate the invoice considering the level of service and penalties.
Analytics	The solution will automate forecasting reports such as budget versus actual costs, potential cost overruns and suggested adjustments.

Remember that the CSI register solution assists in managing records that are ultimately being executed outside the scope of the process. Register records are a placeholder for projects or changes that are to improve the services and are not there to manage the projects or the change.

11.6 COST MANAGEMENT SOLUTION

11.6.1 Overview

SLM, as explained in Chapter 10 on financial management, will be assigned as the owner of activities associated with transparency, which include cost modelling, chargeback, penalties and earn-backs.

Table 11.5 is a list of primary requirements for a cost management solution, but it is not all-inclusive. When developing the use case, consider this list along with the user requirements.

11.6.2 Guidelines and recommendations

11.6.2.1 Avoid working in a void

The SLM cost management activities are closely linked to other areas, including SLA tracking, customer satisfaction and much more. Thus it is advisable to combine the cost management solution with other SLM solutions, thereby illustrating the close relationship between them.

11.6.2.2 Optimizing cost management

It is virtually impossible to achieve a flawless cost model the first time around; it should be viewed as a starting point for an improvement process aiming for a stable and reliable model. This is a significant difference from the deployment of any other software solution. In other solutions, the better you plan and design, the less adjustment and bug fixing you will need to do, whereas in cost management it is anticipated that adjustments will be necessary as an integral part of the deployment.

11.7 SUMMARY

Ideally, one solution can be customized to your needs and that will fulfil the requirements to support the activities of SLM. There are basic elements that are linked among all processes and therefore should be linked within the technology deployed for them. However, budget and technical constraints are factors that we must manage and therefore require us to identify all stakeholders and collect all their requirements, so by the end of the deployment the solution is fit for purpose and fit for use.

PART 3
Service transition

Transition planning

12

12 Transition planning

Transitioning the process into production or into the operational state is a challenging task. Once the process has been designed, documented and approved, an implementation project must take place to bring the process into production. This chapter offers practical guidance on transition for practitioners.

12.1 SERVICE TRANSITION OVERVIEW

At its core, the transition of any process into production is a well-structured project plan with multiple work streams and phases. The plan must address the gaps found during the process maturity assessment, bring the process into practice and work towards changing the way people think, act and approach the services on a daily basis.

In order to build and execute a project plan, one needs a capable, experienced and IT service management (ITSM)-savvy project manager. Certifications and qualifications aside, the most successful project managers for this transition will be leaders who can effectively drive behavioural changes within service providers, operations and the business. Whenever possible, the role of transition project manager should be completely separate from that of the service level manager. The service level manager will have more than their share of the transition tasks and often will not have the time or energy to manage the project. Moreover, the skills required by the project manager and the service level manager are quite different.

Secrets of the trade

We have seen excellent sponsors of service level management (SLM) come from the office of the chief information officer (CIO), the chief operating officer or the IT service manager for the firm. The right executive sponsor for this transition should have as many daily interactions with service providers as with the business function that receives the services.

There are some phases in the project that will be the same for all readers. What we cannot predict is the time it will take for you to transition your organization's services, lines of business or customers into the SLM process. On average, for a larger organization, you should allocate one quarter (i.e. three months) per line of business or service tower – but there are many exceptions to this rule of thumb. Some of your lines of business will be eager to be engaged as a partner and become part of the SLM process. Others will want to be last on the list and may only join the others under duress.

12.2 SERVICE TRANSITION GUIDELINES

12.2.1 A phased approach

As with most major organizational behaviour changes or service deployments, a phased approach is almost always preferred. Identifying a business unit that is 'process friendly' or will be most open and willing to partner with IT is critical. Ensure your pilot or first phase is going to be successful and you will have a much better chance of getting the other parts of your business to follow. If possible, leave the most difficult business units or services until the end of the transition plan. This will hopefully create positive momentum for the transition and produce early results.

Once the plan has been put together, ensure it is reviewed with each major stakeholder from the executive management team and secure their buy-in before any project kick-off takes place. The recommended approach to ensure all of the stakeholders feel as though they have had an opportunity to provide input, voice concerns, steer the project's direction and ultimately agree to the plan is with an envisioning workshop.

12.2.2 What works and what doesn't?

Some of you will have seen many successful and some unsuccessful ITIL process transitions. We will now describe some of the most important characteristics of successful transition programmes, and then discuss some of the lessons learned from the transitions that did not progress very well and were sometimes abandoned.

12.2.2.1 Strong leadership

An SLM transition, as well as the process itself, will often succeed or fail based on the leadership capabilities of the service level manager and the project manager leading the transition. Organizational change is never easy. People inherently dislike and distrust changing their behaviour, especially if the established behaviours have been seen as 'good enough'.

12.2.2.2 Focus on the business

SLM is concerned with building a new partnership between the service provider and the customers. Transitioning the process with the organization will

not be a major obstacle as long as you have the headcount in place to transition and execute the process. The most successful transitions we've seen are heavily focused on the transformation of the business.

If the business is not driven or does not see any value in the process, the transition is doomed.

12.2.2.3 Awareness must be present at all levels

Awareness and education must be a major component of the transition plan. The most successful transitions have a clear, concise, varied and steady stream of targeted communications to both the service provider and the business. Partnering with your company's corporate communications department and centralizing information on the knowledge base portal will ensure the awareness programme is a success.

12.2.2.4 Service improvement feedback

As the transition progresses, feedback concerning the positive improvements being achieved needs to be provided to stakeholders. The service improvements and high levels of customer satisfaction will often not be evident to many resources. When the earliest results or trends are available, these must be shared via the awareness programme, and those responsible recognized and possibly rewarded.

12.2.2.5 Celebrate significant milestones

A critical part of an effective awareness programme is a visible, meaningful and memorable celebration of major milestones being met and the success and benefits that come with these achievements.

12.2.2.6 Centralize information

Successful SLM requires publicity as well as an easy way for process stakeholders to access its information. ITSM portals have become very popular at many corporations, where almost every process has a portal where information can be easily found. The process stakeholders, such as service providers, customers, service desk, end users and SLM staff, may find the information on the portal very useful.

The most comprehensive SLM portals include the following information:

- Welcome message from the service level manager and/or CIO
- Process charter
- Announcements: transition progress or changes to the process
- Service structure document
- Service information, via service level agreement (SLA) or service catalogue
- Report catalogue
- Education materials such as pre-recorded webinars and presentations
- FAQs and how-to documents
- A mapping of how SLM interfaces with other processes.

12.2.2.7 Pilot SLA period

The pilot period for the SLA is when service levels are monitored and reported to verify customer expectations and service baselines. At the end of the pilot period, the SLA is reviewed through the SLA audit process, adjusted if necessary, and then finalized (see section 14.5.4).

12.2.2.8 This process is not just about service failures

Negative news travels fast, is burnt into our memories (when compared with positive news) and often comes to the forefront of our conversations about the service. SLM is not and should not be solely focused on service failures, breached SLAs and service improvement plans (SIPs). While these conversations must take place with the business, the other half of the process and the ITSM philosophy should never be forgotten.

Remember that SLM is meant to foster the relationship between the service provider and the customer to ensure that services are designed and operated in such a way that business needs are met at a cost that is appropriate.

12.2.2.9 Pay attention to the business cycle

One of the auxiliary benefits of SLM should be that the IT function becomes much more aware of the rhythm of the business. The service provider should know when each part of the customer's business is most active, because these critical periods will translate into higher volumes of incidents, problems and changes. This type of period should be minimized with transition activities.

Secrets of the trade

Once, while working with an educational firm, a consultant noticed they were always extremely busy at the beginning of each school term. Admissions, financial aid transactions, enrolment and other business functions kicked into high gear in order to get as many students as possible into class. However, no one in IT could tell me when the beginning of each term was, exactly. What made this more complicated was that the different schools and campuses that the customer managed were all on different schedules (some on quarters and others on semesters).

Putting all of this information on a centralized calendar as part of the SLM portal helped everyone understand and predict when IT services would be pushed to the limit and when a glut of incidents would probably take place. Other business units within this organization were very interested in this calendar and IT got credit for pulling the information together and maintaining it. During a process transition, these busy times are the wrong times to ask the business for help with the transition.

12.3 SUMMARY

Planning the SLM process transition is critical for success. This chapter has provided practical guidance on the critical thinking that should accompany the planning phase of the transition project. Since the process transition is an actual project, good project management practice is also important.

Transition
work streams

13

13 Transition work streams

In the previous chapter, we examined the service level management (SLM) process transition at a high level. Guidance was provided on best practice and the all-important planning aspect of transitioning a process into everyday practice. This chapter goes a level deeper and discusses the actual activities required to execute the transition.

We will approach the transition project by dividing the activities into four sections or work streams. These work streams should be executed in parallel during the transition. The transition plan work streams are broken down into the same four Ps of service design that ITIL introduced: people, process, products and partners.

13.1 TRANSITION ACTIVITIES AND WORK STREAMS

All of the planning has been done except for the last step: creating the process transition plan and executing the activities. The process transition project manager needs a solid, structured and holistic plan to execute in order to bring all the process components and dependencies into alignment. The transition will prepare everyone for the process and will then execute the process for the first time (sometimes called a pilot).

In order to structure the transition in a logical manner, we have divided the transition project activities into four work streams. These work streams have some dependencies on each other but can overlap in the transition. We have:

■ **People** Transitioning the people involved with the process

■ **Process** Transitioning the process into common practice
■ **Products** Transitioning the tools needed to support the process
■ **Partners** Transitioning the external suppliers to ensure they are ready to support and integrate into the process.

Secrets of the trade

All four work streams are critical to the success of the transition. The more time and attention the transition receives, the more smoothly the process operations will go after the transition is complete. Think of the transition time and effort as a bill or invoice. You can pay the invoice now with cash (the cost of a solid transition) or pay later through an instalment plan with interest (the reduced cost of a shorter transition is paid, but the pain and frustration for the first six months of process operations will also have a cost greater than if you had paid cash up-front).

We would advise you to pay up-front and execute an effective process transition now instead of paying for it later. Ultimately, a good transition into smooth operations reflects better on the IT organization.

13.2 PEOPLE

This work stream is associated with the people who work within the process or who must interface with the process on a regular basis. The transition must address organizational change, because customers and the IT function will be asked to change their behaviour.

13.2.1 Process transition awareness

An executive once said that there is no such thing as over-communicating. This might have been true at one time, possibly in the early 1990s, but today end users are likely to discard communications instead of paying attention to them if they are too numerous, complex or seemingly immaterial. It is critical to ensure stakeholders within the service environment and the business are well informed about the SLM transition; but these communications must be clear, concise, targeted and designed to feed the audience information at a steady, manageable pace.

Awareness programmes for new process transitions should include the following:

- **Executive introduction** Introduce the transition programme, major milestones and timelines, and demonstrate that the process has the backing of both the service provider and business executives. List the benefits that the process is expected to bring and provide a pointer to the website or portal where the SLM transition information will be available.
- **Introduction of the service level manager** At the next departmental meeting, take some time to reiterate the main messages concerning the SLM transition and introduce the service level manager.
- **Process implementation status reports** As the transition progresses, there should be communications to stakeholders that describe the status of the transition, congratulate the organization for its successes (e.g. meeting

major milestones), and name areas where improvement is needed or progress is unsatisfactory.

- **Successes celebrated** As stated in the previous bullet point, it is important that the transition programme celebrates major milestones in the transition. Email messages accompanied by cake in the break room (with a card or poster ensuring everyone knows why there is cake) is a way to thank everyone for their time, attention, efforts and willingness to change their behaviour.
- **Roadshow with the CIO** After the first business unit has transitioned to the SLM process, it is a good time to embark on a roadshow to spread the word, emphasize the benefits actually realized in the early transition phases, and prepare the rest of the business for their turn to transition.

One of the keys to success for any process transition is a solid, well-developed and targeted awareness and communications plan. You should ensure that you take the time to develop one of your own that meets the needs of the organization.

13.2.2 Organizational change

In Chapter 2, we spoke about the roles and responsibilities associated with the SLM process and how these roles can fit into a typical IT organization. Assuming that the CIO has made organizational changes and appointed people to the SLM process roles, it is important now to ensure these people are transitioned into their new roles. The roles identified previously include the service level manager, the reporting analyst and the service relationship manager. The procedure you should follow is thus:

- **Create formal job descriptions** Those who have been appointed to the SLM roles must agree to and accept their new roles and responsibilities according to a formal job description.
- **Officially announce the new roles** The CIO should officially announce the changes being made to the organizational structure, announce who is being appointed to the SLM roles, and give a brief synopsis of the responsibilities of the new resources.
- **Introduce the new resources to the business** The SLM resources that will be interacting with the business or customers should be officially introduced to the stakeholders with whom they will be working. The relationships between the service level manager and their counterparts are critical to the success of the process.
- **Review process and RACI assignments** As the resources are settling into their new jobs, the RACI (responsible/accountable/consulted/informed) matrices associated with the SLM process should be reviewed with each person assigned to the process to ensure they are accurate and well understood (see Table 6.1).

13.2.3 Education

Education is critical in order to drive acceptance of the process and proactively prevent circumvention. For SLM, this often means education is needed within the service environment and the business. Stakeholders should be included in the education programme – possibly the resource appointed to work with the service provider on behalf of the business or customer group.

There are many certified IT service management (ITSM) and ITIL training providers in the marketplace. Many training providers offer bespoke training services that include content created exclusively for each customer. Customized training content helps to ensure the education material is directly applicable to an organization and is not simply 'off the shelf'.

13.3 PROCESS

In this section of the transition project, the process itself must be put into regular practice. The process design has been completed, documented in full and approved at this time. This work stream must put the process components into place and ensure the process is executed effectively for the very first time.

For a reminder of what the process might look like, see the Level 1 process flow diagram in Figure 7.1. Just as we divided the SLM process into five distinct components, the transition activities for the process will address one process component at a time (and happen to match those shown in Table 6.1).

13.3.1 SLA management

13.3.1.1 Interface with service catalogue management

SLM works with the service designers and customers to create a formalized service level agreement (SLA) that will be published within the service catalogue. In ITIL, a process has been created specifically for ensuring the service catalogue contains accurate information about the services in production.

13.3.1.2 Ensure SLM is consulted early in the service design process

Now that there is an SLM process, the service level manager must have a view of the new or enhanced IT services pipeline. As services are being requested, analysed and designed, the service level manager must be consulted and become part of the service design process.

13.3.1.3 Create and pilot the SLA template

The definition of services is owned by the service catalogue management process, but the SLA template is owned by SLM. However, the SLA structure cannot be created in a vacuum. The service level manager must ensure that the SLA template does not deviate from the service catalogue's established structure, nor contradict the IT service definitions that are already in place.

13.3.1.4 Finalize the SLA audit criteria and policy

Whenever a customer or the IT governance committee wants to change an SLA, this triggers an SLA audit. An SLA audit should also take place at the end of the SLA's initial pilot period. There may also be other triggers for this event, such as a major change in the IT infrastructure (e.g. due to a merger, acquisition or divestment of assets). Whatever the triggers are, the policy and criteria that launch this part of the process must be documented and agreed.

13.3.2 Monitoring and reporting

13.3.2.1 Identify data sources

In order to create reports that can indicate breaches in SLAs, the SLM process will probably need service reporting data from multiple sources, tools and systems. The transition must identify these data sources and build interfaces that will allow the process to get a continual feed of data on IT services.

13.3.2.2 Turn the data into usable information

The information collected on service levels must then be analysed, massaged and turned into information concerning an IT service's SLA measurements. Once again, this can be a laborious and repetitive task that should be automated wherever possible.

13.3.2.3 Validate accuracy

It is critical that SLM has a way to validate SLA reporting data. If the customer finds fault in any SLM report, they will not trust the service provider or any service reporting. In an outsourcing engagement, inaccurate performance reports – specifically those that are tied to financial penalties – may result in damaged relationships with the customer or, worse, in legal actions.

13.3.2.4 Build SLA reports and analyse the information

Once the SLA data have been validated, the SLA reports for the services must be created. If tools to automatically mine this data and create reports are not available, you may have to import the data into a spreadsheet and manually create historical line graphs that show the service level against the minimum SLA threshold.

13.3.2.5 Establish the interface with other ITSM processes

SLM should establish an interface with several other ITSM processes that should be informed when an SLA is breached. Major interfaces with SLM include:

- **Incident management** The urgency of an incident increases as the clock ticks down to the point where an SLA is breached. SLM must interface with incident management to ensure incident impact and urgency are mapped to SLAs and automated (if possible).

- **Problem management** This is the focal point for any root cause analysis (RCA) efforts. The problem manager must understand the service review process and what their role may be concerning RCA.
- **Service desk** The service desk provides services according to the SLA. Incidents and service requests are responded to and prioritized as defined in the SLA.
- **Availability management** If there is a breach in an availability SLA, SLM must interface with availability management to investigate the breach and bring options for service improvement to the customer.
- **Capacity management** If there is a breach in a performance SLA, SLM must interface with capacity management to investigate the breach and bring options for service improvement to the customer.
- **Supplier management** If there is a breach of an underpinning contract (UC) that may or may not breach an SLA for one or more IT services, the performance of the external supplier should be noted and managed.

13.3.3 Service review

13.3.3.1 Identify customer to pilot a service review

The initial service review meetings are unlikely to be perfect, professional affairs. It will take time for SLM to establish a meeting baseline and momentum. The service level manager should select a 'friendly' customer with whom to pilot the service review meeting.

13.3.3.2 Collect and create service review presentation

Many of the reports needed for the service review should already be available from the monitoring and reporting occurring during the transition (see section 13.3.2). However, the reports needed for the service review should show SLA trends over a longer period of time.

13.3.3.3 Pilot service review

Finally, conduct a pilot service review meeting with the customer. Be sure to keep the conversation formal even if the customer knows this is a sort of 'dry run'. At the end of the meeting, ask the customer for feedback.

13.3.3.4 Perform penalty and earn-back calculations

Examine the reports for SLA violations and then use them to calculate any penalties. If possible, efforts should be made to automate this procedure as much as possible.

13.3.3.5 Implement interface with financial management

SLM must build a process interface and workflow with financial management to establish how the penalties or earn-back calculations are fed into the procedure for customer invoicing or how the bank processes are changed.

13.3.4 Service improvement plan

13.3.4.1 Create CSI register templates

The list of attributes for the continual service improvement (CSI) register should be agreed on. A balance should be struck between a record that provides a quick glance at an improvement task and one that has all the information regarding the improvement.

13.3.4.2 Change management integration

Change management is a key factor in the service improvement plan (SIP) process. Agree with the change manager on activities and integration points between SLM and change management. For more details, refer to Chapter 17.

13.3.5 Continual process improvement

13.3.5.1 Report on process metrics and KPIs

Metrics and key performance indicators (KPIs) associated with the performance of the actual process should be defined, collected and reported on a regular basis. The process's portal should be used as a central storage for these metric and KPI reports over historical periods.

13.3.5.2 Lessons learned

There should be a centralized mechanism, possibly via the SLM knowledge base, where anyone who works with the SLM process can submit ideas for improving that process.

13.4 PRODUCTS

This work stream is associated with the tools and systems that support the SLM process. The transition must ensure that new tools are procured, installed and integrated or that existing tools are configured to produce the products needed by the process.

Products, tools and systems, and the deliverables they each create, are not an end in themselves but a means to facilitate the process. SLM products are going to be a considerable investment no matter what the size of your organization. If your SLM transition plan includes a budget for products, ensure that a careful evaluation takes place against process, business and IT requirements.

The SLM products are generally required to automate the measuring and reporting on service levels and thresholds. The transition plans for new or existing products will vary widely depending on the type of product being implemented, configured and integrated.

13.4.1 Knowledge base products

As mentioned earlier in this chapter, SLM should have its own portal site where process documentation, reports, templates and other information can be centralized and controlled. The service level manager should strive to keep the portal up to date and continually refresh or add to its content.

13.4.2 Service level products

There are multiple products that SLM utilizes to support its activities. Chapter 11 details the common categories of tools required:

- Metrics management tools
- Performance reporting tools
- Service improvement plan tools
- Cost management tools.

The installation of products entails initiation of a separate project, with its own project charter, funding and recourses.

13.5 PARTNERS

Almost all organizations outsource some part of their infrastructure. Just because an organization does not directly design, implement and operate part of its infrastructure does not mean this infrastructure is exempt from SLM. The process's transition must take external suppliers into account and ensure a framework is in place to include them in the transition.

At the core of this integration with partners is the alignment of underpinning contracts to SLAs. As SLAs are being negotiated, they should not surpass the weakest UC supporting the service provided. If a UC is not adequate for the business or an external supplier is not meeting its contractual obligations, SLM must work with supplier management to negotiate a new underpinning contract.

The external suppliers should hold service review meetings and create their own SLA reports for the services that they provide. The service level manager must take this information and incorporate it into a bigger picture for the customers. The service level manager should:

■ **Examine the service structure** For each service within the scope of the process, examine the service structure document to determine how the service maps onto the overall service environment. If any part of the service is under the responsibility of an external supplier, make a note of it. Form a picture of how the external suppliers are involved with the services, and clarify the service structure with the service designers.

■ **Analyse underpinning contracts** Once the external suppliers are known, the existing UCs should be analysed. The SLAs that the external suppliers have signed up to must be well understood. Unless an external supplier is responsible for providing an entire service, it is not enough to simply take note of the SLAs; the SLAs must be mapped onto the service tower and considered as part of a complex system.

■ **Determine reports** Collaborating with supplier management, the SLM transition team should meet with each external supplier to determine what reports need to be provided.

Example

Suppose an important branch office has two diverse WAN circuits from two separate network service providers, where the availability SLA for the first circuit requires 99.9% per month and that for the second circuit requires 98.0%. The service level manager needs to carefully determine the overall SLA for the WAN at this branch office. Are the circuits diversified or do they use the same fibre in the last mile or so? Are there single points of failure?

13.6 SUMMARY

This chapter has provided details on the transition plan needed to move the process into production. The plan was divided into four work streams covering people, process, products and partners. These work streams can be worked in parallel as part of a larger transition programme plan.

Every transition programme will be different for each IT organization. The organization's size, the type of services it provides, the products that are already in place and the organization's use of external suppliers will all impact the size and shape of the transition. This chapter has discussed transition activities that will most likely be necessary.

PART 4
Service operation

Operational service level agreement management

14

14 Operational service level agreement management

Each service level agreement (SLA) has a significant impact on the service environment generally, and specifically on service level management (SLM) as a process. The evolution of the SLA, starting as preliminary descriptions of services all the way through to an agreed legal document, requires a great deal of due diligence, dedication, examination and work with your customers and service providers.

The hard work put into producing the SLA is aimed at 'getting it right the first time', which is a high aspiration but not always achievable. This chapter will provide you with both the tools to produce a solid and close-to-perfect SLA, and the mechanism to adjust the SLA and improve it constantly.

We will also discuss the underpinning agreements for the SLA, the operational level agreement (OLA) and the underpinning contract (UC). These are great tools to support the activities and the process; and although they create additional scope, they will eventually benefit the service level manager as explained in this chapter.

14.1 SERVICE LEVEL AGREEMENT MANAGEMENT OVERVIEW

The stage is now set for SLM operations to complete the SLA by collecting requirements, negotiating its conditions and signing it off.

SLM operations extends into many areas and is responsible for several activities, such as service review meetings, service reporting and the service improvement plan (SIP). The management of the

SLA is an ongoing activity, not limited to the initial negotiation but continually being reviewed and improved (as seen in Figure 14.1 – see section 14.5 for more details).

The SLA, as a contractual document, is supported by multiple artefacts:

■ The service level requirements (SLRs) contain the customer's service requirements. The data captured in the SLRs are a primary input into the SLA.

■ While constructing the SLA, there are two underpinning agreements to be negotiated: the OLA (signed with the internal service provider); and the UC (signed with any external service provider).

In the following sections we detail the elements relating to the use of the above documents, while later, we describe the SLA lifecycle.

14.2 SERVICE LEVEL AGREEMENT

The existence of an SLA does not guarantee the quality of service provision. Service performance depends on many aspects – management, culture, products and much more. So, why is the SLA so important?

Given that the SLA is a signed agreement between the service provider and the customer, it officially defines the expectations from the service provider. An SLA benefits the organization in multiple ways:

- **It formally defines mutual expectations** As IT professionals, we all witness sales managers who over-promise or over-sell on services and products. SLA management defines exactly what the compliance level is, which means that it states clearly what you expect and if you sign the agreement you accept the conditions. At the other extreme, the SLA protects organizations from over-delivering. There is a cost connected with service delivery and, as enthusiastic as the service provider is, the SLA ensures that services are delivered as agreed – no more and no less.

- **It requires service monitoring and improvement** Most people will consider this benefit to be the best-practice purpose of the SLA. Arising from the SLA, there is monitoring of the quality of service relative to the documented service levels in the SLA; and as a result there should be continual service improvement (CSI). Additionally, the practical implementation of an SLA can be used as a marketing tool for further engagements and can be used to prove the efficiency of your organization.

- **It engenders a professional culture** The existence of an SLA enhances professionalism in the service management environment and assists in shaping a culture of accountability in your organization. Rushed agreements and handshake pacts are outdated and create scepticism in the eye of the customer. Well-documented and well-structured SLAs are one of the best ways to impress your customer with your professionalism and efficiency.

The SLA should not hold the service provider and the customer prisoners; rather, the SLA provides the conditions under which services are provided. Many times, the agreed levels and conditions are found to be unachievable. SLA audits are performed to allow mutually agreed-upon changes. To accommodate proactive SLA audits, a pilot period is defined for the SLA.

There are two different considerations, depending on the type of service provider or type of service management environment you are in:

- **Enterprise** This is what ITIL considers as a 'Type I' service provider, such as an IT department providing IT services to other internal departments. The SLA in this scenario is not a legal contract between two companies but, rather, a document that details the expectations from the business of what is needed from the services to support their activities. The process of documenting and negotiating the SLA is limited, generated by the SLRs. The parties involved are the service level manager and the business unit representative(s).

- **Outsourcing engagement** In the case of an external service provider providing services to another organization, the SLA is a legally binding agreement between the customer and the service provider. The SLA becomes an official document included in the master contract for an outsourcing agreement. The SLA will be a sub-section of the master contract, or alternatively a schedule attached to the master contract. This type of SLA will typically include financial consequences to an SLA breach by the service providers. The process of documenting and negotiating the SLA includes many entities – such as sales, account management, legal, the customer, the service provider and SLM.

For further information on SLA structure, content and attributes, refer to Chapters 8 and 9.

14.3 SERVICE LEVEL REQUIREMENTS

SLRs comprise a tool to capture customer requirements for an aspect of a service. They are based on business objectives and are used to negotiate agreed service level targets. Ultimately, SLRs will provide a basis for negotiations linked to the formulation of service level objectives (SLOs). From the SLM perspective, the main purpose of SLRs is to allow the smooth transition of information to the SLA.

Information that is collected into the SLR document should be easily transferable to the SLA. The content edited in the SLR document is not procured merely through discussions with the customer; rather, the content should be based on service options predefined by service level packages (SLPs), metrics and measurements that were designed for the service. For more information, see Chapter 9 on metrics development and the 'solution sets' technique.

14.4 OPERATIONAL LEVEL AGREEMENTS AND UNDERPINNING CONTRACTS

Service providers are dependent on their internal technical support teams or on external partners. They cannot commit to meeting SLA targets unless their support teams and suppliers' performance underpin these targets. Contracts with external suppliers are known as 'underpinning contracts' (UCs), since they underpin the related SLA. Agreements with internal support teams tend not to be legal and are less formal; they are referred to as operational level agreements (OLAs).

The term 'underpinning contract' is used for any type of agreement or contract between an IT service provider and a supplier that supports a service. The term 'service level agreement' is used to refer to an agreement between the service provider and a customer. The general term 'underpinning agreement' is a more generic term and is used to refer to any OLA, and any UC or other agreement that underpins an SLA. So we have:

- **Operational level agreement** An agreement between an IT service provider and another part of the same organization. An OLA supports the IT service provider's delivery of IT services to customers.
- **Underpinning contract** A contract between an IT service provider and a third party. The third party provides goods or services that support delivery of an IT service to a customer. The UC defines targets and responsibilities that are required to meet the agreed service level targets in an SLA.

14.4.1 Guidelines for operational level agreements

Not all companies utilize OLAs. Indeed, many organizations that possess a high level of ITIL maturity do not sign such agreements. These internal agreements are meant to assist with better documentation and service governance and not to create additional work. It is fair to say that highly integrated service provider operations are likely not to utilize an OLA. In contrast, organizations that are based on independent functions are inclined to use OLAs.

When defining an OLA, you need to consider the following guidelines:

- **Be selective** OLAs are not mandatory, so be selective when signing an OLA with an internal function. It is very common to sign an OLA with each support function, such as the service desk, but many feel that OLAs with service delivery functions are not always necessary. Identify the need first, and only after that select the internal functions where an OLA is needed.

■ **Accountability** One of the primary purposes of an OLA is to promote accountability for the supporting functions. Although it is understood that SLM represents the service provider with the SLA, the existence of an OLA affirms the expectations for performance.

■ **Service level** It is a common practice to increase the service levels stated in an OLA relative to those specified in an SLA. For example, if the SLA states that the service provider must resolve Severity 2 incidents within four hours, the OLA within that support group is likely to state a resolution time of three hours. However, please note that this is not ideal. Organizations where service delivery functions work collectively and strive towards the same objectives will prefer to sign OLAs with the same service levels as the SLA. This is a clear sign of trust and a positive relationship between the groups.

■ **Structure and content** Although OLAs focus on one service rather than a complete list of services, as defined in the SLA, it is still recommended to structure the OLA in the same way as the SLA. The OLA must provide guidance to integrate the activities of SLM, the function itself, and agreed processes for service monitoring and review.

14.4.2 Guidelines for underpinning contracts

Unlike OLAs, UCs are mandatory. If a service provider outsources an activity or product to an external service provider, an SLA will be signed between them and this SLA becomes a UC relative to the main SLA. Close integration will occur at this point between SLM and supplier management to ensure that the contract and its conditions will support the required service delivery to the customer.

It is important to note that ITIL indicates that supplier management is responsible for the negotiation of underpinning supplier contracts and agreements, to which SLM provides critical input and consultation. This is due to the fact that supplier management has primary responsibility for the relationship between the IT service provider and its suppliers.

When defining a UC, you should consider the following guidelines:

■ **SLA is the primary input** As a supplier is being considered to support a service, the SLA must be a primary input into the supplier management process. When a request for proposal (RFP) is utilized, the service requirements will accompany the SLA.

■ **Service levels** Unlike the OLA, the service levels agreed with the supplier to underpin the SLA are designed to allow for a margin of error and should be higher than indicated in the SLA. For example, if the internet availability specified in the SLA is 97% of the month and an external supplier is sourced to provide the service, the UC might well require the service availability to be increased to 99%.

■ **Penalties** If the SLA includes service level penalties, it is in the service provider's best interest also to include penalties in the UC. There are two approaches for UC penalties: the first will design a penalties system that is equivalent to the system indicated in the SLA; the second is much simpler, stating that 'any penalties charged that were caused by the supplier's poor performance will be charged to the supplier'.

14.5 SLA MANAGEMENT – THE OPERATIONAL PROCESS

Traditionally, the SLA management sub-process, which we are about to unveil, has been the primary sub-process of SLM. As expressed in this publication, SLM is an integrated process containing five sub-processes, as demonstrated in Figure 1.1.

The sub-process SLA management focuses on the development of the SLA as an agreement and ensures its relevance through continual reviews and audits. As shown in Figure 14.1, it contains four steps:

- Prepare SLA templates
- Collect requirements
- SLA negotiations
- SLA audit.

A common mistake in the IT service management (ITSM) discipline is to negotiate the terms of the SLA and review its performance throughout the SLA lifecycle without questioning its content and conditions. The process outlined below allows questioning of SLA content and permits periodic intervention and audits. This guarantees SLA alignment to actual business requirements and ultimately assists with service performance and customer satisfaction.

14.5.1 Prepare SLA templates and service information

The first activity of the SLA management sub-process is to prepare the documents that act as primary inputs to the process. In Part 2 on service design (Chapters 5–11), we worked hard to define the SLA structure, metrics management and relevant service information. And now, before approaching the customer, we must prepare prerequisite deliverables to initiate the process:

- **SLA templates** In Chapter 8 we developed the structure of our SLA. The SLA structure guides us through the development and editing of SLA content. At this point, we should have other relevant templates prepared, such as SLRs, OLAs and UCs.
- **Metrics and measurements definitions** In Chapter 9 we examined each service and compiled a list of metrics and measurements

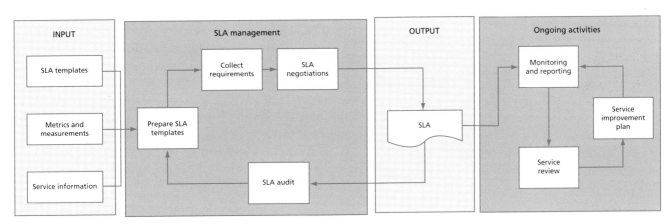

Figure 14.1 SLA management sub-process

appropriate to that service. It is good practice to provide the customer with SLPs which include different levels of service performance.

- **Service information** Preparing for the development of the SLA requires an intimate understanding of the services involved. It is not recommended to meet with the customer and collect their requirements without knowledge of the services. An excellent starting point would be the service structure document detailed in Chapter 8.

Note that the service transition chapters (Chapters 12 and 13) include activities that transition documents and templates, such as SLAs, SLRs, OLAs and UCs, into production. Adhering to this process vastly simplifies this first activity of the preparation.

14.5.2 Collect requirements

There is a misconception about this activity. Collecting requirements regarding service performance expectations does not mean meeting with the customer, getting out a blank sheet of paper, asking the customer what they want and writing it down. The previous step in section 14.5.1, on preparing SLA templates and service information, is crucial. Preparing prerequisite products simplifies this activity and portrays you as the professional that you are.

Collecting requirements is essentially helping the customer identify business needs that are expected to be met from the service. Customers have a tendency to want it all, at any cost. When options are presented that include differential pricing by service levels, the customer will be able to express their business needs more succinctly.

Although the 'collect requirements' activity focuses primarily on the customer, this step necessitates a close working relationship with the service provider as well. The deliverables of this activity, mainly the SLRs, are key inputs into the service specification. You should be able to start to define both of the following:

- **SLR document** The SLRs are the key output of this activity. The document setting out customer SLRs is structured to allow any information regarding service expectations to be recorded. The SLR document must be structured in accordance with the SLA, allowing a smooth transition of content from the SLRs to the SLA.
- **Service specification** The service provider, as part of the service design activity of ITSM, is responsible for developing the service specification, also known as 'spec sheets'. Although the specification is out of scope for the SLM process, it is important to note the integration between the specification and SLRs, as the specification is a formal definition of requirements. The spec sheets translate the customer's SLRs (external specifications) into technical definitions needed to provide the service (internal specifications).

The SLR document, service specification and other documents are dynamic and subject to continual changes. The SLR document is gradually refined as the service progresses through the stages of its lifecycle until it is eventually transitioned into a pilot SLA during the early-life support period. A draft SLA should be developed alongside the service itself and should be signed and formalized before the service is introduced into live use.

14.5.3 SLA negotiations

SLA negotiations include agreeing on the service performance and content of the SLA, finalizing the agreement and signing off.

The scope of SLA negotiations is notably different in an outsourcing engagement in comparison with the enterprise model. In an outsourcing engagement, SLA negotiations entail cost. Many times, the selection of the service provider is heavily dependent on the conditions detailed in the SLA. In the enterprise model, SLM represents the internal IT department and the services it provides. Within the enterprise, the SLA is not a legally binding agreement but, instead, acts as a document that aligns the expectations of the customer with those of the service provider.

For more information on the differences between outsourcing engagement and an enterprise model, refer to section 1.1.5. Even so, as part of the SLA management sub-process it is imperative to detail the activities for both scenarios, which we do next.

14.5.3.1 Outsourcing engagement

In 2000 a study was performed by Nextslm involving 182 executive managers from North America; the purpose of the study was to assess current issues and needs with respect to outsourcing management practices. One of the key findings was that the most important item for outsourcing success is having a well-written, negotiated SLA that effectively addresses roles and responsibilities, goals and objectives, reporting policies, help desk availabilities, penalties, incentives and adjustment procedures.

In outsourcing engagements, multiple stakeholders are involved in the process to ensure that issues are not neglected, particularly where those issues are

expressed in vague terms that must be interpreted and then precisely articulated as contractual elements. There are three groups of stakeholders that provide essential input:

- Business, presented by sales or account management
- Technical, presented by the operational service provider and the customer
- The service level manager as the middleman, providing a channel for communication to ensure requirements by all stakeholders are met.

The negotiation activity is coordinated with the sales team and the conditions, including the service levels, have a direct impact on pricing. The SLA evolves through customer requirements defined in the RFP. Service levels and pricing are negotiated and eventually detailed in an SLA, which is a sub-section or a schedule of the outsourcing contract.

14.5.3.2 Enterprise

Since the SLA is not a legally binding document, the negotiation stage is limited. The service level manager presents the service provider to the customer and communicates the customer's requirements to the service provider.

When the correct SLA management sub-process is performed, long and exhausting negotiations may be avoided. The previous activities, namely the preparation of documents and the collection of requirements, will allow a much smoother transition into the sign-off of the SLA. A well-coordinated SLA process and healthy relationship between the service level manager and customer will result in a formal meeting to sign off the SLA.

Once the SLA is signed and the service provision is initiated, SLM is geared to ongoing operations mode. This activity is a cycle that involves review of service performance reports, SLA compliance reports and improvement of degraded services.

14.5.4 SLA audit

The constant monitoring and reviewing of the SLA by utilizing performance reports and conducting service review meetings does not conclude the SLA management sub-process. The SLA is agreed on assumptions that may not have been accurate or assumptions that do not stand the test of time in the face of changing business needs. The SLA must allow a procedure for it to be reviewed, audited and changed. The final step of the process, i.e. SLA audit, provides the mechanism to review the agreement and the conditions it upholds.

An SLA audit evaluates whether the conditions and targets specified within the SLA still reflect the needs of both the customer and the service provider. The SLA audit involves reviewing the SLA and, if required, recommending changes and renegotiating conditions.

A good practice of SLM is to design the SLA audit process with the customer and, if possible, include it in the SLA as a continuation of or extension to the pilot period clause. In practice, SLAs omit the SLA audit process and simply state that a process will be defined within the pilot to perform an SLA audit.

Secrets of the trade

I was involved with a large-scale outsourcing engagement where the SLA existed as a schedule for the overall contract. The SLA was negotiated and signed in the absence of the service level manager and the customer representative.

As time went by, it became apparent that both sides were expressing concerns about continuing with the current agreement. Some of the metrics had shown a breach of the SLA, while in reality the services were meeting business needs. On the other hand, some metrics met performance expectations, but all the while end users repeatedly complained of service degradation and disruptions.

As I met with both parties, I realized they were under the impression that the SLA is a legal document that cannot be changed until its expiry date. They were reluctant to engage the account management function or the legal department to make changes in the agreement due to a fear of time-consuming bureaucracy.

Studying the SLA, I made the service level manager aware of a clause defining a pilot period. Although the clause did not provide details regarding SLA audit procedure, it opened a loophole for us to work with. Soon after, we worked together to define the missing details for an SLA audit, and the service level manager was thereby able to make the required changes with the customer.

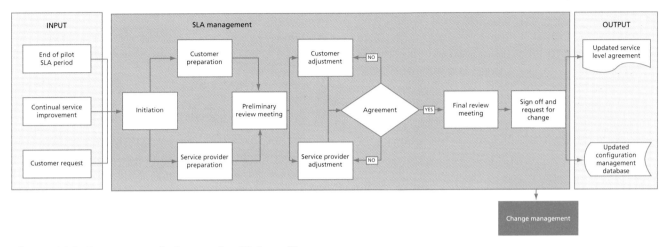

Figure 14.2 Recommended steps for SLA audit

As suggested by Figure 14.2, SLA audits are instigated by three circumstances:

- **End of pilot SLA period** The pilot period for the SLA is when service levels are monitored and reported to verify customer expectations and service baselines. At the end of the pilot period the SLA is reviewed and, where necessary, adjusted and finalized through the SLA audit procedure.
- **Continual service improvement** SLM executes continual improvements by reviewing and evaluating products and activity. Improvements may be initiated by reactive measures coming from some visible lack in the process, or by proactive measures coming from the annual process review.
- **Customer request** The customer may submit a request for SLA changes. It is common for the customer to request changes as a method to enhance, reduce or change the cost of services by adjusting service levels.

14.5.4.1 Initiation

As described above, the request for initiation of the SLA audit process may be submitted by different sources. SLM acts as the single point of contact for the SLA audit request and, as the owner of the process, has the authorization to initiate the process.

The service level manager begins by identifying the type of change that is required. There are three levels at which the change has to be positioned:

- **Overall structure** With the introduction of the ITIL framework into an organization it may be necessary to change the overall structure of the SLA in order to align it with best practice.
- **Measurements and calculations** The SLA provides the calculations for the services to be included on the performance reports. The initial calculations are based on tools and systems in place at the time of the SLA sign-off. Changes in the environment, including replacement of legacy systems, require modifications to calculation design in the SLA.

- **Compliance level** One of the most common requests for an SLA audit is triggered by the requirement to increase or decrease compliance levels. For example, if there is a new business request for the availability of the system/service to be upgraded from 9 a.m. to 5 p.m. to 24 hours daily, this may affect resource allocation, require deployment of new software and hardware, and increase costs.

The service level manager needs to document an SLA audit request detailing the request for change (RFC), and then evaluate its impact. This is a high-level document that defines the scope and provides stakeholders with an overall understanding of what the change will involve. The document is sent to the customer for review and discussed in service review meetings.

Following completion of this document, the customer and service provider are sent individually to work on their requirements and prepare their case before the preliminary review is performed.

14.5.4.2 Customer preparation

The customer prepares information based on the SLA audit request, to be presented in the preliminary review meeting. If the change requires an increase in service compliance, a business case may be needed to gain approval for the additional funding. If changes in SLA conditions such as the measurements are needed, improved conditions should be developed along with reasoning and incentives.

14.5.4.3 Service provider preparation

While the customer prepares their information to support the change that is requested, the service provider evaluates the impact of the change, utilizing the six constraints on change:

- Scope
- Time
- Cost
- Quality
- Risk
- Customer satisfaction.

Note that some changes are considered to be minor and may not require an in-depth analysis. However, the determination of whether the change is minor or not is a result of a study carried out during the preparation for the preliminary review meeting.

14.5.4.4 Preliminary review meeting

The purpose of the preliminary review meeting is for the service provider and the customer to present their cases. When requested changes entail infrastructure modification or affect pricing and service levels, the preliminary review meeting provides a platform for negotiation.

The service level manager should act as a communicator between the sides. The service level manager documents the requirements of both sides and outputs meeting minutes and a meeting summary for the service provider and the customer to support their subsequent adjustments.

The service provider and the customer then set about adjusting requirements and developing a final change request.

14.5.4.5 Customer adjustment

The customer will have collected information in the preliminary review meeting and will now develop their final change request.

If the change entails new funding, the customer will meet with senior management to acquire a budget to increase the service level or obtain additional resources to support the service.

14.5.4.6 Service provider adjustment

Just as the customer assembles their stakeholders to discuss final touches for the change, the service provider meets internally to refine documentation in light of additional data discovered in the preliminary review meeting.

The adjustment period involves continual communication between the service provider and the customer to negotiate and agree on a final draft for the change in the SLA.

The service level manager plays a key role in this adjustment period as the communicator between the parties. The service level manager understands that the changes to the SLA could greatly influence the process, and any unreasonable new requirements will negatively affect many of those involved in meeting customer needs, including the service level manager. For that reason, the service level manager must apply themselves a great deal at this critical phase.

14.5.4.7 Final review meeting

If agreement is reached and no further discussions are needed, the final review meeting is a formality. Some even choose to skip the meeting and rely on electronic agreement or a phone call. If an agreement is not reached, the parties keep meeting and conducting internal discussions until the requirements are adjusted and aligned with the other party.

When a good relationship exists between the parties, the final review meeting is combined with the next activity, which is approval of the new requirements and initiation of the RFC.

14.5.4.8 Sign-off and request for change

Significant changes in the SLA will require the service level manager to lead the SLA audit process and will ensure that primary stakeholders adhere to it. The changes requested are documented through the process. What started as a high-level document at the initiation stage has become an extensive, detailed document that both sides can agree to and approve.

As the SLA is a configuration item, it is subject to change control. The service level manager, as the owner of the SLA, will submit an RFC based on the requirements agreed with the customer.

14.6 SUMMARY

This chapter has detailed two processes that are essential to the management of the SLA.

The first process comprises overall SLA management, which takes us from the basic collection of service requirements all the way to signing off the SLA and continues with the ongoing monitoring of the objectives of the SLA. The second process, SLA audit, is a governance activity that allows changes to occur to the SLA, promoting continual improvement to the SLA and to the SLM process itself.

Service reporting

15

15 Service reporting

This chapter aims to describe the activities under the responsibility of service reporting. Service level management (SLM) uses service reporting either by sourcing reporting work to an external function or by allocating a resource in the form of a reporting analyst. Either way, the activities must be scoped and defined. This chapter provides you with the essentials of service reporting and then concludes with the overall service reporting framework for SLM.

15.1 SERVICE REPORTING OVERVIEW

The service reporting function is one of the essential functions within SLM, not just for SLM, but for the success of service management practice as a whole. Effective decision-making, from high, strategic levels to continual process improvement, is based on the results of the service reporting.

Organizations deploy service reporting differently, depending primarily on organizational structure. Some companies deploy an independent function that is solely responsible for generating reports. This function, sometimes called business intelligence, is normally part of the IT function and works with operations to collect data to satisfy reporting requirements submitted by different groups. Other organizations choose to allocate resources for functions that rely heavily on reports. In our model, SLM will be allocated reporting resources, along with financial and management functions.

SLM as a process depends heavily on service reporting; this dependency creates dilemmas and difficulties. A limited understanding of service management and ITIL best practice encourages managers to allocate a service level manager under the assumption that this is a reporting role. This is a crucial mistake that has the potential to negatively affect the rest of the service management environment. It is strongly recommended to allocate a separate service reporting function, in the form of a reporting analyst who dedicates time to report production. This will allow the service level manager to focus on building the relationship with the customer and the operation, continually improving services and creating a positive perception of service provision.

For more information regarding SLM functions, including the reporting analyst, refer to Chapter 6 on SLM functions and processes (in Part 2 on service design).

15.2 SERVICE LEVEL AGREEMENT COMPLIANCE REPORT

The service level agreement (SLA) compliance report presents the results for service performance specified in the SLA. The SLA details a list of service level objectives (SLOs) and the compliance level expected by the service provider. The SLA compliance report collects relevant data, calculates the metrics and presents the actual (achieved) results, comparing them with expected (compliance) service levels.

15.2.1 Automated versus manual report production

It goes beyond good practice to automate the SLA compliance report. ITIL practitioners are still amazed to find well-established service management organizations that manually generate the report. Set out next are a few of the advantages for deployment of an automated SLA compliance report.

15.2.1.1 Resource utilization

The allocation of reporting resources to creating a report manually each month is costly and inefficient. An automated reporting mechanism requires initial settings and maintenance but the costs thereafter are relatively low. Following the deployment of an automated solution, many organizations use their reporting analysts more effectively, to perform advanced activities such as the examination of information and improvement of service provision.

15.2.1.2 Accuracy

The repeatable data processes of the automated solution prevent potential human error, whereas manually generated reports are typically rushed, error-prone and incomplete.

15.2.1.3 Proactive SLM

Automated solutions collect data over a prescribed interval – the suggested time is at night, when overheads on servers will generally have the least impact. However, it is not uncommon to find data collection on an hourly basis, depending on the requirement. SLA reports that are updated throughout the month allow close tracking of SLOs, enabling alerts in cases of threshold breaches and warnings. This type of proactive management allows service providers to adjust service provision during the month and avoid waiting for the end of the month to discover failures.

15.2.1.4 Scalability

SLM is challenged with constant change, including additional data, metrics and reports. A standard framework in the format of an automated solution relieves those challenges.

15.2.2 Report presentation

In the 2000s, our industry established standards and general guidelines for the SLA compliance report, as described below.

15.2.2.1 Centralization

The reports must contain all the objectives for the relevant SLA, providing one centralized view of the metrics. The SLA compliance report is formatted as a table, listing the objectives categorized by service category/service towers (see Table 15.1 for an example). The report viewer should have an indication at first glance of the services that are degrading.

15.2.2.2 'RAG'

The reported results are marked in 'RAG' (red, amber, green), visualizing the achievement of the SLOs.

- **Red** The compliance level is in breached status
- **Amber** The compliance level is in warning status, or has reached a threshold but has not yet been breached
- **Green** The objective is compliant and is meeting the goal of the service level.

Table 15.1 Example of an SLA compliance report – monthly SLA dashboard

Category	SLA name	Specific SLA	Objective	Goal	SLA % achieved	Data range	No. of missed tickets
Network services	Time to resolve (TTR) SLA solution set	Administrative requests: response time	90% must be responded to within 2h	90%	100%	64	0
		Administrative requests: TTR	90% must be resolved within 8h	90%	86.54%	64	16
		Monitored alarm events: response time	90% must be responded to within 2h	90%	100%	40	0
		Monitored alarm events: TTR	90% must be resolved within 8h	90%	96%	40	14
Help desk	Abandoned calls	Abandoned rate	Must not exceed 7% monthly	7%	6.11%	1636	100
	First-call resolution rate	First-call resolution	70% must be resolved monthly	70%	100%	810	0
Desk-side services	Desk-side service TTR: solution sets	Desk-side campus by severity: response time	90% must be responded to within 2h	90%	100%	656	0
		Desk-side campus by severity: TTR	90% must be resolved within 8h	90%	83.33%	656	293

Table 15.2 Example of an SLA compliance report – specific service level objective

Specific SLA	Objective	Goal	SLA % achieved	Data range	No. of missed tickets
Time to respond for Priority 3 incidents	90% must be responded to within 8h	90%	83.33%	656	293

Secrets of the trade

We argue about one aspect of the RAG approach sometimes at work: should the SLA include definitions of each of the thresholds determined by colours (red, amber, green), or is that a judgement call made by the reporting function?

Definitions of red, amber and green should in our view be specified and agreed to by stakeholders. The clearest definition is a mathematical calculation. Take an example where the SLA is that all Severity 1 tickets must be responded to in 15 minutes. Is 'red' when a single ticket exceeds 15 minutes? Probably not. In this case, defining red, amber and green as a percentage of total tickets may be appropriate. However, what if the one ticket that exceeded the 15 minutes SLA was a ticket submitted by a senior vice president who has a knack for complaining? Having agreed-upon definitions will help in these circumstances. In cases where a mathematical formula is not possible, ensure that all stakeholders still discuss and agree the colour-based status meanings before finalizing the report.

As a rule of thumb, red is when an SLA has been breached. Amber should be set as a threshold for two reasons: the first is to alert the service provider and allow enough time to ensure that actions are taken to remedy the services so that by the end of the review period the SLA is not breached; the second is to highlight borderline cases for the service review meeting, because not all targets are reviewed in the meeting but those that are breached (red) and then those that are in warning (amber) must be looked at and prioritized.

15.2.2.3 Achieved versus expected

For each metric the result (achieved) is positioned next to the expected service level for quick comparison.

15.2.2.4 Report duration

The report allows the user to compare results throughout an agreed period – the previous quarter, six months or year.

15.2.3 Drill-downs

One feature and significant advantage of a robust automated SLA compliance report is the ability of the viewer to 'drill down' to examine further detail for the metric.

There is no single correct way to drill down through the data; the goal is to meet the business needs. When designing the SLA report and its drill-down options, stakeholders must be consulted for feedback on what type of information will be useful for them.

By their nature, SLOs in the SLA are high-level and attempt to measure end-to-end service. Thus, the breakdown of information is beneficial for examination of service performance. Consider the example results for 'time to respond' for Priority 3 incidents, as shown in Table 15.2, where we can clearly see that the service level has been breached. For further examination, we need to be able to drill down to see the underlying data either by location or by category:

- **Drill down by location** The first option we provide is location. This drill-down would answer the question, 'Which sites are not responding well to Priority 3 incidents?' The example report in Figure 15.1 is a drill-down by location, indicating that the New Jersey site is the root cause of the breach, since the other sites are in compliance with the service level.

- **Drill down by category** This drill-down answers an interesting question: 'Which type of incident takes the longest time?' The example report in Figure 15.2 indicates that Priority 3 incidents related to the local area network (LAN) take too long to resolve.

Although we determined the cause of the breach, we are interested to go one step further and see the detail for the incidents themselves. This report will allow us to establish the root cause of incidents that have breached the threshold by a significant margin and will thus assist in defining the action item(s) necessary to address the breach. Table 15.3 provides an example.

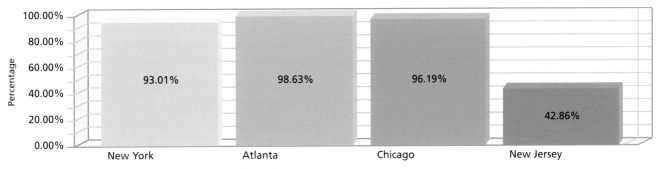

Figure 15.1 SLA report: drill down by location

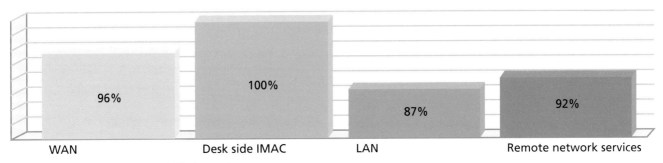

Figure 15.2 SLA report: drill down by category

Table 15.3 Example of an SLA compliance report – drill-down to incident detail

Call ID	Description	Severity	Open	Close	Duration	Suspended	Target
100-01	Application server down	2	03-07-06 10:00	03-07-06 11:34	01h34m	00h12m	01h30m

Secrets of the trade

The number of drill-down levels differs per scenario. In one project, I was asked to suggest drill-downs for an SLA report where it soon became apparent that drill-down by location was the way to go. The support groups were structured by geographical location, utilizing a virtual 'follow the sun' service desk.

To determine the levels of drill-down to view for the performance of the service support, I examined the level of management and interviewed stakeholders to understand what information benefited the business and the customer. We established five levels of drill-down:

1 SLA result

2 Region (North America, South America, Asia Pacific, Europe, Middle East, Africa)

3 Country

4 Site

5 Incident detail.

15.3 SLA ADJUDICATION

SLA adjudication is the process that enables the modification of the SLA compliance report results. The service level manager is responsible for the overall process activities and their outcome. However, service reporting or the reporting analyst is the owner of the process.

The basic idea behind SLA adjudication is that sometimes the results of the report do not reflect the actual service performance. This can be the result of many underlying causes, such as corrupt data, invalid data entry, lack of data, no business impact or any other exception agreed by the customer and the service provider that allows manual modification of the reporting results.

There are two conditions under which the SLA adjudication may take place:

- **Process documentation** The process must be discussed with the business and agreed by the customer. In outsourcing engagements, SLA adjudication should be detailed in the SLA.
- **Technology** There must be tools to support the modification of data to ensure that, following the agreed changes, the data are reprocessed and the results are as expected. The tool must support audit tracking for future reference to understand where changes were made.

15.3.1 SLA adjudication process

The SLA adjudication process is initiated at the service review meeting and, in most cases, is aimed at avoiding service level penalties. While reviewing the SLA compliance report during the service review meeting, the service level manager and the customer may agree that one or more of the breaches was caused by corrupted data and that the SLA results do not reflect the level of service performance.

Although this example may be common, not all SLA adjudications are triggered by bad data. The customer may also agree that the business was not impacted by the breach and thus penalties can be discarded. At the other extreme, the SLA report may show full compliance but, in fact, services were not performing adequately and the report should be modified to show the SLA breaches.

The documented process should include three main steps:

- **Service review** The service level manager and the customer agree to initiate SLA adjudication for one or more SLOs and negotiate on the desired result. Depending on the situation, the service level manager and the customer may also agree on where the data should be modified (see the options for data modification in section 15.3.2).
- **Data modification** Following the meeting, the reporting analyst will modify the data, rerun the calculation and verify that the new results are aligned with decisions made at the service review meeting.
- **Final sign-off** The new products, including the reports, meeting minutes and final results are submitted to the service level manager and the customer for a final sign-off.

15.3.2 Options for data modification

There are three levels where data may be modified to enable the SLA adjudication (see Figure 15.3). Whatever level you decide on, there must be a log file system or audit tracking note left behind for future reference. There are three attributes for tracking: date and time, modifier name, and description. The description field is used to document the reason for the modification.

Although modifying the SLA results simplifies the data processing, it is suggested in some cases that the raw data should be changed to recalculate the SLA result. For example, if you only change the SLA result and in the future go back to analyse the data, you might not be able to understand the disparity between the SLA result and the raw data.

The three levels for data modification are:

- **SLA compliance report** The most common place to modify the SLA result is on the SLA compliance report. In an automated SLA solution the user can navigate to an SLA adjudication screen where a replica of the SLA compliance is presented with additional functions for SLA adjudication. An automated solution controls access to this function and grants only specific users rights to modify the SLA results. When the reports are developed manually, the risk of unauthorized modification is higher and the process must be monitored.
- **Raw data** When data have been identified as corrupt or data integrity requires correction, you are recommended to modify the raw data that were provided to generate the SLA results. In this case the data are reprocessed and the SLA results are recalculated.
- **Original system** In extreme cases the SLA results were miscalculated as a result of data corruptions as early as the system that created the data. For example, the customer relationship management (CRM) system is used to log relevant incidents and service requests. Data are extracted from the CRM system to be used as raw data to calculate the metrics laid down for time to respond or time to resolve. When data corruption is identified in the CRM system, operations and service reporting may

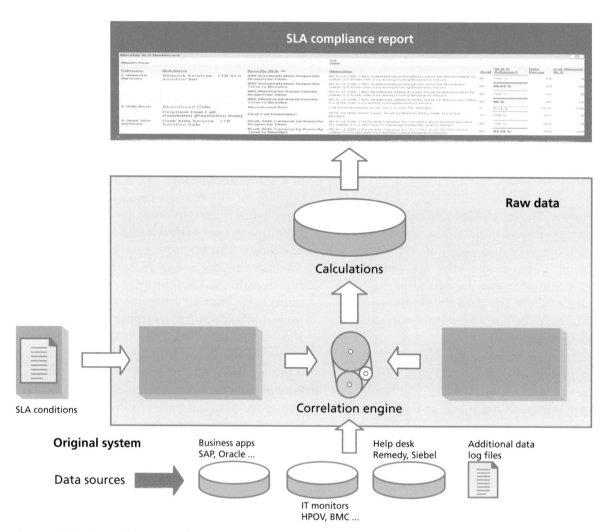

Figure 15.3 Three levels of data

choose to modify the original records and re-extract the corrected raw data for the SLA results to be recalculated.

15.4 DASHBOARDS

A dashboard is an executive information system user interface that organizes and presents the collected information and its analysis in an easy-to-read fashion.

Dashboards provide critical information at a glance and aim to allow managers to step back from the details and see the key trends and relationships between components that make up overall service performance. When required, the user will drill down into further details.

There are techniques that ITIL suggests regarding dashboards: the balanced scorecard and SWOT.

15.4.1 'Balanced scorecard' technique

The 'balanced scorecard' was developed by Kaplan and Norton in the 1990s (see Kaplan R S and Norton D P, 'The Balanced Scorecard: measures that drive performance', *Harvard Business Review*, Jan–Feb 1992, pp71–80) to align business activities to the vision and strategy of the organization, improve internal and external communications, and monitor organization performance against strategic goals. This framework covers four different perspectives:

- **The learning and growth perspective** This perspective includes employee training and corporate cultural attitudes related to both individual and corporate self-improvement.
- **The business process perspective** This perspective refers to internal business processes. Metrics based on this perspective allow the managers to know how well their business is running and whether its products and services conform with customer requirements.
- **The customer perspective** This gives rise to reports focusing on the customer perspective, customer satisfaction survey results and feedback.
- **The financial perspective** The financial perspective examines whether the company's performance is contributing to the bottom line in the financial results.

15.4.2 SWOT technique

This technique is credited to Albert Humphrey and is a strategic planning method used to evaluate the strengths, weaknesses, opportunities and threats involved in a process, service or business performance:

- **Strengths** The elements of the company that contribute to the success of the process.
- **Weaknesses** The elements that are harmful to achieving the business objectives.
- **Opportunities** Internal and external conditions that are helpful for achieving business objectives.
- **Threats** Elements that have the potential to do damage to business objectives.

15.4.3 Choosing your dashboard

The different techniques provide food for thought when configuring dashboards. The guiding principle is to choose the most important elements for the user to manage their function or process.

The reporting analyst works with the main stakeholders to examine the most suitable reports that make up their dashboard. In SLM practice there are three dashboards to consider:

- **Service level manager's dashboard** This dashboard will include the up-to-date SLA compliance report, customer survey results and warnings that may cause an SLA breach.
- **Customer's dashboard** The customer's dashboard is always a tricky one. Providing the customer view of service levels can promote positive relationship building, establishing a partnership between the customer and the service level manager. However, the customer may request reports containing sensitive information, putting the service provider in a difficult position.

- **Service provider's dashboard** The service provider is divided into the functions of IT operations and service owners. This type of audience is looking for information related to them that is more detailed. It is very common for real-time reports to be generated that indicate the current status of the application, services and incidents to be found on the service provider's dashboard.

15.5 DATA SOURCES – CHALLENGES OF SOLUTIONS

15.5.1 Challenges

Those who manage SLM reporting projects experience the sometimes difficult challenge of data collection. There are multiple software solutions that provide valuable benefits for service management, including automated SLA compliance reports, drill-downs and dashboards. Those companies know very well that the reports are only as good as the data they receive. When initiating any reporting activity, service reporting must prioritize the matter of data sources to be resolved before any further actions can take place.

Project managers initiating reporting projects often face data source challenges. To overcome those challenges you will need to anticipate and try to resolve them before they come to the surface and disrupt the flow of the project. The following points are primary concerns regarding data sources:

- **Data source owner** Data source owners are very possessive over their data, frequently stating implicitly or explicitly: 'With all due respect to SLA reports, I have an application to run.' Without the encouragement – and, in

some cases, the enforcement – of senior management, there will be no incentive to data source owners to provide you with access to data.
- **Database overhead** The collection of data from databases requires database resources. SQL queries cause stress on the server, especially when the reports require data collection at frequent intervals.
- **Data integrity** Although the report requirements are complete, they might not have all the data to support them. For example, if a report aims to present service performance by geographic levels (region, country, site) but the data for sites are inconsistent, reports will be corrupted, resulting in misleading information.

Secrets of the trade

I started my career as a database developer, shortly after I started managing SLM reporting projects. Quickly, I learned the unavoidable challenge of data sources and how heavily the success of the project depends on them.

My strategy to defuse the issue was to proactively raise the risk of data sources before the project began. As I assembled my team and signed off the project charter, I made management aware of the issue. I identified the data source owners as resources at risk and kept a close relationship with primary stakeholders until I felt comfortable that all challenges of data sources were resolved. More than once I put projects on hold in an attempt to proactively prevent failure of the overall project due to poor-quality data sources.

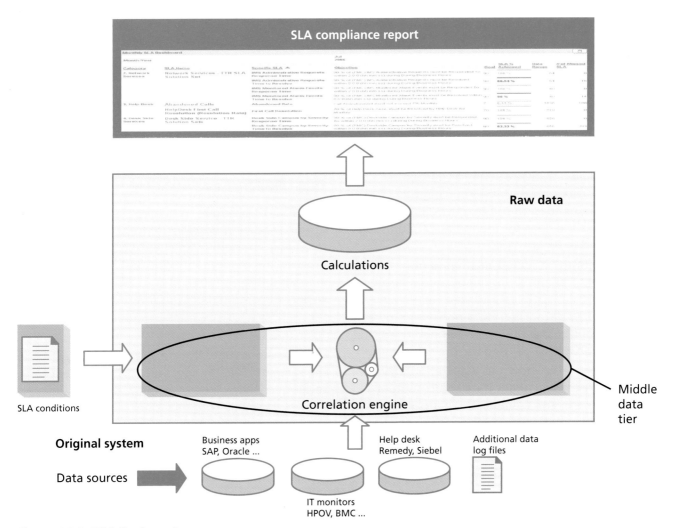

Figure 15.4 Middle data tier

15.5.2 Data processing

Processing data for the reports isn't just about calculating the SLA results – it also includes aligning, massaging and manipulating the data. In fact, the calculation part is the last step in the series of steps that comprise data processing.

When designing the data infrastructure that will support the reports, you must appreciate its complexity. For example, the data sources may be scattered across multiple locations; the integrity of the data may be continually questioned; the data may come in many different formats; essential data elements may be missing; and the only consistency you can count on is that the data are ever-changing.

To simplify the architecture, we can provide you with the steps that need to take place as part of the data processing for reports:

- **Data collection** The first step is tapping into the data source system. For example, the data can be pulled by SQL queries or pushed by agents located on the data source server. You are recommended to utilize a middle data tier to deposit the data for the initial data dump, as illustrated in Figure 15.4.

- **Filtering (also known as qualifying or cleansing)** The initial step deposited a large volume of data; this second step filters out unnecessary data. Filtering is performed by a background process using predefined rules that qualify records to be used for the calculation.

- **Alignment (also known as association)** This step correlates different data sources into a single record. For example, if we are looking to calculate resolution time for an incident, we start with basic information for the incident from the ticketing system; additional information not found in the ticketing system is tracked to other data sources, which are aligned into a single record.

- **Transformation** This step performs the final preparation before the calculations begin. The data format is manipulated to eliminate having to do so in the calculation step – for instance, working hours are edited, date fields are simplified and basic SQL functions are executed. The rule of thumb is to try to complete as many of the data transformation processes as possible prior to the calculation.

- **Calculation** This is the final step in data processing. The results are the data points used in report generation. The calculation, with regard to SLM reports, generates information that helps in comparing actual service performance results with expected service levels and thus in determining whether breaches have occurred.

15.6 REPORT CATALOGUE

The report catalogue details the list of reports that service reporting provides. Since service reporting for SLM is imperative for the support of the process, the report catalogue and its contents are managed through their lifecycle and are reviewed as part of continual process improvement activities.

15.6.1 Owner

Organizations that allocate a reporting analyst for the service level manager will establish a report catalogue that will be owned by the reporting analyst. In smaller organizations where the service level manager has limited resources or works alone, the report catalogue will be limited in its level of detail and will simply list the reports available, with few attributes shown.

15.6.2 Menu

The report catalogue will provide a menu (i.e. a table of contents) for the user. The menu defines a logical structure to catalogue the reports and to allow simple navigation through them. The structure of the catalogue is typically based on the overall categories of reports. The following is a suggested list of reporting categories:

- **SLA reports** This section of the catalogue includes the SLA compliance reports and all linked reports, such as drill-downs and customer surveys.
- **Service performance** The service performance reports are tied directly to the SLA or other contractually bound reports. This section is typically separated into further categories related to an organization, including IT operations, customer, the SLM process, key performance indicators (KPIs) and more.
- **Real time** The real-time reports represent the current status of a service. For example, many IT operations will work together with SLM to generate a report for open incidents judged as Severity 1 and 2. This type of report can be part of the network operations centre's monitor display or the customized dashboard for a service desk manager.

15.6.3 Level of detail

The level of detail for the catalogue will differ from organization to organization. The more mature that service reporting is within an organization, the more detailed the catalogue will be. A 'thin' catalogue will break down the categories and focus on listing all the reports. Its primary goal is establishing an initial list; and minimal attributes are edited for any report, including report name, description, type and owner. In contrast, a more robust report catalogue will include specific and detailed information by report, including (for instance) data source definitions, field calculations and measurements.

Secrets of the trade

The level of detail for the report catalogue has consistently been a question that arises on projects that implement service reporting. The answer has depended mainly on the culture and its ability to maintain a high level of detail per report.

One issue I have always emphasized is that, when initiating a report catalogue, the first goal is to collect all the reports and list them in the catalogue. The information per report should be minimal and should not hold up the first phase of the project, which is identifying the complete scope of reports. This initial step will provide service reporting with the understanding of which reports are redundant or missing. Once the complete list is established, the next phase can begin to provide further details of reports.

The report catalogue is a dynamic tool and should be structured to allow consistent changes. The customer, IT operations and the service level manager will require improvements to reports and the introduction of new reports. New or changed services will trigger adjustments to the catalogue. (And, in these circumstances, an automated reporting solution is beneficial and will make the reporting activity effective and less time-consuming.)

An important strategy for establishing the list of reports is 'less is more'. One of the most important tasks of the reporting analyst is to control the scope of service reporting. Service management naturally requires intensive reporting efforts and, for this reason alone, the reporting analyst will find themselves overwhelmed with a high volume of reports to be satisfied. Close examination of the reporting requirements will reveal redundancies, unreasonable demands and sometimes conflicting requirements and priorities. Adhering to the service reporting framework by establishing a policy and rules for the standard design of reports will provide the means for a coherent and sound platform for service reporting.

15.7 SERVICE REPORTING FRAMEWORK FOR SLM

SLM utilizes an effective service reporting framework that does not begin and end with the SLA compliance report. The framework must establish standards and agreed-upon guidelines through a reporting policy that will steer the reporting activities and align them with SLM.

The ongoing operational activities focus mainly on supporting the service review reporting requirements and should be adequately prioritized. However, continual improvement of the reporting framework should also take place to realign the reports with the ever-changing reporting requirements.

15.7.1 Service reporting policy

The service reporting framework must be defined and agreed through the reporting policy. The policy includes guidelines and rules discussed with the business regarding how reporting will be implemented and managed.

The goal of the policy matches the typical goal of a process charter, which is to define the scope of the process. Since this reporting activity is positioned as a sub-process of SLM, it is particularly important to define whom the reporting framework serves and who the audiences of the reports are. There is constant demand for reports; thus, scoping the reporting activities and goals is the policy's first priority.

The policy should include:

- Targeted audience
- What to report
- Reporting responsibilities
- Data sources and other system dependencies
- Addressing new reporting requirements.

15.7.2 Report design

The foundation of the design work is the report catalogue. The design work is performed in collaboration with the main stakeholders, especially the reporting audience, whether they are the customer or IT operations.

The amount of effort spent on report design depends on the tools that will generate the reports. If a single, central reporting solution is used for service reporting, the effort can be minimized by allowing the use of standards, terminology and templates.

Report design addresses five factors:

- **Purpose** Defines the intended use for the stakeholder
- **Frequency** Defines how often reporting should take place
- **Roles** Defines the audience in terms of stakeholders' roles
- **Content** Defines the elements to be presented in the report
- **Context** Identifies the tools and data sources used to generate the report.

15.7.3 Report development

Service reporting treats the development phase as the transition part of the lifecycle. The development stage is complete when audiences are viewing the reports in the live environment.

The reporting analyst working for SLM may find themselves in a different type of role depending on the maturity of the organization. In smaller organizations or in low-maturity service management environments, the reporting analyst is expected to develop the reports, including data extraction and data mining. In more advanced organizations, the reporting analyst fulfils a more analytical role by examining the information and improving the reporting practice. In this latter type of environment the reporting analyst coordinates the development of the reports, typically completed by an external service provider or a business intelligence type of department.

15.7.4 Service review reports

Service reporting supports the service review process by supplying the reports necessary to examine service performance during the service review meeting. The reporting analyst is often responsible for presenting the findings at service review meetings.

Post-service-review activities include adjusting reports, including SLA adjudication (see section 15.3). The responsibility of the reporting analyst is to complete any necessary adjustments after stakeholder sign-off on the changes.

15.7.5 Continual process improvement

Service reporting is very dynamic. The information that the reports provide is essential in driving the governance of service quality. New requirements are submitted constantly. Any change in the service environment results in a new or a changed report. Service reporting must ensure that the practice meets the business needs by continually improving the service. There are two main triggers for service reporting improvement:

- **Reactive improvements** The reporting analyst may receive feedback from stakeholders on reports that can be better presented, or other comments that can help service provision. The reporting analyst may recognize improvements that should be deployed. All those suggestions should be collected into a registry and prioritized for development at the appropriate time.
- **Proactive improvements** At regular intervals, service reporting must ensure that its policies and standards are aligned with the business needs. The report catalogue should be refreshed and then used to seek service reporting improvements.

15.8 SUMMARY

SLM has come a long way since being an SLA reporting function. Today, the industry realizes that an independent service reporting function must support the activities of the SLM process. However, SLM service reporting has unique activities centring on the SLA compliance report and service reviews. The service level manager examines, defines and assigns those activities to service reporting. This approach allows the service level manager to focus more on the customer's perception of service performance and on building relationships.

Service review

16

16 Service review

This chapter will provide you with an understanding of service review, arguably the most important activity of service level management (SLM). After a full discussion of the service review definition, we will continue by describing the associated processes and tools.

Service review goes beyond working sessions with the customer to review service performance. As we will see, service review aims to build the relationship between the service level manager and the two primary actors in the IT service management (ITSM) environment, namely the customer and the service provider.

16.1 SERVICE REVIEW OVERVIEW

Service review is the focal point of the operational activities of the SLM process (see Figure 16.1). A great deal of work was put into the strategy and into positioning it properly within the organization's overall functionality. The design work, including documentation and measurements, will have already been completed and the service level agreement (SLA) will have been negotiated and approved. From this point onwards, service review meetings are the main focal point for the service level manager.

Service review initiates the service improvement plan (SIP) and establishes chargebacks and service level penalties. Service review is the process around which all other activities rotate.

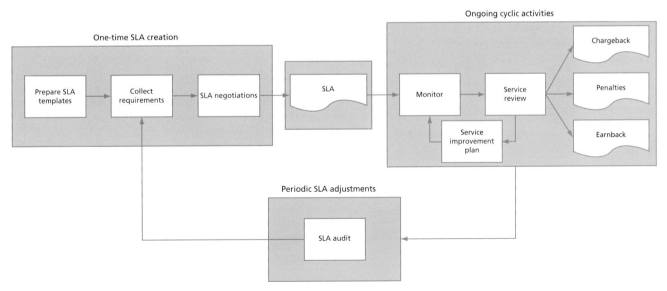

Figure 16.1 Service review within the SLM process

Service reviews are defined as meetings held on a regular basis with customers to review the service achievement in the last period and to preview any issues for the coming period. Service review meetings are time based and aligned with the contractually agreed service levels. Since most service levels are based on monthly measurements, it is recommended that service reviews are performed on a monthly basis.

Secrets of the trade

Many service providers on outsourcing engagements practise early-life support (ELS) following transition of a significant release into operational mode. This practice is exercised typically at the initial period of the contract and aims to provide extra resources to support services that are under deployment or change and also to provide an immediate response to end user queries. The primary goal of ELS is to establish a high level of customer confidence in the initial stages of the relationship. In this period it is customary to perform the service review meetings on a weekly basis to allow the customer to express concerns or provide feedback on a more frequent basis.

16.2 INPUTS AND OUTPUTS

16.2.1 Inputs

Inputs to the service review sub-process are as follows:

- **SLA compliance report** The report represents the complete set of objectives in the SLA and provides a view of service provision quality at first glance.

- **Service performance reports** Standard predefined reports, including availability reports, incident reports and trend reports, will be needed.
- **Change schedule** This input provides information regarding changes for the forthcoming period and their business impact.
- **Minutes from previous service review** The service level manager will prepare responses for issues raised at the previous meeting.
- **CSI register** The continual service improvement (CSI) database or structured document is used to record and manage improvement opportunities throughout the lifecycle.
- **Presentation** It is good practice to consolidate all inputs into one set of presentation slides to allow better management of information, thereby promoting an effective meeting.
- **Service level agreement (optional)** The SLA can be used as a reference for any dispute regarding service performance where more detail for examination is required.

16.2.2 Outputs

Outputs from the service review sub-process will comprise the following:

- **Meeting minutes** Summary minutes of the service review meetings – including agreed action points, customer concerns and issues to be followed up – need to be documented for future reference.
- **Updated CSI register** Action items are discussed and negotiated with the service providers and, when appropriate, are recorded in the CSI register for operations to plan and execute service improvements.

- **Updated service performance reports** Although the reports are based on automated data, at times the customer and the service level manager may agree to change the results shown in the reports.

16.3 SERVICE REVIEW PROCESS

The service review activities do not begin and end with the meeting itself. They require careful planning, execution and post-service-review activities. Adhering to the process and perfecting it determines the overall success of the SLM process. We should always keep in mind that the main objective of service review meetings is establishing and maintaining the customer relationship by means of attaining a high level of customer satisfaction.

Service reviews are made up of four steps (see Figure 16.2):

- **Planning** This step includes reviewing previous meeting minutes and determining whether any issues require special attention. Based on your analysis, invite the appropriate stakeholders to discuss the topic and request for information to be prepared.

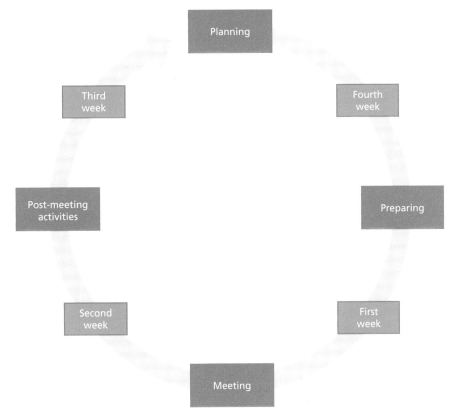

Figure 16.2 Service review within the monthly cycle

- **Preparing** The meeting involves the review of performance reports, SLA reports and other supporting evidence. Preparation entails generating those reports and collecting and collating information from external functions. A slide deck (of presentation slides) should be created to organize the speaking points and data.
- **Meeting** This step comprises conducting the meeting and executing the agenda as planned. The result of the meeting will deliver action items for service improvement, via the CSI register.
- **Post-meeting activities** Most of the activities following the meeting involve updating products such as the CSI register, SLA reports and meeting minutes, and issuing them to the appropriate stakeholders.

Data from the previous month are collected and compiled from the first day of the following month. The first week of that month is spent preparing for the meeting, after which it is held. Post-service-review activities are completed during the following week. As soon as the cycle ends, determined by the final issue of the updated CSI register, the planning for the next service review begins.

The four steps are described in greater detail next.

16.3.1 Planning for service review

Planning for the next service review meeting starts as soon as the post-meeting activities of the previous one are completed. As a service level manager you should have in mind the main issues to address in the next meeting and what resources you will need to support the discussion taking place within it.

Planning does not include preparation of reports and collection of information. The task of planning is for the service level manager to strategize for

the next service review and initiate activities required to execute that strategy. The agenda may indicate an item that requires longer preparation time, such as inviting additional audiences or additional presentations; the planning exercise will provide sufficient time for preparation.

16.3.1.1 Create the meeting agenda

The standard agenda is reviewed, and improved if need be. Topics that require special attention are added. For example, if a service has been lacking and needs to be monitored; if previous meeting minutes have indicated a follow-up; or if an upcoming change has been identified by the forward schedule of change (FSC). It is also recommended to add an item to the agenda that does not address degradation of service or any requirement for improvement. This additional item can take the form of a guest speaker, a discussion on new technology, or an exploration of new opportunities.

16.3.1.2 Submit special requirements

Agenda preparation may reveal requirements that are not the standard service review deliverables. Special reports may need to be developed or resources may need to be reallocated for specific tasks. This activity aims to identify all the non-standard elements required for the upcoming service review and to initiate their preparation.

16.3.1.3 Schedule the meeting and invite attendees

The above activities may identify additional attendees for the upcoming service review. The service level manager will select a date for the meeting and submit the necessary invitations, including the proposed agenda. The date for the meeting should provide enough time for preparation but should be as close as possible to the end of the previous month – it is usual to hold service review meetings during the first 10 days of the next month.

16.3.2 Preparing for the service review meeting

Preparation for the service review meeting includes report generation, material preparation, research and presentation development. Those activities are refined until they are perfected.

16.3.2.1 Prepare service reports

Reports are generated, collected and analysed. Reports include SLA compliance reports, service performance reports and customer satisfaction surveys. Organizations that use an automated reporting solution will benefit at this stage by avoiding the manual labour required to create the reports.

16.3.2.2 Examine service performance deficiencies

The reports may identify abnormalities in service performance that require further analysis. The first report to analyse is that for SLA compliance. Obvious SLA breaches or warnings need to be singled out and analysed. The deficiencies should be listed, examined and, most importantly, explained.

16.3.2.3 Calculate penalties

In the event of an SLA breach, penalties may occur. The penalties are calculated and totalled, although the service level manager may well continue working on an examination of the penalty in order to attempt to reduce the amount involved. If the service level manager convinces the customer that the SLA breach does not reflect the level of service provision or that the service degradation did not impact the business, the customer will be inclined to negotiate downwards the penalty amount or cancel it altogether.

16.3.2.4 Prepare root cause analysis for major incidents

It is good practice to generate a root cause analysis (RCA) in the case of a major incident. SLM will collaborate with the support groups to establish the RCA and make recommendations for mitigating the risk of recurrence.

16.3.2.5 Consolidate service improvement plan

Many organizations utilize multiple CSI registers addressing different types of services or geographical sites. The master CSI register should be consolidated once a month by the service level manager in order for it to be reviewed with the customer. Even where there is a single CSI register, the document must be reviewed periodically and kept up to date.

16.3.2.6 Acquire change schedule

The change schedule lists the changes that are planned to be implemented, and it provides the users with notice of interruptions to services. The change schedule is commonly communicated to the end user through the service desk. The service level manager, in accordance with the change manager, reviews the FSC to identify major changes and rollouts that need to be pointed out to the customer during a forthcoming service review meeting.

16.3.2.7 Compile final presentation

A template for a standard service review presentation is populated with the above deliverables. It is suggested to use one set of presentation slides for the whole presentation and not to shift to multiple presentations. The overall presentation must be coherent and follow the logical structure of the meeting. The presentation will be issued to stakeholders as part of the post-service-review activities.

16.3.3 Conducting service review meetings

The success of SLM is measured by customer perception. Positive customer perception of service performance is the primary goal of the process. The service review meeting is therefore your chance to either develop customer perception or, on the contrary, destroy it. The service level manager is the ambassador, representing the service provider, and must use the meeting to listen to the concerns of the customer and act on them.

The agenda of any particular service review meeting is heavily dependent on who attends the meeting. The basic assumption is that the presence of the customer and the service level manager is mandatory. Regarding the rest of the attendees, typically there are two philosophical approaches that are adopted by organizations:

- **Minimal participation** In organizations where the service level manager is a strong figure who possesses authority in the service environment, the service level manager is the sole representative of the service provider at the service review meeting with the customer. Action items can be agreed without the need to have service owners and the operations function present at the meeting, assuming that the service level manager has the knowledge and ability to understand the detail and make sensible decisions.

- **Extended participation** SLM is perceived by some organizations as the process that maintains the SLA, reports on its results and discusses service provision with the customer during service review meetings. In an organization where the service level manager has limited authority of this kind, the service providers take an active part in the meeting. Their participation is essential to present findings concerning service performance and to suggest action items for improvement.

The standard agenda items for a service review meeting reflect the business need and the two approaches detailed above:

- **Customer feedback** The meeting should begin by setting the stage for the customer to express their concerns and comments. No SLA report can provide you with better feedback regarding service performance than what will come out of the customer's mouth. Responsiveness and the resolution of customer feedback must be proven by the next service review.

- **Review of the previous period** By reviewing the previous meeting's minutes, the service level manager will demonstrate that issues that were raised are now resolved or undergoing improvement.

- **Review SLA compliance report** Review of the SLA compliance report provides a quick view of service provision quality. If any breaches or warnings are showing for a metric, further detail will be provided to examine where and when the service was lacking.

Secrets of the trade

The 'topic of the day' idea was introduced to me while I was providing ITIL consultancy for a large service provider. I was asked to perform a gap analysis and recommend actions for improvement of ITIL processes.

I attended the service review meetings as a guest. Observing the meeting, with its presentation and interaction between the parties, I gathered the information as evidence for my final gap analysis. Although I was not familiar with the 'topic of the day' idea until then, I discovered that adding an item to the agenda that does not address service performance had great value. The service level manager and the customer 'negotiated' which interesting topics should be discussed during the topic of the day, which guest speakers should be invited and much more. During the meeting itself, the topic of the day – which was always the last subject on the agenda – shifted the atmosphere from a service performance and technical discussion to a more relaxed and friendly atmosphere.

- **Review of performance reports** The service level manager or the reporting analyst will present standard reports that focus on specific metrics such as call volume, availability of critical services, trend analyses, and incidents per site or per service.
- **Preview of next period** This is the opportunity for the service level manager to make general announcements concerning changes in the business or resources. The service level manager precedes the discussion by reviewing the change schedule and focusing on major changes that may affect the business.

- **Compile a summary of actions items** The service level manager and the customer will compile a summary of action items through the SIP process via the CSI register.
- **Topic of the day** It is good practice to add one more topic to the meeting, in the form of a guest speaker, a discussion of new technology, or an exploration of new opportunities. The objective is to avoid the negative atmosphere that can develop when the service level manager is on the stand being cross-examined for most of the meeting.

16.3.4 Post-meeting activities

The scope for post-meeting activities differs depending on the relationship of the service provider with SLM.

In some organizations, the service level manager and representatives of the service providers/ operations take part in service reviews. They join forces to prepare for the meeting and attend the service review meeting as one unit. This type of collaboration results in agreeing together, with the customer and the service provider, on action items. The negotiations and agreements are thereby completed during the meetings themselves, avoiding subsequent discussions. In this scenario, the post-meeting activities are reduced to merely updating and issuing documents.

At the other extreme, some service management organizations choose to separate SLM from the service provider. According to ITIL best practice, the service level manager is the go-between communicating between the customer and the service provider. In this scenario, immediately after the service review meeting, the service level manager must review with the service provider the action items that were agreed with the customer.

16.3.4.1 Conduct service provider review

As explained above, in a case where the service provider does not take part in the service review meeting, the service level manager must communicate with the service provider following the meeting. The service level manager and the service provider review customer concerns and prioritize the CSI register and action items for service improvement.

16.3.4.2 Update and issue documents

After discussions with the customer and service providers are complete, the associated documents are updated and finalized. The documents are then posted on an agreed central location accessible to stakeholders, or sent to them directly.

16.4 EMERGENCY SERVICE REVIEWS

Emergency service reviews are performed under unique circumstances and are rare. The assembly of the meeting is quick and typically addresses a specific, urgent issue. The customer may submit a request for an emergency service review, but it is recommended that the service level manager proactively arranges the meeting, proving prioritization of the matter at hand.

A lot like dealing with emergency changes in the ITIL change management process, emergency service reviews are not ideal but are, at times, unavoidable. The conditions for initiation and the procedures of emergency service reviews must be predefined with customers.

Secrets of the trade

Although the conditions for initiation of an emergency service review are defined and agreed upon, it is suggested to allow such a meeting on any occasion that the customer calls for it – even if the situation does not fulfil those conditions. It is important to note that the objective of the emergency service review is to promote positive customer perception, and so responding adequately to the customer takes a high priority.

16.4.1 Conditions

The conditions under which an emergency service review is performed must be documented in the process documentation in accordance with what has been agreed with the customer. Typically, the emergency service review is instigated by a major incident or anticipation of a change that may heavily impact the business. The service level manager and the customer may decide together that the customer is permitted to call for an emergency service review meeting when a significant concern arises regarding service provision, even if an actual threshold has not been breached.

16.4.2 Attendees

Owing to the urgency of the matter under consideration, it is not uncommon to hold the meeting virtually rather than wait for all stakeholders to be available at the same location. The service level manager and customer, or their representatives, attend the meeting. The service level manager will seek to include the service owner or the service provider that is directly involved with the matter at hand to provide immediate response, avoiding unnecessary follow-up communications for this urgent matter.

16.4.3 Inputs

The service level manager will prepare evidence regarding the matter to be discussed in the meeting. For example, if the meeting addresses a major incident, then relevant reports, log files, root cause analysis and incident records should be prepared for review at the meeting. The CSI register is used to review related action items.

16.4.4 Outputs

An updated SIP is the main output of the meeting. Ideally, the service owner will commit to changes or improvements to eliminate recurrence of similar incidents. If the service review addresses a significant change, the service level manager will produce a plan to mitigate risks regarding the change.

The most important output of an emergency service review meeting is a satisfied customer. Let's remember that at the beginning of the meeting the customer had heavy concerns regarding service provision, otherwise an emergency service review would not have been requested. So the service level manager's objective is to conclude the meeting with the customer's perception that the issue is being addressed and is soon to be resolved.

16.5 SUMMARY

When I am asked to provide consultancy services in relation to SLM, my customers are always surprised to find the emphasis on service review rather than on SLA reports.

Service reviews determine the success of SLM and have a significant impact on service provision as a whole. Service providers feed off the service review meetings, and many of the service improvement activities are steered by the products of service reviews.

Service
improvement plan

17

17 Service improvement plan

The service improvement plan (SIP) refers to the process that is executed when a gap materializes between the expected quality and the actual quality of a service, as measured and reported against service level targets. While service level management (SLM) documents, monitors and reports on quality of service, including gaps in service, the process of identifying and reviewing service quality gaps needs an underlying process to demonstrate to the customer that corrective actions are carried out to continually improve the quality of services – specifically, those that are not meeting agreed targets. All SIP items are recorded by means of the continual service improvement (CSI) register.

This chapter introduces the concept of CSI through the SIP, an essential element of best-practice service management. We explore the structure and components of the CSI register as the main information repository for service improvement. We conclude by describing the underlying SIP process, detailing its activities and its relationship to service review.

17.1 SERVICE IMPROVEMENT PLAN OVERVIEW

The SIP and the service review are two processes that go hand in hand. The SIP and its CSI register are, together, one of the most important inputs into service review. Service level managers spend time on compiling and updating the CSI register for service review meetings, tracking and documenting actions that are required to improve

services and eliminate service quality gaps. At the other end of the service review process, an updated CSI register is produced with a new set of prioritized actions. It is good practice to attach an updated CSI register to each service review meeting set of minutes, since the CSI register encompasses most of the decisions made in that meeting.

The CSI register encapsulates the overall plan of prioritized improvement actions, together with the associated owners of improvement activities and the current progress status. The CSI register is customer-focused and service-oriented, focusing on actions to improve the quality of services as experienced by the customer.

Everyone is involved in the SIP process and all sides should have access to the CSI register itself. In a well-established SIP process, the majority of service delivery and support functions have an interest and are involved in the content of the CSI register. Although the service level manager, customer and service provider utilize the CSI register as a working document for negotiating and prioritizing service improvement actions, other functional groups will accommodate the CSI register to support their activities. Change management uses the CSI register to forecast future request-for-change (RFC) submissions; the service desk and others use the CSI register to track and review required service improvements within their environments. Hence, it is essential to develop an easy-to-read and easy-to-access CSI register.

The SIP process has gained popularity in recent years and has become an integral part of service management best practice. Although the majority of service providers have traditionally documented and tracked changes within their environment, the process and associated documents were focused on technical activities and shared mostly with internal operational groups only. The SIP process detailed in this publication engages both the customer and internal technical staff in an inclusive process that focuses technical activities on improving services to the customer.

There are three main benefits in adopting a customer-focused SIP process:

- **Cost** The SIP process is fairly simple to implement and does not require an expensive software solution to support its activities. A robust software solution has the ability to send alerts when an activity threshold is reached, and it can tie together related incidents and problems. But it will cost you.
- **Prioritization** In complex service environments, the list of activities quickly increases and becomes difficult to manage. Service review meetings provide the opportunity to discuss with the customer the priorities for service improvement.
- **Standardization and centralization** The CSI register must be accessible to all relevant parties in the service environment, with a high degree of transparency regarding the progress and status of service improvement activities. A central location for planned service improvements, progress reports, risk registers and resource allocations is beneficial to all stakeholders.

17.2 CSI REGISTER OVERVIEW

The CSI register is not to be confused with project plans or any other documents that detail changes within the service environment. The CSI register is merely a list of action items, aimed at promoting an illustration of current and future service improvements, including their prioritization. For this reason, as we develop the structure of the CSI register we will attempt to minimize the number of components/columns in the plan. A simple and minimized structure will avoid overwhelming our target audience and will encourage stakeholder participation.

The CSI process manager should own the CSI register. Improvement initiatives are triggered from multiple processes and functions, and it is logical that the CSI process manager will collect, coordinate and communicate all those initiatives.

In the absence of a mature CSI process, SLM will own the CSI register – mainly because service review meetings are likely to generate improvement initiatives, but also because the SLM function interfaces with the customer and the service providers. An effective CSI register becomes the interface, where customers are informed of actions executed to improve services and service providers deal with essential information such as customer expectation and prioritization of items.

17.2.1 Overall structure

Before diving into the details of the components that comprise an effective CSI register, we will first consider the overall structure and organization of a SIP. The objective of the CSI register structure is to allow easy navigation and updates to the plan, and so the overall structure of the CSI register must reflect the service delivery environment.

Documents such as the service structure, service catalogue and service level agreement (SLA) provide the blueprint for the CSI register structure.

There are two prevalent approaches to the CSI register structure, although your options should not be limited to these two approaches and you should consider the most appropriate structure based on your specific service environment and customer needs:

■ **Service structure** Your service structure document groups services into categories, or service towers, e.g. WAN, LAN, application, voice, video and more. The service structure provides the underlying structure for other service-related documents such as the SLA and service catalogue. The CSI register is no different: it too can share this common underlying structure.

■ **Geographical organization** A common practice in SLM is to allocate service relationship managers to own the CSI register relevant to them. In a large-scale organization – specifically, where the customer resides in different geographical locations – service relationship management (SRM) is often structured accordingly. In this latter case, the global service relationship manager will interface with the service level manager and will coordinate the different service relationship managers for each region; furthermore, the service level manager will choose to structure the CSI register by geography, allowing easier compilation of items, in preparation for a service review.

The main disadvantage to choosing a fixed structure for the CSI register is that it can obscure the prioritization of service improvement activities. If service improvement activities are grouped by

service towers, for example, it may be impossible to view activities by priority. An automated software solution may solve this dilemma by providing reporting capabilities to view CSI register information in different perspectives. A software solution simplifies the entry process of new and updated records, avoiding manual labour to support data integrity.

17.2.2 CSI register attributes

The CSI register is a database outlining the list of agreed activities that are considered to be opportunities for service improvements. As mentioned earlier, the CSI register does not include detailed work instructions, as captured in the RFCs, and should be kept simple and minimal. The following are typical components of a CSI register (and Table 17.1 gives an example showing some of these attributes):

■ **Opportunity number** An indexing sequence for the improvement initiative

■ **Service tower** Indicating the function that the service is categorized under

■ **Name** A short title for the record, i.e. 'Severity 3 resolution time', 'VPN slow connectivity'

■ **Description** Short description of the issue, i.e. '80% of Severity 3 incidents are resolved within two working days, while the SLA compliance level is 95%.'

■ **Raised by** The resource that suggested, requested or discovered the need for the opportunity – it is important to keep track of the person who raised the issue for later clarification of the improvement

■ **Date raised** The date when the issue was discovered, suggested or raised

Table 17.1 Example of a CSI register

Number	Service tower	Name	Description	Raised by	Actioned by	Priority	Date required by	Status	Record update
1	All	Service Desk; Reporting; Training	Train staff handling repairs reporting to log repair requests under improved mechanism. Refer requests for pre-inspection if required, and liaise with change management.	DE	SM	3	07-01-2012	Open	04-01-2012
2	IPT	Priority Category	Substantially revise the current 7 priority categories down to 5. This will establish simplified and clearer priority criteria for effective performance management.	JC	MJ	2	08-04-2012	Open	04-01-2012

■ **To be actioned by** An owner responsible for resolving the issue and providing ongoing updates – it is customary to indicate the job title and name of the owner

■ **Priority** The priority is different from the severity or impact of the issue. 'Priority' indicates the order in which the CSI register activities will be implemented. Agreeing priorities is a sensitive process as the impact and importance of service improvement activities are often different for the service provider and the customer. For example, CSI register activities to restore service level targets that incur service penalties are likely to be of a higher priority for the service provider. This column is subject to negotiation and constant change

■ **Date required by** The activities' owners provide an estimated date for completion that is tied to the priority of the item. This column is also subject to negotiations

■ **Status** The status tracks progress of service improvement activities. It is customary to use a list of values for this field – e.g. open, closed, or in progress. It is also good practice to provide a percentage of completion, from zero to 100%

■ **Comments** Also referred to as 'comments of fulfilment' or 'status comments', these are tied to the status column, detailing the progression or delay of the improvement initiative

■ **Record updated** A time stamp indicating when the CSI register record was last updated.

The attributes discussed are highly recommended but you should nevertheless customize the CSI register to meet your needs. There are other attributes that are useful, such as justification, key performance indicator (KPI) metric, size (of the project), timescale etc.

Secrets of the trade

The CSI register is developed to meet an organization's specific needs. It is common to adjust the structure of the plan according to the internal needs of SLM and requirements from external functions utilizing the CSI register to support their activities. In one SIP process implementation project I was involved with, the change manager had asked to add the RFC number and project management number to the CSI register for cross-reference purposes. Although the latter attribute did not offer any benefit to the service level manager, we welcomed the suggestion as it promoted input and participation from other processes.

One interesting component in a CSI register that I have seen was 'success criteria' (also referred to as 'KPI metric'). Such a column would stipulate the conditions against which a record can be closed. Interestingly enough, this addition to the register is almost always declined. Managers are hesitant to include success criteria in the CSI register because of their concerns surrounding subjective measurement of success, and overlapping or conflicting criteria set by change management for connected RFCs.

17.3 SERVICE IMPROVEMENT PLAN PROCESS

The SIP process is a cyclical process without clearly defined start and end points. The CSI register is constantly being updated and used as input to many processes, with the service review process intersecting with the SIP process to keep the CSI register up to date. The prioritization of CSI register activities is discussed and negotiated among the parties to provide the operational teams with the necessary guidelines for required changes to the service delivery environment. The SIP process is composed of five basic steps, as illustrated in Figure 17.1 and described in greater detail below.

17.3.1 Service review output

As described more fully in Chapter 16, service reviews are meetings that are held on a regular basis with customers to review service achievement. Service review outputs include such products as meeting minutes and updated service performance. However, the most important output from service review is the updated CSI register.

Many items on the service review meeting agenda have an impact on the CSI register. When the customer provides feedback on service delivery, action items are agreed and documented in the CSI register. Furthermore, prioritized CSI register activities are considered during the meeting's review of the previous period. The most crucial activity during the service review meeting is to prioritize and summarize action items, at which point the CSI register is reviewed and discussed in detail. The priorities are renegotiated based on new facts and changing customer business requirements.

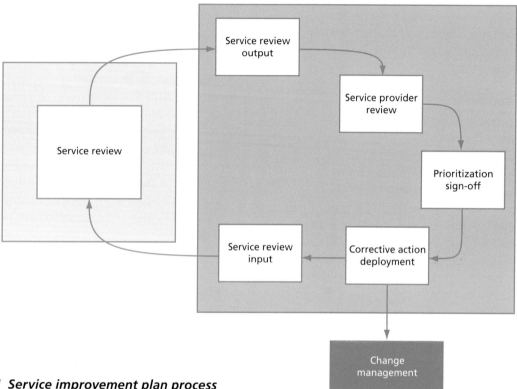

Figure 17.1 Service improvement plan process

In a service review meeting where the service provider participates, the CSI register may be agreed and finalized in the meeting. In a scenario where the service provider does not participate in the meeting, the CSI register will be reviewed and agreed separately in the next activity of the process.

17.3.2 Service provider review

During the service review meeting, the service level manager and the customer will have discussed service performance, identifying and tracking gaps in service quality. Service improvement activities are defined and tracked in the CSI register.

However, the CSI register is not finalized until the service provider has the chance to review the register and provide feedback. To this end, the service level manager meets with the service provider to go over the main discussion points from the service review meeting and to discuss service improvement requirements.

The service provider might not agree with the customer's requirements and priorities. The corrective actions discussed in the service review meeting may be too costly or risky and, according to the service provider, should be re-examined and reprioritized. In this scenario the service level manager acts as an intermediary between the customer and the service provider until an agreement is reached.

17.3.3 Prioritization sign-off

During the service review meeting, CSI register entries will have been updated, including new corrective actions and changes to activity prioritization. The negotiations, related discussions and the service provider review (see section 17.3.2) accumulate to give a final and agreed-by-all CSI register.

We identify the prioritization sign-off step in the process separately because at this point the CSI register is transitioned and compiled into actionable project plans. Just as it is essential to provide a platform to agree on the action items, it is just as important to agree on the order of their execution.

It is good practice to formalize this sign-off activity, making clear that an agreement has been reached on the priority of service improvement implementation and ensuring that this final version is accessible to all.

17.3.4 Corrective action deployment

The CSI register records are converted into actionable plans through a statement of work, project plan, RFC or (sometimes) emergency change, depending on the organization's existing processes and protocols. The activity of service deployment of corrective action is outside the scope of SLM. In general, though, it can be stated that each organization will choose to deploy service improvements differently and there are three typical courses of action:

- ■ **Request for change** Submit an RFC in order to implement the corrective actions outlined in the CSI register. The change management function will oversee the change through deployment and release, perform the post-implementation review, and inform the service level manager of the change result.
- ■ **Emergency change** If further investigation and diagnosis of the service improvement proposal – usually done by the problem management function – concludes that the risk is serious and an immediate response is required, a request for an emergency change is submitted. This may also occur if there is a significant commercial risk for the service provider in not implementing the service improvement in a timely manner.
- ■ **Risk acceptance** If no satisfactory solution is found, the risk may be accepted, which means no action will take place. Risk acceptance is a decision made by the customer following presentation of evidence by the service provider or the service level manager. The CSI register record is closed with a comment describing risk acceptance after customer approval.

17.3.5 Service review input

As explained earlier, the SIP process has no definitive starting and ending point. Although the service review input is the last step in our process description, it does not close the process but, rather, provides the input into the service review meeting, resulting in a cyclical flow and a continual SIP process.

Throughout the measurement period, and before the next service review, the CSI register undergoes continual change. In large-scale organizations specifically, where the customer resides in different geographical locations, each region is managed by an individual service relationship manager – see Chapter 6 for more information on this role. As each service relationship manager works with their customers, the CSI register is changed accordingly, creating different versions of the CSI register per region.

The service level manager, as part of the preparation for each service review meeting, compiles a single version of the CSI register providing consistent and uniform information. The process of compiling the CSI register not only collates all the data into one master register but is also used to update the CSI register regarding the status of outstanding service improvement activities.

At this point of the process, the CSI register is ready for the next service review meeting. The process then continues, with the service review output becoming input to the upcoming meeting – see Chapter 16, and in particular sections 16.2 and 16.3 within it.

17.4 SUMMARY

The SIP is an essential process within SLM, specifying agreed activities to improve service delivery. The service review meetings are where the customer and the service level manager review service provision and identify and track gaps in the quality of service. It is at this intersection between the two processes that the CSI register begins and ends (although it is generally an iterative cycle).

The CSI register lists the required improvements and outlines the priority of the improvement implementation. The register is accessible by all parties and provides a channel of communication between the customer and the service provider, ensuring that service improvements are implemented efficiently but, equally importantly, in accordance with business needs.

Service relationship management and customer satisfaction survey

18

18 Service relationship management and customer satisfaction survey

The service level management (SLM) process utilizes service relationship management (SRM) to develop a positive perception by building a relationship with the customer, performing customer satisfaction surveys and creating a channel for the customer to express their experiences and concerns regarding service provision.

This chapter lays out the responsibilities of SRM and describes its typical role and responsibility in the service management environment. Using a customer satisfaction survey to establish customer feedback falls under the scope of SRM, and so this chapter defines the process related to the survey and provides general guidelines regarding its execution.

18.1 SERVICE RELATIONSHIP MANAGEMENT OVERVIEW

SRM provides the human element in IT service management (ITSM). Studies indicate that, in times of crisis, service desk call volumes increase by 20–50%, with no clear business or technical reason behind the increase. The studies also show that the length of calls increases, mainly as a result of callers expressing personal concerns along with their business concerns. The conclusions of the studies did not only focus on the productivity of service desk support but also proved that service management is about human emotions as much as it is about service performance and product support.

SLM as a core process of ITIL utilizes two functional areas: service reporting and service relationship management (see Figure 6.1). In large organizations, SLM will be organized as an independent function. The service level manager heads up the function while managing the service reporting and SRM. In multinational companies, SRM is responsible for different geographical locations.

Practically speaking, and generally owing to a lack of resources, it is common for the service level manager to fulfil the role of the service relationship manager as well. Although the process does not allocate dedicated resources for SRM, it is essential for the process to take responsibility for the SRM activities detailed below.

Before going into the activities of SRM, let's distinguish between three different terms that are often confused:

- **Business relationship management** Business relationship management is the process that enables business relationship managers to provide links between the service provider and customers at the strategic and tactical levels.
- **Service level management** This is one of the core processes of ITIL, responsible for negotiating achievable service level agreements (SLAs) and ensuring that these are met. It is responsible for ensuring that all ITSM processes, operational level agreements (OLAs) and underpinning contracts (UCs) are appropriate for the agreed service level targets.

- **Service relationship management** As an extension of SLM, SRM is dedicated to building and maintaining a relationship with the customer by working with that customer on an ongoing basis to improve service provision.

As Figure 18.1 suggests, the business relationship management function is positioned high up in the organization hierarchy, and it communicates with senior management and makes sure that processes and functions are aligned with the business requirements. SLM has both strategic and operational elements: it is required to receive strategic decisions and work with account managers; and at the same time it works closely with service providers and operations to ensure that services are provided appropriately. SRM is limited almost wholly to operational activities, working with end users and surveying customers to understand their levels of satisfaction.

18.2 SERVICE RELATIONSHIP MANAGEMENT ACTIVITIES

The nature of SRM is to work together with the customer and to build a positive customer perception. The service relationship manager pitches in and helps the customer as much as possible. The service level manager scopes out the work of SRM at the design phase, by ensuring that SLM activities that involve close work with the customer will fall under the responsibility of SRM.

Set out next are the common activities that fall under the responsibility of SRM.

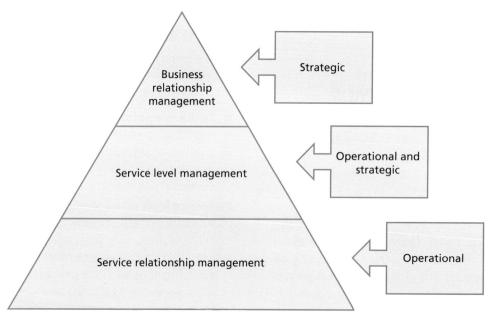

Figure 18.1 Business relationship management, service level management and service relationship management

18.2.1 Incident management

During a major incident it is essential to keep close communication with the customer to limit any types of concern that the customer might have. In a high-impact incident, the customer will tend to speculate and make false assumptions that may lead to loss of confidence in the service provider. The main objective of the service relationship manager is to continually communicate with the customer, and through that rebuild any lost confidence.

SRM comprises two main activities that are performed in conjunction with incident management, and are defined in the process documentation and work instructions of incident management. The two activities are:

■ **Incident escalation** Incident management defines what a major incident is – for example, Severity 1 or 2 incidents. This type of incident typically involves an impact on many end users or disruption to critical services. It will be serious enough to trigger hierarchical escalations (also known as management escalation), typically alerting the service desk manager, IT operation managers and service relationship manager. The service relationship manager will then immediately undertake the following activities:
  ● Communicate with the customer, providing a status update and initial assessment.
  ● Continue delivering updates on any changed status.
  ● Update the customer at intervals even when there are no changed statuses.
  ● Assist in incident closure (by ensuring that the end user can go back to work), gain approval from the customer that the situation has been dealt with satisfactorily, and pass that approval to the service desk.
  ● As good practice, conduct a short customer survey and receive feedback from the customer on how the service provider performed during the incident resolution.

■ **Root cause analysis (RCA)** The closure of an incident does not necessarily recover the customer's confidence that was lost due to a major incident. The service relationship manager will collect data regarding the incident and meet the customer to provide an explanation of the event through root cause analysis.

18.2.1.1 Handling complaints and compliments

SRM must establish a mechanism for the service desk to log complaints and compliments. The end users should know that their feedback counts, and a designated channel needs to exist to record their complaints and compliments. The service relationship manager would be advised to review the complaints and compliments on a monthly basis, as preparation for the service review, and present the findings to the customer.

18.2.2 Service review

Although the service level manager coordinates and leads the service review, the service relationship managers take an active role in preparing and conducting the service review meeting.

18.2.2.1 Preparation

The service level manager coordinates the service relationship managers, typically throughout the sites of the customer as broken down by geographical location. The service relationship managers may own a designated continual service improvement (CSI) register for each geographical location, all of which must be compiled by the service level manager into a master CSI register as part of the preparation for the service review. The service level manager communicates with the service relationship managers prior to the service review to collect relevant information.

18.2.2.2 Presentation

Depending on the relationship between SRM and SLM, the service relationship manager may be required to take an active role in conducting a service review meeting, particularly presenting reports and information relating to customer satisfaction surveys, service improvement plans (SIPs) and root cause analyses.

18.2.2.3 Root cause analysis

On an as-needed basis, root cause analyses may be on the service review agenda. If in the current period a major incident has occurred that requires discussion with the customer and service provider, the service relationship manager will present an assessment and lead the root cause analysis efforts during the service review meeting.

18.2.3 Customer satisfaction survey

The customer satisfaction survey is the primary instrument for SRM to build and maintain a relationship with the customer. It is another important activity undertaken by the service relationship manager.

Sections 18.3 to 18.5 deal with this topic and aim to give guidance on the major aspects of conducting a customer satisfaction survey.

18.3 CUSTOMER SATISFACTION SURVEY OVERVIEW

One of the core concerns of SLM is customer perception. But how do we know what our customer perception is? How do we find out whether our customers are satisfied? The best way to find out whether your customers are satisfied is to ask them. What to ask the customer and how you ask it are just as important, and it is essential to know what to do with the answers.

In an outsourcing engagement, the customer satisfaction survey is crucial for long-term profitability. In this type of competitive environment, unsatisfied customers will look for alternative service providers. So senior management and account management will dedicate resources to perform customer satisfaction surveys and continually improve processes and services.

The ownership of the customer satisfaction survey, in large organizations, is given to quality functions on the corporate level. This means the policy, definitions, method and questions are developed and reviewed by the quality function. The execution of the survey is performed by SRM, and the examination of the answers and the resulting action items are carried out in coordination with the quality function.

18.4 CUSTOMER SATISFACTION SURVEY – METHODS

SLM commonly considers two methods for obtaining feedback from users. Both methods should be performed and their results should be aggregated, with action items defined against them. The two methods are as follows:

■ **Customer satisfaction survey** This type of survey is commonly conducted once or twice a year. It requires a cyclical process to be defined and optimized. This process is detailed in section 18.5.

■ **End user satisfaction survey** SLM is also concerned with end user perception and satisfaction. The customer is the person who buys the services, signs the SLA and represents the end user. The end user is the person who uses the services on a day-to-day basis, and therefore their perception of service provision is important as well.

The end user satisfaction survey is conducted through the service desk, typically after a major incident has been closed, or at random intervals when the end user is asked a series of questions while on the phone to the service desk. Common questions for the end user satisfaction survey are:

■ Are you satisfied with the overall handling of the incident?

■ Are you satisfied with the time it took to restore the service?

■ Was the representative courteous?

■ Did the representative demonstrate technical competency?

■ Do you have any additional comments regarding this incident?

■ Do you have any additional comments regarding the overall quality of services?

18.5 CUSTOMER SATISFACTION SURVEY – PROCESS

The process detailed below does not attempt to cover best practice for the customer satisfaction survey, nor will it cover all that you will need in order to perform the survey. But it will outline the steps of the process and will point out important guidelines regarding the special needs of SLM.

It is recommended to use a third-party vendor which is an expert in the field of customer satisfaction surveys to develop a survey methodology and a suitable questionnaire. These professionals can help in the development of a design that meets the objectives of your survey.

Secrets of the trade

I interviewed the quality manager in a large organization to establish a better understanding of the background processes for a customer satisfaction survey. We talked about the use of consulting companies for the survey, and I expressed my reservations about outsourcing resources that are not intimately familiar with the internal affairs and culture of the client company. The quality manager answered that she was the one leading the efforts for the development of the survey while using the experts as a sounding board, to rephrase sentences, and to provide general comments.

18.5.1 Define the survey's goal

The goal of the survey differs on a case-by-case basis. Even within SLM, defining the goal as 'asking the customer whether they are satisfied with the services' is simply not enough. Clearly articulated objectives guide the design of the survey and the development of the questions included in the survey.

In an outsourcing engagement, SLM needs to go beyond determining whether the customer is satisfied or not. In this type of competitive environment the customer satisfaction survey is aimed at examining the customer loyalty index.

This means that the service level manager does not only want to know whether or not the customer is happy, but whether or not the customer would continue buying products and services from the service provider. The customer loyalty index aims to group the customer into one of the following categories:

- **Loyal advocates** Comprising customers who view the service provider as a partner or an entity with which they have a very good relationship
- **Hostage** Comprising those who want to stay with the service provider not least because they like the brand – but who are currently being let down by basics elements such as sales, service or billing
- **Ambivalent** Comprising those customers whose expectations are being met and who have some loyalty to the service provider – but who are unsure how the service provider can help them in the longer term
- **Vulnerable** Also considered to be exit bound, these customers have some satisfaction with the service provider, but little engagement or loyalty – and, most importantly, are open to switching.

In less competitive environments, such as enterprise, where the service level manager represents the internal IT department, the survey will aim to understand the satisfaction level of the customer, will allow them to express or vent their feelings, and will focus on issues that are specific to the organization.

18.5.2 Identify the survey population

The goal of the survey assists in identifying the survey population, i.e. those who will be surveyed. This population will vary, depending on the survey's objectives. For example, if you are measuring the satisfaction of the customer from the billing process point of view, end users are not the proper survey population.

Also, consideration needs to be given to the sample size necessary to meet the data requirements of the survey. With larger samples there is greater confidence that the findings are representative. However, larger samples entail additional costs, complications and time for the survey process.

Secrets of the trade

Selecting the survey population is one of the trickiest tasks in this process and can determine the success or otherwise of the survey and its results. On one of my projects, the account managers were asked to select those customers that should be surveyed for the quarterly customer satisfaction survey. The results of the survey presented a high satisfaction from the projects, services and products provided by the service provider. The quality department, after examining the results, determined that the scores were unusually high and required further investigation. After a great deal of research, it was established that since high customer satisfaction scores were tied to the account managers' bonuses, the account managers had selected those customers who were most likely to mark high levels of satisfaction.

18.5.3 Develop the questionnaire

The questions in the survey must be properly written so as to yield meaningful data. When questions are poorly worded or biased, the responses are likely to be inaccurate or uninterpretable. The survey questions should be designed to address the survey's goal as defined in the earlier stages.

The number of questions chosen for the survey should be balanced between collecting as much information as possible and being as short as possible. Customers should not perceive the survey as an assignment. For additional guidelines on the questions in the survey, see section 18.5.4.

18.5.3.1 Satisfaction rating

It has been common practice to rate the answers to questions in the questionnaire on a five-point scale, but many surveys have more recently converted to a 10-point scale. The rating system is not set in stone; some experts will say that a 10-point scale is too spread out and confuses the interviewee, while others will say that a scale of span five is not extensive enough, especially given the fact that people are accustomed to measure in scales of 10 or 100.

18.5.3.2 Free-text answers

Although compiling multiple-choice answers is simple and provides a more accurate picture, it is recommended that you include some questions that allow free-text answers. The customer satisfaction survey professional believes that sometimes those answers reveal more, since they allow self-expression and provide a place to complain about an issue that is not addressed just by multiple-choice questions.

Example

1 Based on your overall relationship with ABC and with the services it provides, please rate your level of satisfaction with ABC in these areas (1 being very dissatisfied and 10 being very satisfied):

● Understands your business needs – [radio button 1–10]
● Provides timely responses to your questions – [radio button 1–10]
● Provides timely responses to service disruptions – [radio button 1–10]
● Demonstrates technical competence – [radio button 1–10]
● Is proactive in providing information that you need – [radio button 1–10]
● Is effective in managing changes – [radio button 1–10]
● Has an effective billing process – [radio button 1–10]
● Works with you to attain your business objectives – [radio button 1–10]
● Is easy to do business with – [radio button 1–10]

2 Please rate your overall satisfaction with ABC – [radio button 1–10]

3 Please indicate the likelihood that your company would:

● Recommend ABC to your colleagues in the industry – [radio button 1–10]
● Choose ABC again – [radio button 1–10]

4 What would you recommend that ABC focuses its improvement on?

5 What would you say are ABC's strengths that it should continue to enhance?

6 Please provide additional comments:

18.5.4 General guidelines

The following are general guidelines for customer satisfaction survey questions:

- **Avoid ambiguity** Make sure it is absolutely clear what you are asking and in what form you want the question answered.
- **Avoid conjunctions** Do not construct a sentence with more than one topic. Avoid using the word 'and' unless it is absolutely necessary.
- **Avoid double-negative questions** The people who will take the survey may be confused about what 'yes' or 'no' means with double-negative questions. For example: Should the service provider not be allowed to disregard complaints?
- **Avoid false premises** For example, in 'What should we do regarding the poor provision of internet services?', not all people might agree with your premise that internet services are poorly provided, and so will find it hard to answer.
- **Include free-text questions** It is recommended to add questions which allow those who are being surveyed to express themselves freely. Free-text questions should be placed towards the end of the survey.
- **Aim for consistency** Those who develop the questions will often change the questions from survey to survey as an act of improvement. However, consider the reuse of questions for consistency and trend analysis for future reference.

18.5.5 Test a prototype

Testing a prototype of the planned survey consists of all the transitional activities of the process. These include:

- **Checking technical performance** This aspect includes quality assurance of the survey application. Since nowadays most surveys are conducted over the web, the link must be tested to ensure it works. The survey must also have a user-friendly interface, and it must provide accurate collection of data into a database.
- **Running the prototype** The prototype of the survey must be tested as well. This means checking that the answers that are collected provide the correct information. This activity may well result in refining the questions or rephrasing them.

18.5.6 Conduct the survey

An invitation is sent to the selected survey population to conduct the survey. Although the survey population is confirmed and contacted beforehand, it is recommended to send an email invitation accompanied by the link for the survey questionnaire.

Those organizations that use a third-party consultant for the customer satisfaction survey will have the invitation sent through the vendor to the customer. This will provide the customer with a sense of the objectivity and professionalism of the service provider.

Example: invitation

Dear John

At ABC, we continually strive to improve our services to better meet your needs. Your thoughts will help us gain insight into our customers' current and future requirements and should take no more than 10 minutes of your time.

We would appreciate your valuable input on your experience with ABC. To complete the assessment, please visit our online customer satisfaction survey.

If you need assistance or you have any questions, please contact us by replying to this email.

Thank you for your time and responses.

Yours sincerely

Kathy Steinway

Service relationship manager
ABC Corporation Inc.

18.5.7 Examine the results

This activity involves compiling the results of the survey and generating meaningful reports. The results act as the primary output of the customer satisfaction survey process to a larger service improvement process. Thus, the generation of action items to repair low customer satisfaction is out of scope for this process and handled by the service improvement process.

The survey results should be presented on a dashboard including findings and conclusions. The survey report should contain a full description of the methodology, the response rate, and a copy of the survey itself.

For scaled questions, it is recommended that the responses are processed to provide the distribution of responses. In the case of the 10-point rating scale, the deviation or percentage answering 1–6, 7–8 and 9–10, as well as the average response, are all useful statistics. Those organizations that answered within 1–6 groups must be highlighted for further examination.

Table 18.1 Example of customer satisfaction survey results (expressed as percentage response)

Question/score	1–6	7–8	9–10
Understands your business needs	–	12	88
Provides timely responses to your questions	–	8	92
Provided timely responses to service disruptions	–	12	88
wDemonstrates technical competence	25	–	75
Is proactive in providing the information that you need	–	–	100
Is effective in managing changes	–	6	94
Has an effective billing process	–	11	89
Works with you to attain your business objectives	–	13	87
Is easy to do business with	–	6	94

From the example shown in Table 18.1 we can quickly conclude that the customer is rather satisfied with the service provider. With the exception of 'Demonstrates technical competence', the average score is 9.15 and all the questions apart from the exception score at least 7.

For 'Demonstrates technical competence', 25% of the scores fell between 1 and 6, which is the lowest category, while 75% of the scores fell between 9 and 10. The average is therefore well under the 9.15 scored on average in other areas.

18.5.8 Implement corrective actions

The results of the previous activity are compiled and summarized. This analytical activity will feed into the management level, which generates decisions on how to address the survey findings and improve customer perception. These decisions may differ depending on the position of the customer survey owner in the organization.

If it happens that the owner of the customer satisfaction survey is service level management or any other operational function, action items resulting from the survey will be documented in the CSI register and continually monitored by the service level manager.

18.6   SUMMARY

SLM does not always utilize SRM, due to resource, cost or culture constraints. However, the activities of SRM are embedded in our process, and are essential for the success of the SLM process.

The service relationship manager has the task of achieving a number of activities in the role, all of which aim to help sustain a good relationship between the customer and the service provider. One particularly important activity is the conducting of customer satisfaction surveys, together with the analysing and reporting of the results of those surveys to higher management and SLM.

Stakeholder management and risk management

19

19 Stakeholder management and risk management

Although the ongoing operational processes of service level management (SLM) include activities such as monitoring and reporting, service review and the service improvement plan (SIP), the service level manager as the process owner must execute process control activities as well.

The first is stakeholder management, which is the process that communicates with and influences internal and external environments by creating a positive relationship with stakeholders. The second is risk management, which aims to identify, manage and prevent uncertainties.

Although these two activities are related to the project management discipline, they are highly effective for service level managers who seek to manage their processes better.

19.1 STAKEHOLDER MANAGEMENT OVERVIEW

Stakeholder management includes activities such as identification of stakeholders, determining stakeholder requirements, continual communication and managing stakeholder influence.

Stakeholder identification includes the compilation of the list of names, roles and responsibilities of the stakeholders. This list is dynamic and, in reality, evolves as the process itself does. The identification of stakeholders is reviewed and refined periodically. The following is a typical list of stakeholders to be considered for the SLM process:

■ **Customer and service providers** As primary stakeholders in the process, we must first list the official representatives of the customers and the service providers. Those representatives are involved in the service review process.

■ **Account management** In an outsourcing engagement, the account manager must be identified initially and managed throughout the lifecycle of the engagement. The customer's satisfaction with financial implications is a high priority for the account manager.

■ **Reporting function** The service level manager must identify the function that will support the reporting activities. SLM as a process relies heavily on reporting, and as such the reporting responsibility must be defined. If a reporting analyst is allocated and dedicated to SLM activities, it will simplify the management of the process.

It is also typical for SLM stakeholders to include data source owners, the service desk, SLM staff and other ITIL process owners.

You should allocate time to creating a complete list of stakeholders from the start. Realizing, in future, that a stakeholder has been missed means that new requirements may need to be added to accommodate the needs of the additional stakeholder.

Secrets of the trade

In one of the largest IT service providers in the United States, I helped implement a reporting system for the service level manager. As part of good project management practice, we identified the stakeholders and kept in close communication with them. The initiation of the project was considered to be successful; the pilot was presented to senior managers, who gave their approval, and the project was transitioned into the live environment.

As transition activities progressed, we realized that we had failed to identify an additional stakeholder, who became a primary disruption to the project. This junior database administrator (DBA) was the gatekeeper to crucial data sources required to generate reports. Any requirement submitted to the DBA was immediately rejected and dragged through bureaucracy that appeared to be aimed at putting off any changes to the database. The DBA quickly became a primary stakeholder and primary risk to the project. This issue was escalated to senior managers and was defused as the project went on.

19.2 RISK MANAGEMENT

Managing a process as complex as SLM always comes with risks – the risk of changes failing, the risk of reports not being prepared on time, the risk of service level agreements (SLAs) being breached, and so on. Some studies quote that 90% of a project's problems are decreased through the process of risk management.

First of all, let's try to understand what risk is. ITIL defines risk as a possible event that could cause harm or loss, or affect the ability to achieve objectives. It is measured by the probability of a threat, the vulnerability of the asset to that threat, and the impact the risk would have if it occurred. Risk can also be defined as uncertainty of outcome – and can therefore be used when measuring the probability of positive outcomes as well as negative ones.

This means that there can be positive risks – negative risks are threats, while positive risks are opportunities. Examples of positive risks can be that service performance improves faster than expected, or that an SLA compliance report indicates that all service levels are complied with and there are no additional comments or complaints from the customer.

Risk management planning defines the methodologies, roles, responsibilities and risk categories involved. One of the most important outputs of the planning stage is the scope for which the service level manager takes responsibility. Consider the risk of incidents breaching their threshold for resolution time. Is it an SLM risk or is it an incident management risk? There is no correct answer. During risk management planning, each organization will determine the responsibilities for every process.

19.2.1 Risk categories

Some risk registers for SLM focus only on report generation and its delivery, which is a common mistake. The selection of risk categories is important and should occur in the risk management planning phase, prior to identifying the actual risks.

The typical risk categories for SLM are:

- **Customer** Including all the risks that relate to service performance and SLA breaches
- **Technology** Excluding reporting, since reporting has its own category
- **Reporting** Tool failure or calculation error
- **Transition** Comprising all SLM activities or tools that are in the course of being deployed
- **Service provider**

- **Supplier**
  - **Cultural risks**
  - **Resource allocation risk**
  - **Unforeseen** Including all the risks that cannot otherwise be categorized.

Further information on risk management can be found in *Management of Risk: Guidance for Practitioners* (TSO, 2010).

PART 5
Continual service improvement

Continual service improvement for SLM

20

20 Continual service improvement for SLM

This chapter focuses on how to improve service level management (SLM) as a process. Although we are performing daily tasks at an operational level for the process, we must set aside some time and resources to improve the capability of SLM. Activities should be reviewed, process documentation ought to be examined, and training should be provided – all so as to enable SLM to become a more effective and efficient process.

There are many methodologies and approaches for process improvements, but this chapter aims to simplify the topic for you. It describes the tools needed for process improvement, and it focuses on procedures tailored to meet the specific needs of the service level manager. The process model illustrated in this chapter distinguishes between reactive and proactive corrective actions and guides you through the steps required to improve activities in your business environment.

In this chapter we also help you address 'extreme makeover' for the process: a scenario where the process must undergo fundamental changes because simple improvement patches just will not suffice.

20.1 CONTINUAL SERVICE IMPROVEMENT OVERVIEW

We have come a long way. In accordance with the ITIL service lifecycle, we began our journey by strategizing SLM; we then discussed the design of the process function, and service level agreements (SLAs); and after that we considered the tools to support these activities. We transitioned our process into the live environment and began executing activities such as service review and the service improvement plan (SIP) on an operational basis.

As the process owner, the service level manager leads all operational activities while continually improving the process. The service level manager must guarantee that services are being provided as agreed, while simultaneously ensuring that the process is executed as perfectly as possible.

To improve the process efficiently, we must have a structured approach, not a fire-fighting attitude. Some organizations will brag about process improvement activities, whereas in reality they have implemented a patch to solve a local issue. Although circumstances will have us react to issues and fix them, the preferred way is to approach service improvement proactively with a strategy and a plan. Continual service improvement (CSI) will transfer you from being a fire fighter to being a fire preventer.

To improve your process, you must be prepared to perform both of the following improvement actions:

- **Reactive corrective action** An action taken in order to implement a response to a threat or opportunity that has already occurred
- **Proactive corrective action** An action taken in order to implement changes to avoid a potential threat or capitalize on a potential opportunity in the future.

The challenge is to find the balance between addressing reactive and proactive improvements. Ultimately, a successful continual improvement process plays on both fields.

Secrets of the trade

A famous statement from Charles Sturt University in Sydney, Australia, reads: 'The road to continuous improvement and ultimately perfection runs on a Möbius ring where reactive and proactive improvement, although each clearly taking a presence on its own individual plan, are playing a never-ending game of contention on the same shared plane.'

Reactive corrective action versus proactive corrective action: should we solve problems or improve the process? When reacting to a problem in the process by making a change, have you improved the process? Yes, you might have solved a local problem, but improvements in the process can benefit all parties on a holistic scale. Solving problems is resolving local issues, and many times this happens with a disregard of supportive processes (internal and external) that are interacting with the process. Thus solving problems fails to take a holistic view. After the fix has been implemented you might conclude that the fix was successful, but by failing to take a strategic approach to process improvement you might discover in the future that the overall situation only gets worse.

Process improvement means adopting a structured process with a framework, objectives and measureable activities. SLM process improvement must focus on the end result, namely customer perception and customer satisfaction.

20.2 PROCESS IMPROVEMENT – METHODOLOGIES

When you finally realize that the problem-solving approach should be abandoned (or at least minimized) in favour of process improvement, the first thing you'll need to do is to choose a methodology to help you define your activity and monitor your progression.

There are many frameworks and good practices for improving processes, and whether you choose one or another is entirely up to you and the needs of the business. The important thing is to choose a framework, use it consistently, and continually monitor and improve the process.

Set out next are some methodologies that you may consider for your process improvement.

20.2.1 SWOT analysis

'SWOT' stands for strengths, weaknesses, opportunities and threats. This technique involves the review and analysis of four specific areas of an organization or a process: the internal strengths and weaknesses, and the external opportunities and threats.

Once these areas have been analysed, actions should be taken to:

- Develop, exploit and capitalize on the process strengths
- Reduce, minimize or remove weaknesses
- Take maximum advantage of opportunities
- Manage, mitigate and eliminate threats.

SWOT analyses can be performed quickly and can be used to target a specific area rather than looking at an entire enterprise. They are a strategic planning tool used to evaluate a process, a business venture or any other situation requiring a decision. Sizing up a firm's internal strengths and weaknesses and its external opportunities and threats provides a quick overview of a firm's strategic situation.

20.2.2 Control charts

Control charts are used to routinely monitor the quality of manufacturing or business processes. Sample 'mean and range' charts are used to detect when a process is not under control – see Figure 20.1, for instance. The causes of the variations that exceed the upper control limit (UCL) and lower control limit (LCL), as indicated by point A in Figure 20.1, must be eliminated in order to bring the process back into statistical control.

Control charts assume that the process has predefined key performance indicators (KPIs) and tools to measure its performance. In Chapters 8 and 9 we provide guidance on the development of those KPIs.

20.2.3 Six Sigma

Six Sigma is a disciplined approach to problem-solving and continuous process improvement, which identifies and removes the causes of defects. The technique employed is commonly referred to as MAIC (measure, analyse, improve, control).

An additional step was later added to this methodology, namely 'define', which re-established the process as DMAIC (define, measure, analyse, improve, control). Many professionals felt that you need to define the right process and strategy, since effort can easily be wasted on poorly selected processes.

20.2.4 Total quality management

Total quality management (TQM) is a management technique to improve the quality of processes, reduce operational costs and increase customer satisfaction. Important aspects of TQM include customer-driven quality, top management leadership and commitment, continual improvement, fast response, actions based on facts, employee participation, and a 'TQM' culture.

20.2.5 The Deming Cycle

W. Edwards Deming is best known for his management philosophy leading to higher quality, increased productivity and a more competitive position. As part of this philosophy, he formulated 14 points of attention for managers. Some of these points are more appropriate to service management than others.

He also proposed the Deming Cycle (see Figure 20.2). The four key stages of the cycle are Plan, Do, Check and Act – after which a phase of consolidation prevents the circle from 'rolling back down the hill'.

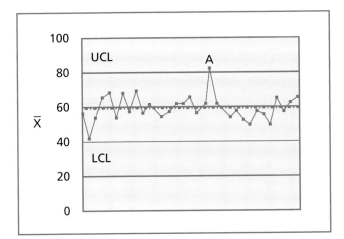

Figure 20.1 Example of a control chart

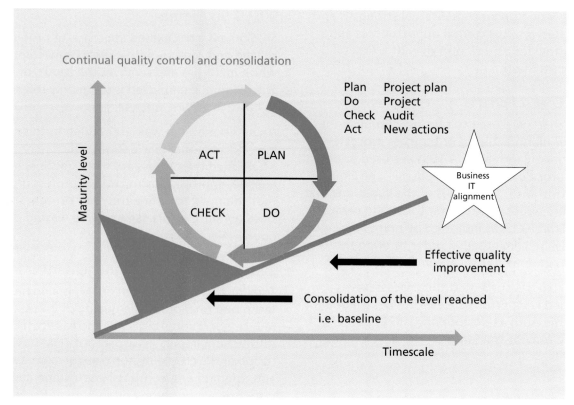

Figure 20.2 The Deming Cycle

20.3 PROCESS IMPROVEMENT – MODEL FOR SERVICE LEVEL MANAGEMENT

The model presented here is customized specifically for improving SLM, blending concepts and activities from business process management, Deming and other process improvement methodologies. Note that you need to distinguish between this model for process improvement and that for service improvement (via the CSI register) detailed in section 20.7.1.

This process improvement model is utilized for both reactive and proactive activities. The entry point may differ, as Figure 20.3 illustrates;

however, it is essential to adhere to the specified activities in order to promote consistency and efficiency for future improvement activities.

Proactive improvement activities start with preparation and examination of the process. Those activities will reveal disparities that will require corrective actions, and the corrective actions will need to be prioritized and implemented. With reactive improvement activities, the disparity is apparent and will be automatically transitioned into the prioritization phase.

The process improvement model activities, as shown in Figure 20.3, are set out in more detail next.

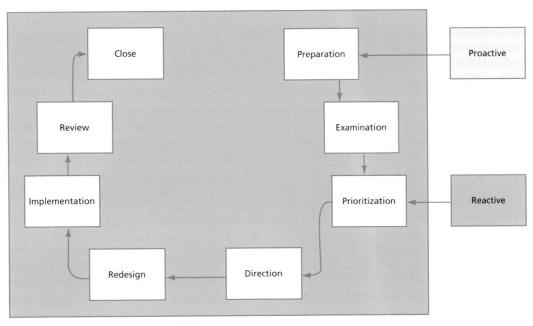

Figure 20.3 Process improvement model

20.3.1 Preparation

Proactive improvement activities are set by intervals – typically an annual improvement programme. The preparation stage includes:

- Gaining senior management's commitment and sponsorship
- Aligning with the organization's improvement strategy
- Initiating a project – organizing a team and developing a project charter.

As part of the preparation, the service level manager should develop reusable templates for the improvement process by identifying the needs of each activity in the model and the tools it requires. For example, the prioritization activity requires a tool that assists with predefined specifications and other documents. Although the development of templates is a once-only task and, as good practice, they are developed as a service transition activity, the templates should be reviewed at the start of a new cycle. Chapter 13, on service transition work streams, provides a list of tools that must be developed during the service transition phase to produce the products needed by SLM.

20.3.2 Examination

This is the core of the proactive improvement activities. Here we assess, review and conclude what improvements are necessary. For the complete list of sub-activities relevant here, see section 20.5 on proactive process improvement.

20.3.3 Prioritization

Although practitioners have a tendency to overlook the prioritization stage, it cannot be stressed enough how important this activity is. Process improvement is about prioritizing problems and fixing only those that provide significant outcomes; it is not about fixing any problem that arises. In fact, you may be better off leaving some problems because there are more important uses of your time.

Prioritization analysis is completed using predefined specifications, of which the most common are impact and urgency. This activity should be completed in conjunction with the primary stakeholders and using a standard template.

Elements to consider during prioritization include:

- Impact and urgency
- Cost
- Risk
- Duration of implementation.

An example of prioritization is given in Table 20.1.

20.3.4 Direction

The overall vision and strategy have been established during the preparation. However, now that the corrective actions have been prioritized, we need to ensure that those that are queued up for redesign are aligned with the vision for the organization and the correct intention for the new or redesigned process. The following three aspects need to be considered during the direction activity:

- New critical success factors (CSFs) and KPIs
- Return on investment, and return on value
- Benchmarking.

The direction activity finalizes the list of corrective actions for the process improvement and promotes confidence in decisions made during the prioritization activity.

Table 20.1 Example of prioritizing continual service improvement activities

Index	Name	Description	Priority	Estimated cost	Duration of implementation
1	Reporting solution	Currently we use Excel spreadsheets. The customer has made several complaints about presentation and the response time of the reports. On top of that, we employ a number of resources that could be allocated to other tasks if an automated tool were to produce those reports.	1	$400,000	6–8 months
2	Service review	The service review process is lacking and requires redesign. The current process does not follow ITIL best practice. External functions that are necessary to complete tasks are not integrated efficiently into the process.	1	$50,000	2–3 months

20.3.5 Redesign

Now that we have a list of corrective actions to be implemented, we go back to the drawing board and redesign the associated processes, procedures, activities and tools. Core processes, such as service review and the SIP, may need adjusting too, along with reporting tools, communication plans and any other activity that was identified during examination and prioritization. For further guidelines on specific steps of process redesign, see section 20.6.

A common mistake is to start the process activities at redesign. The main goal of this chapter is to provide you with a structure and standard improvement process, including prerequisite steps, such as preparation and prioritization. Adhering to this methodology, even at the cost of time and effort, guarantees not only the improvement of process activities but also avoiding any negative impact of parallel process activities.

20.3.6 Implementation

This activity takes the form of transition processes, submitting requests for change, and the initiation of the release management process for deployment of new or changed items.

Note that this activity includes standard transition tasks, such as pilot testing, training, revision, tracking, evaluating, post-implementation review, and approval.

20.3.7 Review

A review needs to take place after all corrective actions have been implemented – individual reviews for single corrective actions are undertaken during the implementation stage. The goal of the overall review is to ensure that the changes implemented did not negatively impact services or parallel processes, that overall integration occurred and that no items have been left behind.

The review typically addresses:

- Stakeholder feedback
- Monitoring of performance and reports
- Continuous training and support programmes
- Adjustment to the process as required.

20.3.8 Close

Closing the improvement process is an internal activity, completed by the service level manager (sometimes possibly involving their staff members). Similar to project management closure, this activity includes:

- Confirmation that the work has been completed as required
- Development of a 'lessons learned' knowledge base
- Communication of the results to stakeholders, especially senior management.

20.4 REACTIVE PROCESS IMPROVEMENT

In the previous section we laid out the process model for you to establish a framework for process improvement. It is time to get more specific and anticipate elements within SLM that may be subjected to improvement.

Process improvement methodologies emphasize the importance of a strategy to proactively improve processes rather than wait for failure to occur and then reactively attempt to resolve the problem. All theories aside, as ITIL practitioners we face the reality that failures occur and that at some point we have be prepared to get to work.

However, it is important to note that performing a reactive corrective action does not mean incompetent, high-risk activity. A lot like incident management, which itself is typically a reactive process, our reactive process improvement is structured within a specific strategy with roles and responsibilities, inputs and outputs. As explained in the previous section, reactive corrective action must follow the process model illustrated in Figure 20.3.

Set out below are common items in SLM that may require improvement, triggered by customer, service provider or merely local failure. These items could well initiate a reactive corrective action.

20.4.1 Service level agreement audit

The SLA audit involves reviewing the SLA, recommending changes and renegotiating conditions. This process is described in greater detail in section 14.5.4, which sets out all that you need in order to perform the audits.

An SLA may need to be improved from time to time. After its creation, it is typically subject to a pilot period, which is the initial period (usually six months to a year) of the agreement. At the end of this period the SLA may need adjustment as a result of what came to light during the pilot period. Furthermore, it may be necessary to adjust an SLA not only after the pilot period but as the service changes over time.

Organizations resist change and SLAs are no different, especially as SLAs are quasi-legal documents that impact on many functions, processes and stakeholders. Anticipating change requests for an SLA is crucial. Agreeing with the stakeholders, especially with the legal department and the customer, on the initiation procedure for a change will overcome that resistance.

An SLA audit is considered to be a reactive improvement activity, mostly because it is difficult to foresee most changes required as a result of the audit. The best way to prepare for an SLA audit is to follow the guidance in Chapter 14 and design an SLA audit process that documents the conditions for initiation, develops templates for negotiations, and contains activities to ensure agreement by all sides to proposed SLA changes.

The following are tools to support the improvement of the SLA:

- **Service level requirement (SLR) document** The SLR document is used to provide a record of the customer's service requirements and to negotiate agreed service level targets. The SLR document is a useful template that lists all the conditions that are prerequisites for change in the SLA.
- **Structured SLA** This publication dedicated a complete chapter to helping you establish a structured SLA – see Chapter 8. One of the goals of the chapter is to create an easy-to-use and easy-to-navigate SLA in order to support changes requested throughout the lifecycle of the agreement.

20.4.2 Reporting, metrics and calculations

One of the most common reactive improvements in SLM concerns the tools that support the monitoring and reporting activities. Reporting solutions may experience degraded performance or the output of inaccurate calculation results. A change may be requested by the customer for new or changed reports, and changes to an SLA may impact the calculations and reporting of service performance.

To be able to address the improvement of reporting and calculations, you need a flexible platform that can be used to respond to reporting requests in a professional and timely manner. There are two tools that support that platform:

- **Metrics management solution** Detailed in Chapter 9, the metrics management solution consists of the metrics, measurements and calculations required to manage the services. This library organizes all your calculations across your service environment and possesses the flexibility to allow changes and improvements.
- **Report catalogue** Owned by the reporting function of SLM, the report catalogue maintains a list of reports and their definitions that have been discussed, analysed and agreed with the customer and the service provider.

20.4.3 Service review

To improve the service review process, you will need a solid baseline. The baseline is your process model. The service review process is arguably the most important process in SLM, and we must assume that even if we initially designed a perfect process, it will be adjusted continually. There will be unforeseen occurrences – such as the time to complete the preparation of reports or the compilation of the SIP – that will require you to go back to the beginning and re-examine the activities and their time intervals.

The goal of the service review process is to produce high levels of customer satisfaction. You should always allow input from the customer regarding the service review process, and any criticism or comment from a customer should be seriously considered and evaluated as a means of improvement.

20.4.3.1 Service review meeting

The meeting itself is the best source of input for improving the process. The service review meeting will typically address the services that are being provided, but attendees are likely to comment on the effectiveness of (and preparation for) those services. The service level manager may note that these activities can be improved for the next cycle of the service review meeting.

20.4.3.2 Service review documentation

An efficient process does not just happen; it requires design, documentation and constant improvement. As this publication has argued more than once, the service review process is the core of SLM, and as such it requires process modelling and precise documentation. This type of process development is important not only for performing the activities of the process, but also for assisting with improving activities by visualizing the process and revealing weaknesses that require further examination.

20.4.4 Service improvement plan

Experienced service level managers will tell you that the SIP process demands constant improvement. The SIP process is dependent on many external elements: service providers, problem management, change management and many more – any changes in the change control policy, for example, will have an impact on the SIP process. You will receive requests for changes from different functions to allow them to improve their work relevant to the SIP, and these all have to be harmonized.

20.4.4.1 Integration

To improve the SIP process, you will first need to identify the stakeholders of the process. This process is also linked to many other processes and functions, each with their own stakeholders. A prerequisite to improving this process is to understand the various stakeholders' interests and the constraints of the process.

20.4.4.2 SIP documentation

In similar fashion to the service review process, for the SIP process to improve you will need solid documentation, including process modelling, activity descriptions and work instructions.

20.5 PROACTIVE PROCESS IMPROVEMENT

Proactive process improvement activities are performed through periodic process reviews. It is good practice to set annual intervals for such reviews. The goal of each annual review is to allow the service level manager to take a step back and view the process from a holistic point of view in order to answer questions such as:

- Is our process aligned with the business needs?
- Are we performing according to best practice?
- Can we do things better?

Secrets of the trade

To begin process improvement, we look for the root causes of problems that have arisen. A reactive approach seeks to understand and resolve the problem in the process, while proactive process improvement seeks to understand the cause and prevent a recurrence of an undesirable event. The only way to stop a recurrence is to change the design itself.

Many organizations choose to outsource this activity to industry experts, who will perform a review and examination of the process and present their findings. Although this entails cost, it generates two significant advantages. The first is avoidance of the reallocation of resources within the organization from their daily tasks by bringing in consultants for a defined short-term period. The second advantage is to bring a fresh outlook on the process, in order to generate new ideas and knowledge of your organization's practices.

As explained above, both reactive and proactive improvement activities follow the standard process improvement model, illustrated in Figure 20.3; they differ only in their entry points. Proactive activities are initiated at 'preparation', which consists of logistical activities and project initiation. The next step, 'examination', is the core of the proactive improvement activities and it is at this stage that we assess, review and conclude what requires improvement and what does not. The main activities of the 'examination' stage are detailed next.

20.5.1 Gap analysis

Gap analysis is performed using the service management process maturity framework, based on the well-known Carnegie Mellon Capability Maturity Model Integration (CMMI) and available as an appendix in *ITIL Service Design*. The assessment compares current process activities with best practice. The key outputs of a maturity assessment are a comparison analysis and suggested roadmap to close any gaps. For complete guidance on SLM maturity assessment, refer to Chapter 4.

The gap analysis is an excellent approach to initiating process improvement. When hiring experts, you will receive suggestions and recommendations to improve your process based on best practice and on the past experience of those experts.

The most important output of the assessment is the roadmap that specifies the required remediation and corrective actions. A well-structured roadmap will provide prioritization and a breakdown of the activities into three time categories: short term, medium term and long term. This type of roadmap can give direction and guidance for the remaining activities of process improvement.

20.5.2 Business realignment

Business realignment is an activity that ensures that the process meets the specific needs of the business. The activity is attributed to the business relationship management process.

SLM must review, during the annual process improvement exercise, the overall goal of the process, communicating with senior management and gaining their support. In a case where organizational strategy has changed – for example by aiming at a different marketplace – SLM must realign its goals to meet the new business objectives.

On a practical level, the process charter must be reviewed and any business realignments must be reflected in that charter.

20.5.3 Review CSFs and KPIs

One of the most common practices in process improvement is a review of the CSFs and KPIs used by the organization. In Chapter 6 we saw how to develop CSFs and KPIs. Now is the time to review them and make appropriate adjustments.

CSFs are elements necessary for the process to achieve its mission. They are typically high-level statements based on the goals of SLM. For

example, if one of the goals of SLM is to 'Improve the relationship and communication with the business and customers', then a CSF is the existence of a communication plan. KPIs are more specific and measurable. Such measures are commonly used to help an organization define and evaluate how successful its processes are. An example of a service level management KPI is 'Reduction in requests for SLA changes and audits'.

There are two activities concerning CSFs and KPIs:

- **Review annual results** The CSFs and KPIs were developed not just to be included in the process charter but instead to be reviewed and acted on. Data from the measurements yielding the KPIs must be collected, compiled and presented in a report. The reports should provide any noticeable discrepancies. If too many issues were raised by this activity, they should be prioritized so as to enable a focus on those that require immediate attention.
- **CSF and KPI adjustments** Any business realignment will have a significant impact on the CSFs and KPIs already specified. Any change of company strategy is examined by the process and considered to be included in the CSF and KPI adjustments. It is plausible to assume that even in a scenario when no organizational changes occur, the CSFs and KPIs are subject to annual review in order to ensure that they still reflect major elements of the process.

20.5.4 Refresh process design

During the service design stage, we developed multiple documents detailing the processes of SLM, including SLA management, service review and the SIP.

The annual process review is an excellent opportunity to brush up the documents. Start improving your process design documents using the following steps:

■ Analyse your existing processes to reveal elements for improvement
■ Prioritize processes for review
■ Modify your process to reflect existing activities.

Use the guidelines set out in section 20.6 to help you.

20.5.5 Improve operational capabilities

SLM operational capabilities are all the elements that support and enable the daily activities of the SLM processes.

The process capabilities to be reviewed are:

■ **Management** The service level manager, service relationship manager and other function heads are capable of improvement as well as the SLM process itself. This self-improvement can be performed internally and externally. The managers may review their performance throughout the year, go through process KPIs, discuss with their managers and list components where they may improve. Managers may participate in external IT service management (ITSM) training, ITIL certifications and other related topics.

■ **Organization** In organizations where SLM has evolved into a structured function with managers, hierarchy and staff, it is beneficial to re-examine the way the process is organized and suggest improvement. Changes in the function's structure may be triggered by changes to processes and tools, and therefore it is recommended to consider structural changes in a later part of process improvement.

■ **Knowledge** A knowledge base should be established for every process, and SLM is no different. The knowledge base should be in a centralized location and contain documents regarding best practice, lessons learned, personal performances, process documentation, relevant diagrams and other tools. During improvement activities, the knowledge base is refreshed; documents are updated and new materials are added.

■ **Staff** Human resources are the most important resource of the SLM process. The service level manager reviews the performance of staff and identifies components for improvement. The review includes discussion regarding training for members to strengthen their skills and knowledge.

Good practice is to collect staff's input on the process during the review. Understand their difficulties and what can be done to improve the environment, to enable them to do their job better.

■ **Applications** Technology to support the activities of the process needs to be explored. Review the current applications and consider new ones. A list of issues or suggested improvements regarding SLM tools can build up through the year; now is the time to review the list and make decisions.

The main consideration is automation, in order to create a more efficient environment. In SLM, the reporting process is commonly prioritized for automation. When a strategic decision is made to mature the process by deploying an advanced reporting solution, the service level manager will calculate the return on investment and value of investment, and will then present the results to senior management.

Secrets of the trade

It is not uncommon for organizations to confuse process improvement with deployment of technology. They can easily say: 'How do I improve my process? I will just purchase a really expensive software solution.'

More than once I have been called into an engagement to assess elements for improvement. As an expert in the field of SLM, the expectations were for me to recommend a new and advanced SLA reporting solution. In extreme cases, the basic assumption was that I would present options for acquisition.

It is not coincidental that the discussion regarding applications occurs at the end of this chapter. Deployment of technology must come subsequent to a sound process. This statement is not theoretical and does not belong in books alone. Rather, it is totally practical. A process that deploys technology prematurely will suffer later – by backpedalling, redesign, rework and, most importantly, over-spending on the estimated budget.

A process must be designed, deployed and adjusted before technology is considered.

20.6 GUIDELINES FOR IMPROVING THE REDESIGN PROCESS

During the redesign stage, organizations need to allocate sufficient resources to complete this task. Many organizations choose to hire external consultants to assist with documentation and design work. There are documented guidelines provided by best practice that should be taken into account during redesign work, and these are as follows:

- **Understand process design** Always keep in mind the ultimate goal of a process, which is to produce outcomes that are expected, are efficient and increase customer satisfaction. This should always be the guiding light through process improvement.
- **Eliminate unnecessary steps** Allow yourself to think outside of the box. Although we initially designed the process with documented activities, now at the redesign stage we need to reconsider steps of the process. For example, the service review process includes many steps to negotiate between the customer and the service provider. Based on your experience, you may expose some steps that are not valuable and that can be eliminated.
- **Define standards at integration points** Be specific in decision points to avoid different interpretations. When the process indicates integration with external functions – for example, receiving performance reports – ensure that all sides agree on deliverables, duration and procedures.
- **Consider the automation of repetitive steps** When a process is initially established, it is likely to be assumed that most activities are to be performed manually unless an automated tool is already in place. As time progresses and the process is advanced, we should consider utilizing technology to automate activities. Two of the most common automation targets in SLM are:
  - Automation of reports development
  - Automation of the CSI register via integration with the change management systems, allowing alerts and the updating of CSI register records.

- **Reduce activity duration** At the process design stage we estimate the duration of each activity, while adding to the overall duration a potential margin of error. During the redesign activity, we base the duration of activities on actual durations, allowing us to identify the activities with the longest durations.

- **'Fast tracking' and 'crashing'** These two terms are borrowed from project management methodologies. Both are techniques to improve the time taken for completion of a process. 'Fast tracking' addresses activities that are normally done in sequence but which, with suitable redesign, can be performed in parallel. 'Crashing' the schedule means increasing the number of resources responsible for the completion of the task.

- **Redesign documents** SLM requires the use of many documents. Virtually every task is based on a document: CSI register, project plan, process charter, service level agreement, operational level agreement (OLA), underpinning contract (UC) and many others. Maintaining these documents at a high quality may come at a cost. As the process progresses, you may find redundancies in documents that may be combined or eliminated.

Looking back at the guidelines you might identify a common principle running through them: simplification. Eliminating faults and variance or reducing activity duration requires simplifying the design of the process. The challenge, as in any attempt at change in an organization, is the related cultural change and the external dependencies.

When redesigning a process, you will identify changes depending on other processes or those that require the reallocation of resources or even additional resources. This situation does not mean

you should deviate from the plan or the redesign of the process. The situation demands hard work, business cases and determination.

20.7 SERVICE LEVEL MANAGEMENT – EXTREME MAKEOVER

This section assists practitioners who are looking to revolutionize the existing SLM process. The preceding sections assume that a process is established and is in an operational state, with reactive improvements addressing local failures and proactive improvement eliminating risks to the overall process. However, there are some cases where organizations are in need of fundamental changes and will require an extreme makeover for their process.

This 'extreme' type of process improvement is typically initiated as a result of one of the following two triggers:

- **Low ITIL maturity level** We see more and more organizations realizing the value of adhering to ITIL best practice. If, historically, organizations were satisfied with service desk and basic processes to resolve incidents and transition changes, today those organizations strive for a completely integrated framework to help them become more cost-effective and improve their processes to become as effective and as efficient as possible. Regarding SLM, SLAs and performance reporting are simply not enough. Organizations are curious to discover how SLM can establish a healthy relationship between the customer and the service provider, and how to provide services that are aligned with true business requirements. In short, organizations are looking to convert SLM into a proactive process that will have a significant impact on the service environment.

■ **Fundamental business change** In order to be more profitable or more effective, organizations may choose to undergo fundamental changes involving their organization structure and marketplace. Organizations must adapt to constant change; they must battle to defend their markets and their margins against pressures, including new competition, over which they have no control. Any type of 'snoozing' will result in disastrous losses. One famous example is Kodak's loss of

market share to Fuji, and its failure to adapt to new business rules, new customer profiles and more. Kodak turned from leader to follower. Changes in the organization will also require service delivery changes. Specific to SLM, changes to service level targets will not suffice. In this type of extreme business change, the vision and strategy of the process must be reviewed and modified, a complete new set of CSFs must be assembled, and stakeholder identification must be performed in order to understand the new service environment.

The above are typical instigators for process transformation where documentation reviews or tools enhancement will surely not suffice. This

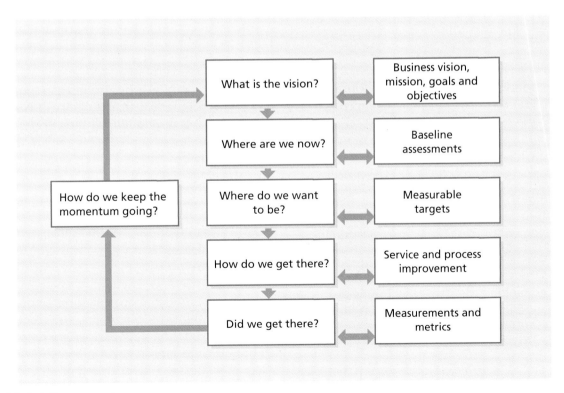

Figure 20.4 CSI approach

requires a long and hard look at your process, establishing a new vision and working from the ground up to make fundamental adjustments. In the remainder of this section we will provide you with two methods for a structured framework to plan your steps to improve and re-establish your process. The two methods are:

■ **CSI approach** A structured approach including six steps to guide you through the improvement of the process, including a 'keeping the momentum' step to ensure that process improvement becomes second nature to the organization.

■ **ITIL lifecycle approach** Implementing the activities according to the ITIL lifecycle: service strategy, service design, service transition, service operation and continual service improvement.

20.7.1 CSI approach

The CSI approach described here is very close to the DMAIC (define, measure, analyse, improve, control) methodology in Six Sigma (see section 20.2.3). The model will help us improve our process by taking a wider look at the overall mission and how it will relate to the activities of the process.

Figure 20.4 describes the steps of the CSI approach, which comprises a constant cycle for improvement. The improvement process can be summarized in six steps:

1 **What is the vision?** Embrace the vision of SLM by understanding the high-level business objectives and how SLM will underpin them. The vision should align the business and the process activities.

2 **Where are we now?** Assess the current maturity level of SLM by executing the ITIL gap assessment.

3 **Where do we want to be?** Understand and agree on the priorities for improvement, based on a combination of a development of the principles defined in the vision and the roadmap resulting from the gap assessment. A full implementation of the vision may be years away but this step provides specific goals and a manageable time frame.

4 **How do we get there?** Detail the roadmap to plan how to achieve an advanced SLM process.

5 **Did we get there?** Verify that KPIs and metrics are in place to ensure that milestones were achieved, process compliance is high, and business objectives and priorities are being met by SLM.

6 **How do we keep the momentum going?** Finally, the process should ensure that the momentum for improvement is maintained by establishing the CSI activities detailed in this chapter.

Although the model is positioned at a high level and seems theoretical at first glance, it becomes practical as it is developed, with concrete activities and deliverables. In Table 20.2 we relate the model steps to activities detailed in this publication and their output deliverables.

20.7.2 ITIL lifecycle approach

Drastic times call for drastic measures. An ineffective process is not just a waste of resources. An ineffective process, especially a process as important as SLM, will actually damage the most crucial interests of the organization, undermine the relationship with customers, and result in a lack of coordination between service providers and an ungoverned service environment. Sometimes even an immersed improvement programme, including a CSI approach, will not suffice.

Table 20.2 CSI approach steps

Step	Action	Deliverables	Chapter reference
What is the vision?	Establish the vision and strategy of the process according to the business needs	Envisioning the process charter	Introduction to process strategy (Chapter 2)
		CSFs	Envisioning value creation (Chapter 3)
Where are we now?	Define a baseline for the process via ITIL gap assessment	ITIL gap assessment	SLM process assessment based on capability maturity (Chapter 4)
		Roadmap	
Where do we want to be?	Create a practical roadmap with activities on how to progress from your current position to your goal position	Detailed roadmap	SLM process assessment based on capability maturity (Chapter 4)
		Prioritized activities (short, medium and long term)	
How do we get there?	Develop a project plan to transition and implement the roadmap	Service transition	Transition planning (Chapter 12)
		Project plan	Transition work streams (Chapter 13)
Did we get there?	While implementing, ensure that activities provide the value that they were intended to. Perform post-implementation reviews and measurements of process KPIs at intervals	Service transition	Transition planning (Chapter 12)
		KPI performance reports	Continual service improvement for SLM (Chapter 20)
How do we keep the momentum going?	Provide a platform for continual improvement of the process	Methodology for process improvement	Continual service improvement for SLM (Chapter 20)
		CSI approach	

To build a new structure, you will need to remove the existing structure; you will need to start from the beginning. This publication provides comprehensive guidance for implementing SLM. It does not necessarily assume that the implementation will start from scratch, in the sense that the organization is assumed not to possess any SLM activities. On the contrary, it understands that the majority of organizations indeed perform some SLM activities. These organizations will consider the implementation of the process, even a large-scale one, to be a process improvement programme.

If you are a decision maker (i.e. process owner, senior management) or even a consultant who is faced with a variety of approaches for potential process improvement, you might want to consider a complete implementation of the process, according to the guidance documented in this publication.

This approach surely requires additional resources, such as money and people, and may even entail a long approval process. However, the advantages are numerous. The ITIL lifecycle approach ensures that the design of the process is based on strategic decisions that align the process with business needs. The ITIL approach continues with best-practice activities that rely on proven field experience.

Implementing SLM from top to bottom by adhering to the chapters of this publication guarantees that nothing will fall between the cracks.

20.8 SUMMARY

Process improvement does not only mean fixing local problems. Adhering to the concepts of this publication you will come to a realization that structured practices are beneficial for short- and long-term benefits.

It is difficult to dedicate time for process improvement unless it was predefined by the initial process plan. Yes, if a fault has risen to the surface, it must be addressed and resolved; but, again, it must follow predefined procedures. On the other hand, initiating proactive improvements will eliminate many of those faults before they even arise.

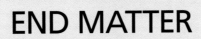

END MATTER

Conclusion

21

21 Conclusion

Service level management (SLM) aims to generate positive customer perception through continual communication with the customer, enquiring about services provided and improvement where needed. The five phases recommended in this publication guarantee achievement of this aim. In other words, if you define your strategy, detail your design, plan your transition into the live environment, execute activities within your operation and continually improve your process, you will ensure the success of SLM, and ultimately the service environment and the business it supports.

A common misconception regarding guidance books such as this is to approach it with 'It's just a text book; it is theoretical and detached from the real-world practices.' The shrewd reader will quickly discover that this publication is based on good practice supported by real project experiences. It is not a theoretical book intended to be taught in the classroom; rather, it is based on the practical experiences of consultants and practitioners. Follow its guidance and it will help you avoid the costly pitfalls that often underlie service process improvement projects.

As a seasoned veteran in the service management arena, I am well aware that implementing all the activities suggested here is 'mission impossible'. The reality is that our working environment is permanently challenged by budget, resources and time constraints. Management will not always support the implementation of processes and tools that do not generate an immediate return on investment. But then again, if it was that easy to implement, you would not be reading this guidance and I would not have needed to write it.

As a project manager or even as a service level manager, it is unlikely that you will be starting with a clean slate, meaning that you will start your job within an established environment where the organizational culture will not always be aligned with the philosophy I have laid out before you. For that reason, I have suggested that you start with basic activities such as process assessment, critical success factors and service structure. I have also structured the publication in a way that allows you to choose a topic and focus on that topic alone. The assumption is that practitioners will find ways to introduce improvements to the process in due course.

SLM is much more than a technical process or a process focused on technology. It differs from other service management processes because it focuses on perception, satisfaction and other concepts related to customer emotions. Those who can combine their technical and management experience with their interpersonal skills will be most likely to succeed in implementing and operating SLM.

Index

Index

Bold page numbers indicate figures, *italic* numbers indicate tables.